Resisting Boundaries

LATIN AMERICAN STUDIES
VOLUME 6
GARLAND REFERENCE LIBRARY OF THE HUMANITIES
VOLUME 1865

Latin American Studies

David William Foster, *Series Editor*

The Contemporary Praxis of the Fantastic
Borges and Cortázar
by Julio Rodríguez-Luis

Tropical Paths
Essays on Modern Brazilian Narrative
edited by Randall Johnson

The Postmodern in Latin America
edited by Claudia Ferman

Readers and Labyrinths
Detective Fiction in Borges, Bustos Domecq, and Eco
by Jorge Hernández Martín

Magic Realism
Social Context and Discourse
by María-Elena Angulo

Resisting Boundaries
The Subject of Naturalism in Brazil
by Eva Paulino Bueno

Lesbian Voices from Latin America
by Elena M. Martínez

Resisting Boundaries
The Subject of Naturalism in Brazil

Eva Paulino Bueno

Routledge
Taylor & Francis Group
LONDON AND NEW YORK

First published 1995 by Garland Publishing, Inc.

Published 2019 by Routledge
2 Park Square, Milton Park, Abingdon, Oxon OX14 4RN
52 Vanderbilt Avenue, New York, NY 10017

Routledge is an imprint of the Taylor & Francis Group, an informa business

Library of Congress Cataloging-in-Publication Data

Bueno, Eva Paulino.
Resisting boundaries : the subject of naturalism in Brazil / by Eva Paulino Bueno.
p. cm. — (Latin American studies ; vol. 6. Garland reference library of the humanities ; vol. 1865.)
Includes bibliographical references (p.) and index.
ISBN 0-8153-1789-1 (alk. paper)
1. Brazilian fiction—19th century—History and criticism. 2. Naturalism in literature. I. Title. II. Series: Garland reference library of the humanities ; vol. 1865. III. Series: Garland reference library of the humanities. Latin American studies ; vol. 6.
PQ9601.B84 1995
869.3—dc20 95-3923
CIP

ISBN 13: 978-0-8153-1789-0 (hbk)
ISBN 13: 978-1-138-86425-2 (pbk)

Series Preface

The monographs in Garland's Latin American Studies series deal with significant aspects of literary writing, defined broadly and including general topics, groups of works, or treatments of specific authors and movements. Titles published have been selected on the basis of the originality of scholarship and the coherency of the theoretical underpinnings of the critical discourse. Cognizant of the fact that literary study is an ongoing dialogue between multiple voices, established topics and approaches complement attempts to revise the canon of Latin American literature and to propose new agendas for their analysis. Studies will also focus on interdisciplinary approaches, the bridging of national and linguistic divisions, subaltern studies, feminism, queer theory, popular culture, and minority topics. The series includes only studies written in English.

David William Foster

To my daughters Virgília, Sara and Lucília
and to my son Daniel

CONTENTS

FOREWORD

This book consists of the study of five Brazilian novels produced in the last decades of the nineteenth century: *O mulato* (1881), *O cortiço* (1890), both by Aluísio Azevedo, *A carne* (1888), by Júlio Ribeiro, *Bom-Crioulo* (1895), by Adolfo Caminha, and *Dona Guidinha do Poço* (1897) by Manoel de Oliveira Paiva. These novels, traditionally considered naturalist, portray tensions caused by the realignment, or, better still, the sudden visibility of people such as strong women, blacks, mulattoes, and homosexuals in Brazilian fiction. The standard reading has seen their appearance as a mere function of a "mechanicist" view of existence, or of naturalism's preference for the ugly, lowly, and revolting aspects of life. These novels are, at once, the product and the reflection of a very complex moment in the constitution of the nation: for late nineteenth-century Brazilians the *idea* of Brazil was becoming undone precisely because the political moment—the beginning of the republican regime—necessitated the call for a centralized idea of Brazil which could be summarized under the positivistic motto "Order and Progress."

Of course one question is begged here: *whose* idea of Brazil was going out of control? It was not the peasants, nor the masses of illiterate provincial people, nor the slaves, nor was it the idea of those provincial intellectuals who viewed with suspicion the machinations engendered in the capital. For these groups, what mattered respectively was the notion of their family, or of their immediate community, or of their household/plantation, or of their provincial intellectual centers. The nation as such, a Brazil with its official history and celebrated historical figures, was perhaps more distant a reality than the spatial distance between these people's homes and the capital of the country, Rio de Janeiro, to which most Brazilians had never traveled in their lives. At this crucial moment, the Brazilian elite (and elitist Brazilians) were acting in concert in an effort to add another chapter to Brazilian history. The writing of this chapter, and its addition to an "official history," was being done on behalf of those who could not, or would not, participate in it. This book is a study of the counter-hegemonic resistance to the writing of this official history.

But another question is necessary here: how do we recover these moments of resistance when we know that historical documentation is the product of the dominant classes, or, in the Brazilian case, by the empowered classes stationed in the capital of the empire? And, of course, how can we avoid falling in the trap of easy categorizations of "good" and "bad" guys? I am aware that these categories not only do not do justice to the often contradictory political situations through which relations of power are processed, but also, and especially, these categories mask the crucial, even if subtle, moments in which domination and subordination under the guise of "order," faced a no less subtle resistance in several forms. These novels, *O mulato*, *O cortiço*, *A carne*, *Bom-Crioulo*, and *Dona Guidinha do Poço*, themselves fraught with contradictions, are nonetheless examples of such resistance.

I have framed my discussion of these novels on three main issues: the problem of literary history, the status of the literary text, and the nature of literariness itself. The problem of literary history which concerns me here is, first of all, related to the location of naturalism between romanticism and realism. Of course this is a matter of periodization itself, and I am much indebted to the critique of Fredric Jameson, who argues that the very idea of periodization

> tends in spite of itself to give the impression of a facile totalization, a seamless web of phenomena each of which, in its own way, "expresses" some unified inner truth—a world-view or a period style or a set of structural categories which marks the whole length and breadth of the "period" in question. (*The Political Unconscious* 27)

In order to avoid the temptation to assume that these five novels constitute a "seamless web of phenomena," I want to state at the outset that my choice of these canonical novels is propositional. That is, I want to investigate the ideological stance each novel takes toward the social and historical conditions which have been used by Brazilian critics in order both to circumscribe the period known as naturalism at the time the novels were published, and to continue to reproduce it in present-day criticism. It may be, as Jameson suggests, that any such totalization is "facile." My central concern, however, will be how this totalization is accomplished, text by text, and what "seams" in each one are subject to periodizing operations that conceal or efface more than they reveal.

Their status as canonical representatives of naturalism was not given to these novels without struggle. The critics of the time, Sílvio Romero, José Veríssimo and Araripe Júnior among the most prominent, debated, sometimes heatedly, the question of which novels were deserving of the title of "naturalist," and what naturalism entailed in a Brazilian context. The category may indeed be the most contested one in Brazilian literary history. This brings us to my second point which concerns this history: both the internal differences—a literature produced in the center of the country versus one produced in the distant provinces, and the external differences—Brazilian practice versus French and, especially, Portuguese practice. Few periods in Brazilian literary history provoke more difficulties over what in a nation's literature is internal to itself, what is external, and, most importantly, what clear basis can be employed to tell the difference. I will suggest that the practice of Brazilian naturalism is more discontinuous with itself than it is proper for one practice in a literary period to be.

In part this is so because the very definition of a literary text is insistently raised by the novels I want to discuss. First, of what subjects would a literary text consist? Are there subjects, on the other hand, which must be excluded? These are urgent questions, and what all critics of naturalism (and not merely those of the nineteenth century) seem to have missed in *O cortiço* or *Bom-Crioulo*, for example, is their discontinuities and even inconsistencies regarding what may be spoken about and what may not. My own discussion emphasizes the historical occasion in all cases: that is, the situation of a nascent republicanism anxious about its own ideological authority and eager to establish a stable, unified national identity for the whole of Brazil. What we find in the conventional critical treatment given to these texts by, among others, Sílvio Romero and José Veríssimo in the nineteenth century, and Lúcia Miguel Pereira, Nelson Werneck Sodré, and Flora Süssekind in the twentieth century, however, is an even more conventional discourse about texts simply "influenced" by history and authors whose meanings are (at the least) under the control of their intentions. Consequently, I will at times have to talk about individual authors because the criticism of the nineteenth century especially—after all the founding moment of literary criticism in Brazil—addressed these authors very pointedly, often noting, for example, the regions where individual writers came from as crucially informing their view of the country. So, what Jameson terms a "set of structural categories" produces a period, if not periodization itself. I hope it will be clear, on the other hand, that my own theoretical persuasions run counter to this unproblematic discourse of authors. I aim, instead, to resituate the idea of regionalization within the larger formation of what it means in the first place to presume a centralized Brazilian subject.

In this study of five novels, therefore, each one functions as a representation disclosing various tensions and ruptures implicit in the necessarily ideological project of how the Brazilian identity was formed after the fall of the monarchy. I am interested in each less as a "literary work" than as a heterogeneous example of cultural production (explicitly modeled on languages other than Portuguese in one case, and implicitly completed by a contemporary editor in another case) which can be understood as, in addition, an oppositional production. I will be looking at the terms of this opposition, and trying in the process to discuss what they commonly opposed: the same male, white, republican hegemony which manifested itself, in part, by appropriating the very alignments of gender, race, and class so relentlessly vexed, dissolved, and challenged in these very novels. I should make clear that my interest is not finally in the literary production of the naturalist period just because naturalist texts provide unusually instructive examples of how texts are undone by their own heterogeneity. Any period in Brazilian literature—even romanticism—could be selected if I wanted to content myself with such a formalist reading. Instead, their very nature as naturalist texts expresses the more rich, diverse, and ideologically inflected portrait of the Brazilian subject which it is ultimately my aim to investigate. As Edward Said suggests, "[T]he realities of power and authority—as well as the resistances offered by men, women, and social movements to institutions, authorities, and orthodoxies—are the realities that make texts possible, that deliver them to their readers, that solicit the attention of critics" (*The World, the Text, and the Critic* 5). It is important to recover these moments of resistance; Brazilian identity remains, I believe, one in which too many have been excluded by too few in the name of power and authority.

To state it once again: an oppositional, counter-hegemonic dimension is crucial to my analyses of these novels. Brazilian naturalists were the first group of writers to turn a de-centered, or ex-centric, gaze at the totality of the Brazilian society of their time, and to attempt to represent it as a whole composed of contradictory parts, each highly intensified and exacerbated, consisting of blacks, mulattoes, masculinized women and homosexuals or feminized men. The world of naturalism is a densely peopled one, and its characters previously enjoyed no privileged position in any aesthetic dispensation in Brazil. What I want to try to do is to explain, first, what historical circumstances produced these novels. That is, precisely what aesthetic agendas came after romanticism, and what role did these agendas have in the production of Brazilian nationhood? Secondly, how might positivism be distinguished from naturalism in this agenda, and what class interests are entailed in the distinction? Finally, what does a study of Brazilian naturalism suggest about the relation between what is foreign to Brazil and what is not? My purpose throughout will be to locate areas of resistance to hegemony represented by the "nation," and to stipulate precisely what forces—regional, sexual, racial—need to be realigned in order that what is both most radically unsettling as well as conserving for the idea of nationhood in the naturalist text can be more acutely understood.

The idea of the need for a unified entity had a historical urgency in the moment these texts were produced. The nation Brazil, with its various and different regions sometimes practically out of reach, with its racially unstable population, with its social and political problems resultant from slavery, and with its dependence on foreign trade, was an extremely fragile concept at the end of the nineteenth century. To describe Brazil at this moment, we can borrow what Anthony J. Cascardi describes as the culture of modernity: a divided, fragmented whole which could only be "unified through the powers of an abstract subject, or its political analogue, the autonomous State" (*The Subject of Modernity* 179). Of course, one can immediately remark that Brazil was already an autonomous State at the end of the nineteenth century. Independence from Portugal had been obtained in 1822. However, as I understand it, the Brazilian monarchy, since 1822 surviving in Brazil mostly under the aegis of the Portuguese Bragança family, was at a turning point. A modern State, which would equate Brazil with the other republics of South America, was overdue. The modern State, which, Cascardi says, "embodies a series of positive goals" premised on "the rejection of social hierarchies," on "the equality of all before the procedures of the law," and on "the accession to a realm of subjective freedom founded on reason" (180), would be exactly what Brazilians needed and expected with the change from a monarchic to a republican State. However, as Cascardi points out, "the authoritarian structure of the State reflects the fact that the subjects are radically uncertain about the nature of virtue and values; as a result, it indicates their susceptibility to manipulation and control" (180). To what extent, we might ask, were the Brazilians of the end of the nineteenth century aware of the reach of the processes of manipulation and control which the new republican State would inevitably need to submit them to in order to take hold? Of course the visible signs of these processes, namely, the use of the armed forces to repress regional rebellions, are easy to recognize. Nevertheless, as Mary Poovey correctly remarks, "repression is not always conscious, nor is it always attributable to identifiable individuals. Instead, this process of repression, which produces and proceeds by exclusions, is a function of any process of definition in an epistemological system that depends upon non-contradictory logic and unitary identity" ("Cultural Criticism" 619).

It interests me to study how this repression was textualized in late nineteenth century Brazilian culture. More importantly, however, I want to uncover totalizing and homogenizing practices and, finally, I want to demonstrate how they have been constitutive parts of a whole ideological apparatus aimed at neutralizing the differences. Obviously, some of these differences are those the naturalists insisted on pointing at, referring to, and building their works upon. As Poovey says, repression is not always attributable to identifiable individuals. In this case, the critics who commented at the time on naturalist novels were participating "in the ideological masking of the system of relations in which readings and textual productions take place" (Poovey 618). What I attempt to do is to bring to visibility the network of repressed relations and to unmask these processes, which include a whole set of institutional practices related not only to the literary text as a stable cultural object, but also to its grounding in the complex cultural system of composition, publication, dedication, and, in different times, of reviewing, treatment in specific editions, Editor's notes, and, in one case, of work notes accompanying one of the novels.

One last note on procedure. Although some of these Brazilian novels and critical texts have been translated to English, I use my own translations throughout. All other translations of Spanish texts, unless otherwise noted, are also mine.

ACKNOWLEDGMENTS

When I started writing this book, wonderful people lived close to me. Now, most of them are far away in their native countries, or in New York, which, some argue, is very much a foreign country. I want to use this opportunity to record my gratitude to these friends' kindness and willingness to talk literature when there was so much else requiring their immediate attention. To Michelle Soriano, Victorien Lavou, Michelle Ortuño, Marina Catzaras, Peter Gaines, Raúl de Aguinaga, my gratitude for the many wonderful hours we spent together in Pittsburgh. My thankfulness goes also to my former house mate, Michael Aronna, who shared with me not only many viewings and discussions of *Star Trek* (the original and the new generation), *Pee-Wee* and assorted Weather Channel shows, but also books, magazines, recipes and his wonderful sense of humor. John Beverley, Bobby Chamberlain and Cornejo Polar also helped me with their comments, encouragement and important books throughout this project. Marie Novak, even though she has a house full of little children, was kind enough to help me put the manuscript in presentable form. Marie Fortis helped me understand some French texts and the politics of small towns in America. Connie Tomko cheered me up and invited me to lunch when all I needed was some friendly chat. Lidia Díaz, María Franco, Zuli Segal and Carlos Orihuela were always good and reliable friends. My eternal love and gratitude to Francisco Caetano Lopes Júnior, *amigo de fé, irmão, camarada*, who, even during his battle against a painful and fatal illness, continued to be a source of inspiration and consolation. Finally, I want to acknowledge the confidence and support given to me by my husband, Terry Caesar, a superb reader of my texts and my moods, my best friend, my co-conspirator, without whom this book and many other things could not ever have become reality.

INTRODUCTION

I

From approximately the beginning of the nineteenth century, Brazilian literature was dominated by romantic aesthetics, which helped establish a readership for distinctively Brazilian themes, Brazilian names, and, more importantly, anything which resembled a glorification of Brazilian nature. The country proclaimed its independence from Portugal in 1822. The fabrication of Brazilian symbols was not just a matter of literary concern, but more urgently of the formation of a national identity separate from that of the mother country. Antônio Cândido remarks that the development of the Brazilian novel, from Joaquim Manuel de Macedo to Jorge Amado, "shows how our literature has been conscious of its social role and of its responsibility in the construction of a national culture" (*Formação da literatura brasileira* 115). This work of construction, however, started before the Romantic period. Cândido argues elsewhere that the work done in the Academies that flourished during the eighteenth century in Bahia and Rio de Janeiro paved the way for nationalist sentiment. These Academies—Academia Brasílica dos Esquecidos (Salvador, 1724-25), Academia dos Felizes (Rio de Janeiro, 1736-40), Academia dos Selectos (Rio de Janeiro, 1751-52), Academia Brasílica dos Renascidos (Salvador, 1759-60), Academia Científica (Rio de Janeiro, 1772-79), and Sociedade Literária (Rio de Janeiro, 1786-94)—were founded and protected by viceroys and magistrates, and their members were "persons of eminence in society," and, obviously, they "encouraged in literature the frank glorification of the established order, works praising the norms of civilization, defending the efforts of the colonizers, and echoing the words of the authorities" ("Literature and the Rise of Brazilian National Self Identity" 30). However, as Cândido points out, "the Portuguese colonial process was, as is inevitable, creating its own contradictions, as it changed in order to adapt itself and consolidate the dominant classes of the colony " (31). The Academics, because they concentrated in an effort of historical and scientific inquiry, ended up "exalt[ing] the role of certain Brazilians, dr[awing] importance to their achievements, accent[ing] the particular characteristics of the country, and thus prepared the way for nationalistic attitudes" ("Literature and the Rise of Brazilian National Self-Identity" 31). The Romantic writers,

> [L]evados à descrição da realidade pelo programa nacionalista...eram contudo demasiado românticos para elaborar um estilo e uma composição adequados. A cada momento, a tendência idealista rompe nas junturas das frases, na articulação dos episódios, na configuração dos personagens, abrindo frinchas na objetividade da observação e restabelecendo certas tendências profundas da escola para o fantástico, o desmesurado, o incoerente, na linguagem e na concepção. (*Formação da literatura brasileira* 115-16)[1]

In the words of Sérgio Buarque de Hollanda, romantic literature was aimed at making Brazilians feel "less exiled in their own land" (*Raízes do Brasil* 3).

Romanticism did not die easily in Brazilian literature. The literary production of the nation throughout the whole nineteenth century can be fairly characterized in terms of its derivation from European, especially French, models. As Lúcia Miguel Pereira points out, Flaubert published *Madame Bovary* in book form in the same year one of the milestones of Brazilian romanticism, José de Alencar's *O guarani* (1857), was published; Zola started his *Rougon-Macquart* series (1871-93) when Taunay wrote *Inocência* (1872), a classic of romantic regionalism, and Machado de Assis published his first novel, *Ressurreição* (1872) (*Prosa de ficção* 119). In other words, the most advanced European literary, philosophic and social concepts took twenty years to reach Brazil. In 1873, Machado de Assis wrote that "the books of a certain French school, although very much read among us, have not contaminated Brazilian literature; and I also do not feel in [Brazilian literature] any tendency to adopt this school's doctrines. . ." (qtd. in Pereira, *Prosa de ficção* 120). The school Machado is referring to is what twentieth century critic José Guilherme Merquior calls "the literary extension of the scientific mentality" (*De Anchieta a Euclides* 109): the naturalist school.

But Machado is a realist whose first works have clear roots in romanticism. For him, Brazilian literature still derives its inspiration from the" Victor Hugos, the Gautiers, the Mussets, the Gozlans, the Nervals," and its principal elements

---

[1][L]ed to the description of reality by a nationalist program, were nevertheless too romantic to be able to elaborate adequate style and composition. At every moment, the idealist tendency arises in the structure of the sentences, in the articulation of the episodes, in the configuration of characters, thus opening gaps in the objectivity of information and reestablishing some deep tendencies of the school for the fantastic, the immeasurable, the incoherent, both in language and in composition.

are "the picturing of habits, of passionate struggles, of nature's landscapes; once in a while [it depicts] a little study of feelings and of personalities" (qtd. in Pereira, *Prosa de ficção* 120).

The fact is, however, that while the European literary and philosophical landscape was being reconfigured, Brazil, although so eager to imitate Europe, fell inevitably behind. Lúcia Miguel Pereira remarks that "the delay in adopting the realist aesthetics here is a symptom of the writers' alienation not only from the world, but from the very conditions of the country" (*Prosa de ficção* 119). The last romantics, alienated from the political world, were outdated while the country lived out its turbulent passage from monarchy to republicanism. Hence, we need to understand the establishment of a new Brazilian aesthetic practice in two fundamental ways. First, as a delayed response both to the romantic aesthetics and to the "realist" one already rationalized at least a decade before in France, by Zola, and in Portugal by Eça de Queirós,[2] among others. Secondly, as a direct response to contemporary history.

When the new aesthetics finally appeared in Brazil, the very fact of its emergence revealed the existence of a series of anxieties and representational crises which could no longer be accommodated within an idealistic practice. This practice, furthermore, had been distinguished by its appropriation by the elites, aristocratic or merely academic, stationed in the capital of the empire. Writers needed not only "a new way" to express what they saw and felt about Brazilian history during the last decades of the nineteenth century. They needed terms for a profound crisis in national ideology. In the new republican era even elites could no longer continue singing the beauty of Iracema, whose main claim to life was

[2]Alexander Coleman says that Eça de Queirós's literary allegiances would qualify him not as a mere follower, but as "a synthesist of the various kinds of imaginative bifurcation that Romantic, Realist, and Naturalist theory and practice have come to mean for us" (5). However, synthesist or not, Eça's work was not easily accepted in Brazil. An interesting proof of this is Machado de Assis' 1878 highly critical review of Eça's *Cousin Bazilio*. This review seems to have not only wounded Eça deeply, but also attracted ill-feelings among Eça's admirers in Brazil. In the second installment of his review, published two weeks after the April 16, 1878 commentary, Machado writes: "As far as Sr. Eça de Queirós and *his friends on this side of the Atlantic* are concerned, I will repeat that the author of *Cousin Bazilio* has in me an admirer of his talents, but an adversary of his doctrines. . . (my emphasis). Machado's criticism was originally published in *O Cruzeiro*. Later it appeared in Alberto Machado da Rosa, *Eça, discípulo de Machado?* 212-13 (qtd. in Coleman 127).

anchored in her death.[3] The sentimental intrigues of the kind portrayed in, for example, Joaquim Manoel de Macedo's highly popular *A moreninha*, or *O moço louro*,[4] could no longer absorb the presence of highly sexual "Lenitas," who chased men rather than surrendering to them, or urban sub-classes who gossiped about a bourgeoisie that grew to fear them. A far more heterogeneous society challenged known taxonomies and modes of representing them. A new aesthetic procedure had become imperative.

Provincial arrivistes, professors and men of letters bent on establishing themselves in the capital of Rio de Janeiro, sprang up to mediate what "literature" was for men of republican inclinations anxious to make their own hegemony continuous with that of the aristocratic elite which they wanted to replace. What kind of authority empowered the critical discourse of this new group? Its vocabulary needs to be carefully considered, if only because it cannot be easily separated from the literature which they presumed to authorize. In addition, both the new group and their alliances were inseparable from the larger discourse of Brazilian nationhood.

---

[3]Here I refer to José de Alencar's Iracema, heroine of the novel *Iracema*. The character's death, at the end of the novel, opens the road for her Portuguese lover to go away with their son, Moacir. As brilliantly argued by Doris Sommer, *Iracema* is about losses: "Iracema's losses of virginity, community, love, and finally her life. But mostly . . . it is about Martim's loss of cultural moorings, the one loss that transmutes all the others into a gain. . . . The Tupí princess . . . is the object of his European desire only after she is missing" (*Foundational Fictions; The National Romances of Latin America* 169-70). Indeed, Iracema has become a very important symbol in Brazilian literature. Her figure will be played out against others that I discuss in this book.

[4]Antônio Cândido says that Joaquim Manoel de Macedo's works were adjusted to techniques of easy communication, and that their little literary value is due to the fact that Macedo tried to represent the scenes, human types, and the life in a society in process of stabilization: "While he used elements which pleased the public's sensitivity, [Macedo] extracted from them consequences which do not occur in daily life, and, this way, [he] influenced [the public's] taste, gave style to the literary aspirations of the carioca bourgeoisie. . . ." For Cândido, Macedo's work—in which he succumbed to his impulses to chit-chat—served to invent a sentimental myth, the Moreninha, "patroness of young loves who still makes adolescents dream" (*Formação da literatura brasileira* 138).

The participation of fiction in national formation has become a compelling object of study in recent years. Benedict Anderson, writing about the origin and spread of nationalism, defines a nation as "an imagined political community—and imagined as both inherently limited and sovereign" (*Imagined Communities* 15). But how does a nation come to imagine itself? What role does the institution of literature play in this process? Cornelius Castoriadis argues that history is impossible and inconceivable outside the "productive" or "creative" imagination. He observes that "nation" performs the role of identification for a triple imaginary reference to any history which wants to understand itself as "common": triple because actual history is always past, because it was not so *common*, and finally because what can be known about it now acts to support the collectivizing identification in people's consciousness which, in turn, partakes mainly of myth (*A instituição imaginária da sociedade* 179). Mythology is central to Doris Sommer's argument about the absence of novels in South America generally before independence because "they would have been politically premature well into the nineteenth century" ("Irresistible Romance" 78). Sommer continues that these subsequent fictions, when they occurred, projected ideal states which were, despite their variety, patriarchal or hierarchical. Because so many of the authors of romance were in fact the founding fathers of their countries, narrators could project an ideal future in the "epistemological gaps that the non-science of history" left open (76). Prose fiction, in other words, was both concurrent and congruent with legislative action or military campaigns (73).

It is all very well, then, that history in South America was unusually available for the resources of fiction in the nineteenth century, or that myth was peculiarly suited to be a compensation for history. But was this foundational fiction based on a consensus of what emerging nations should be? On this point, Sommer states that,

> [I]n the particular case of Latin America's nineteenth-century "historical" novels, the nagging insecurities that writing produces only peek through the more patent and assertive inscriptions [of the more general process of nation-building]. The tensions exist, of course, and they provide much of the interest in reading what otherwise might be an oppressively standard canon. (78)

How can we understand such insecurities? What idea of a nation allows us to recuperate them? There is of course the available notion of a nation's "biography" as discussed by Antonio Gramsci in *El "Risorgimiento"*, in which he links the writing of politico-constitutional history as a periodizable narrative to the moment of the birth of national feeling. This feeling is a powerful political tool for the manipulation of the masses under the power of a central biographical project established, a priori, by intellectual and political factions in charge of writing history. The national identity proceeds to organize themes that, in turn, allow the state to be legitimized. Therefore, the adoption of such ceremonial events as "discovery," "independence," "proclamation of the republic," etc., can be taken as imaginative topoi organized with the intention of building the nation's memory. However, they are articulated according to centralized political principles whose job it is to dismiss supplementary information.[5]

I take such information to be another name for Sommer's insecurities. Taken together, these antecedents would provide what Dominick LaCapra calls an "intercontextual horizon": "a set of contexts in mutual and often tense interaction. Typical members of the set include the writer's intentions, life and corpus, societal conditions, cultural contexts of production and reception, and longer range traditions such as those of genre and mode of discourse" (*Rethinking Intellectual History* 138). The set could be fleshed out within the horizon given by any individual nation. The crucial question, however, is this: who proposes the set? Perhaps it is an easy enough question to answer: anyone who represents hegemonic interests. I think we can further presume that these interests will be best represented if the "interaction" of "contexts" is smoothed out according to an ostensibly univocal, pre-established voice which will organize, edit, and suture all facts so that they are variously beneficial to a continuous national story, or "biography" in Gramsci's sense.

To address the question of who proposed the set in Brazil at the end of the nineteenth century I will begin by considering the example of the new professoriate who took itself to be nationalistically empowered in the latter decades. It may be argued that, under the auspices of a collective biography, the personal biography of some members of the Brazilian Imperial capital was also advanced. Foremost among the members of this professoriate was the critic José Veríssimo, born in the northern state of Pará in 1857. In "Nota bibliográfica sobre José Veríssimo," Wilson Lousada says that, when he emigrated to Rio de Janeiro in

[5]In "Fictional Formations and Deformations," Mary N. Layoun stresses that "if nationalism (and national culture) arises as a means for unity and cohesion in the face of particular social and historical conflicts, it brings with it a whole new set of problems. Something of the contradictory impulses of this solution are apparent in a consideration not only of what and how nationalism/national culture unites, but also of what and how it represses" (55).

1891, Veríssimo had already published *Primeiras páginas* in 1869, *As cenas da vida amazônica*, in 1886, and had also founded the *Revista Amazônica* and a school—Colégio Americano. When Veríssimo established himself in Rio, he worked as a teacher at the Colégio Pedro II, as a journalist, and principally, as a literary critic. His critical works, *Estudos de literatura brasileira* and *História da literatura brasileira*, constitute classics in the genre (x-xii). For João Alexandre Barbosa, Veríssimo's work is deeply connected with the transformations "of taste and mentality which start appearing in Brazil around 1870" (Introdução xi).

Veríssimo himself called this new literary procedure "Modernista," and stated that the historical facts which determined or facilitated the adoption of a new aesthetics were the following:

> a guerra do Paraguai, [que acordou] o sentimento nacional... a questão do elemento servil, comovendo toda a nação, e lhe despertando os brios contra a aviltante instituição consuetudinária; a impropriamente chamada questão religiosa, resultante do conflito entre as pretensões de autonomia do catolicismo oficial e as exigências do tradicional regalismo do Estado...e, finalmente, a guerra franco-alemã com suas conseqüências, despertando a nossa atenção para uma outra civilização e cultura que a francesa, estimulando novas curiosidades intelectuais. ("O modernismo" 169)[6]

This is an excellent example of creative imagining under the sponsorship of historical causality, and historical causality, in turn, in the interests of national ideology. Veríssimo in fact offers a set, whose purpose is to dispose of history as if its fictions already partook of a "horizon" circumscribed by the national idea. Veríssimo lists factors as if they are all finally of equal importance; in fact, he is only curious about them insofar as they contribute to a narrative of progressive national "awakening" from the slumber induced by slavery, religion, and

[6][T]he Paraguay war, which woke up the national feeling . . . the matter of slavery, which moved the whole nation and provoked a revolt against that debasing institution; the improperly called religious question, resulting from the conflict between the intended autonomy of official Catholicism and the demands of the traditional royalty of the State . . . and, finally, the Franco-German war and its consequences, [which] awoke our attention to a culture and civilization other than the French, thus stimulating new intellectual curiosities.

French culture. Of course, any historical account will lack its own power if it fails to acknowledge that concrete ideological work is always being done on the basis of what factors are selected, and not only how they are related. Let me propose three separable contexts for the complicated "intercontextual horizon" that Veríssimo condenses: *intellectual history*, *class formation*, and finally *literary practice*.

The intellectual history of Brazil is highly determined by the fact that, unlike the other Spanish American countries, which had universities created in their territories as early as 1551 (Peru and Mexico),[7] the creation of universities was forbidden by Portugal until after the arrival of the Portuguese court in Brazil (Carvalho, "Elites and State Building: Brazil" 383). Only in 1828 two law schools were opened in Brazil. During, and even after the colonial times, rich families sent their sons to study abroad, especially in Coimbra.[8] The members of this elite, according to José Murilo de Carvalho "came from all parts of the huge colony" (385) and "a substantial part of [this elite] at least at the time of independence, was . . . recruited among the dominant class" (397). Even though Carvalho acknowledges that data on the social origin of the elite are "extremely scarce and not very reliable," he believes that "around 50 percent of the elite had some sort of connection either with the landed or the commercial upper class" (397).

Carvalho argues that the cohesion and ideological homogeneity of the intellectual elite was one of the most important reasons for maintaining the unity of the country: "[A]s it turned out, a substantial part of the leadership involved in the independence movement at the national level, as well as the majority of the national political elite in the three decades that followed, was drawn from this

---

[7]José Murilo de Carvalho writes about this difference between the history of the university in Brazil and the other Latin American countries: "[in Spanish America] it was the consistent policy of the colonial government to encourage the organization of universities under the aegis of the State or of the Church. The royal universities were modeled after the University of Salamanca, the religious ones mostly after that of Alcalá. At the end of the colonial period, twenty-three (or twenty-five, according to some authors) universities had been created" ("Elites and State Building: Brazil" 384).

[8]See pages 395 and 387, tables 1 and 2 in José Murilo de Carvalho's "Elites and State Building: Brazil" for the percentages of place of higher education and field of higher education of cabinet ministers in the period between 1822 to 1889.

group of university graduates" (384).[9] A. J. R. Russell-Wood points out that, in Coimbra, these law students came in contact not only with Europe, but mainly with their fellow Brazilians from regions practically unknown to them when they were in Brazil. It was at this opportunity, according to Russell-Wood, that these students could "appreciate the vastness and diversity of [their] own country. It was this understanding which contributed so decisively to the ideology behind the movement toward independence in Brazil" ("Preconditions and Precipitants" 23). These former Coimbra law students later became cabinet ministers, state councilors, and senators, and they constituted, according to Carvalho, a homogeneous group which shared what Gerald Michael Greenfield calls a "common mental universe" (Greenfield 378) and which would, ultimately, contribute to the establishment of a centralized monarchical system after independence.

As E. Bradford Burns stresses, it is difficult to define the category of intellectuals precisely. In Brazil,

---

[9]A. J. Russell-Wood writes that the first major blow to the colony's intellectual life was the expulsion of the Society of Jesus from Portugal and her dominions in 1759. The Jesuits' departure from Brazil resulted in the secularization of the missionary *aldeias* and in the overnight destruction of the educational programs of the Jesuit colleges throughout Brazil, "which had become centers of intellectual and cultural activity." The crown's repeated rejection of petitions for the establishment of a university in Brazilian territory led to the sending of an increasing number of Brazilian men to study in "universities in Montpellier, Coimbra, Edinburgh, and Paris, and it was this generation of graduates who imported into the colony the ideas of the Enlightenment in eighteenth-century Europe and publications prohibited by crown censorship" ("Preconditions and Precipitants of the Independence Movement in Portuguese America" 20). On this point, José Murilo de Carvalho contends that the Coimbra institutions were far more conservative, because they "managed to isolate their students from the most dangerous aspects of the French Enlightenment, admitting only the reformist and Christian version of the *Lumières*" ("Elites and State Building: Brazil" 384). Carvalho points out that "several students who went to France or England, and even some priests trained in the colony . . . were more influenced by the subversive ideas of the time and more willing to put them into practice through political action than were their Coimbra fellows" ("Elites and State Building" 384-85). On the matter of the radical priests' involvement with the ideas of the Enlightenment, see Eduardo Frieiro, *O diabo na Livraria do Cônego*; Emília Viotti da Costa," The Political Emancipation of Brazil," *From Colony to Nation* 63-70; and E. Bradford Burns, "The Enlightenment in Two Colonial Brazilian Libraries."

> We can use the term "intellectuals" in a general sense to refer to all the educated elite, the teachers, doctors, lawyers, bureaucrats, some military officers, merchants, those who engaged in literary conversations, read European authors, exposed themselves to new ideas or methods emanating from Europe, and concerned themselves with the world around them. ("The Intellectuals as Agents of Change" 224-25)

This small group of intellectuals made up for their size both by their ability to express their ideas "in public oratory, in the classroom, in conversation, and later in books and newspapers," and by their location in the cities "near the decision making process" (225). By the second decade of 1800, an important group within the intellectual elite began shaping up and gaining influence: the writers. For these intellectuals a formal diploma, much less a diploma from Coimbra, was not necessary. What we have here, then, is a split within the category of intellectuals in Brazil: on the one hand, there were the "traditional" intellectuals, wholly enfranchised within the political system—the Coimbra graduates—who participated in decision making and overall historical shaping of Brazil. On the other hand, there were the "new" intellectuals, represented not by a unified front, because they did not constitute what Stanley Aronowitz calls "a distinct discursive community" capable of generating unique subject positions ("On Intellectuals" 11). Although these new intellectuals had a philosophic program in common—positivism—their role in political life established a rift in their capacity to generate actual power.

Furthermore, besides their class difference from the somewhat unified front composed by the magistrates, senators, and other former Coimbra graduates, the group composed by the intellectuals recruited from the middle class and the petite bourgeoisie had to contend with still another problem within their own group in their process to gain respectability: other writers from different places in the country.[10] The attempt to ascend in social status was in itself a divisive

---

[10]Writing about Brazilian intellectuals in the period between 1920-1945, Sérgio Miceli makes the interesting distinction between the intellectuals who were "poor relatives" and the "heirs." For Miceli, the "poor relatives" "seem more inclined to bargain their scant troops for professional refuges," whereas the "heirs" "try to reproduce their families' positions within their own intellectual group" (*Intelectuais e classe dirigente no Brasil* xxi). It can be argued that among the Brazilian intellectuals of the nineteenth century, the Coimbra graduates constituted the group of "heirs," and the writers, mainly those who were originally from regions other than the capital, were the "poor relatives." It seems

factor among writers. As national ideology fostered, the struggle for recognition and fame already facilitated the rivalry among the writers from the provinces and those of the capital; after all, unlike the former Coimbra graduates, none of these writers had had the privilege of a common place of study, and were, therefore, less willing to consider a more comprehensive view of a totalizing entity called Brazil. José Guilherme Merquior writes that, at this time,

> a condição de escritor...foi uma posição cobiçada por muitos filhos da classe média... a origem social dos principais autores literários do período pós-romântico revela que a percentagem dos escritores saídos da classe média, até mesmo da baixa classe média, aumentou consideravelmente em relação à era romântica... Para esses *self-made men*, a vitória nas letras equivalia a uma promoção social... a estética pós-romântica ...exercia uma função heráldica, hierarquizante, conferindo *status* aos talentos de estirpe média e pequeno burguesa. (*De Anchieta a Euclides* 107)[11]

One could inquire whether mere *status* sufficed for these intellectuals. It seems clear that, more than just *status*, what they sought was participation in Brazilian history making, just as the Coimbra graduates enjoyed before them. To do so, however, they needed a basis from which to operate, or a constituency that would legitimize their discourse and would give their knowledge the value of truth. In other words, these writers had to link themselves with "real" agents, or

---

almost too fitting, in this context, that the "heirs" took positions of power within the administration as magistrates, senators, etc., whereas the "poor relatives," at least the brightest and most successful ones (Machado de Assis, Joaquim Manuel de Macedo, José de Alencar, and Aluísio Azevedo, for example) landed bureaucratic and/or politico-administrative jobs.

[11][I]n the second half of the eighteen hundreds, in Latin America the writer's condition . . . was sought by many children of the middle class . . . the social origin of many authors of the post romantic literary period reveals that the percentage of writers from the middle class, and even from the low middle class, increased considerably in relation to the romantic period. . . . For these *self-made men*, the victory in letters was equivalent to a social promotion. . . The post romantic aesthetics . . . had a heraldic, hierarchic function [which] conferred *status* to talents of the middle and the petite bourgeoisie origin.

what Gramsci and other Marxists call "classes."[12] To speak about classes in the Brazil of the late nineteenth century is of course to deal with a most difficult subject.[13] In the chaotic political situation at the end of the empire, we can distinguish several groups of people: the masses of illiterate people (white and black) scattered all over the country, the bourgeoisie concentrated mostly in urban areas, the pseudo aristocracy that purchased titles from the crown, and the military that were engaged in arguments about the unfair promotion practices as well as in further dissensions over differing philosophic and political beliefs (Dudley 44-65). One reads about the "growing middle class," and the "military class" in nineteenth century Brazil (Nachman 1; Dudley 59). However, to my knowledge, no such thing as a "slave," or a "peasant," or a "feminine," or a "homosexual," or a "mulatto" class ever came into existence. It may be that, as the French peasants Marx discusses in "The 18th Brumaire of Louis Bonaparte," these people were never able to form a community, never developed a common culture, and therefore, were never able to represent themselves as classes. Somebody had to represent them. As I see it, those Merquior calls the "self-made men" took as their mission to accomplish this representation. And, to do it, they

---

[12]In "On Intellectuals," Stanley Aronowitz reads Marx's "18th Brumaire of Louis Bonaparte," and, by altering the language of a passage in Marx's text, offers a formulation of class: "Classes come into being under conditions of (1) the occupation of a common structural space; (2) a common discursive (cultural) position that, however, is not presupposed by structural unity; and (3) political organization exemplified by political parties and national trade unions that also function discursively" (8).

[13]I do not mean to imply that only in nineteenth century Brazil the subject is complicated. What I mean is, rather, that the specific situation of a society which is finally constituting a new set of free citizens with the abolition, and changing from a monarchic to a republican regime, makes the subject of class *even* more difficult to talk about.

had to articulate themselves through some intellectual or philosophical project.[14]

At the end of the nineteenth century, intellectuals did not suffer from lack of choices. A wide range of new ideas and intellectual developments begged the attention of these new writers. Foremost among the "new intellectual curiosities" mentioned by Veríssimo is positivism. How may we define the vexed space of this area for intellectual inquiry? Luiz Costa Lima, writing about Euclides da Cunha—military man, engineer, writer, and, above all, positivist—maintains that

> Comtean positivism had been only one of several currents that had swept the country into favor of "the great liberal conquest of our century" . . . despite the small number of their adherents, evolutionist currents played a decisive role not only in the character of intellectuality at the end of the nineteenth century and beginning of the twentieth but also in the very fall of the monarchy. (*Control of the Imaginary* 156-57)

It is clear, then, that positivism did not manifest itself among Brazilian intellectuals at the end of the nineteenth century as a single theory; rather, it constituted a group of ideas developed by Kant, Spencer, Taine, and Darwin, as well as, especially, Comte. Positivism did not attract all intellectuals at the same time. Robert Nachman points out that, initially, it was popular in the

> generally upper-class law schools at the time that the rising middle class was first becoming vocal. The *bacharéis*, trained in consensus politics, saw positivist ideas not only as beneficial to the nation, but as a practical means to incorporate the growing middle class into the national system. As time passed, the elite discarded positivism, leaving it to the middle-class engineers, professors, and military officers. ("Positivism, Modernization" 7)

---

[14]Aronowitz discusses the circumstances under which intellectuals perform specifically political functions. He stresses that intellectuals "begin to occupy a unique political position when the question of the 'masses' enters political discourse. On the whole, the masses appear in the context of the bourgeois revolutions as a necessary but not central participant and are first articulated in the form of the 'social question' at the moment they acquire their own voice, whose first expression coincides with the proclamation of universal rights by their new patrons, the bourgeoisie" ("On Intellectuals" 12).

Leslie Sklair traces the influence of positivism in several countries in Europe, in the United States, and in South America. He writes that

> It was in Brazil . . . that Comtean positivism and the Comtean theory of progress had its greatest actual triumph. Under the influence of Benjamin Constant and Pereira Barreto the Republic of 1889 adopted positivism almost as its official ideology, and went so far as to put the Comtean motto of "Order and Progress" on the flag of the State! (*The Sociology of Progress* 46-47)

From its first appearance in Brazil in the 1870s, through French translatio' Darwinism attracted the attention of several intellectuals, who, accordinp .o Gerald Michael Greenfield, shared one trait:

> "an exaggerated concern" with finding some philosophical or scientific approach that could both explain Brazilian reality and provide positive prescriptions for achieving progress. Brazilian Darwinism also settled into an intellectual milieu in which a broad "scientism" stressed the application of scientific knowledge and approaches to the solution of national problems. ("The Great Drought and Elite Discourse in Imperial Brazil" 396)

All these men were in fact on the agenda of the several schools which appeared in the capitals of some Brazilian provinces, the interior of the Northeast and of Rio Grande do Sul (Nachman 6). These schools provided a space for intellectuals interested in studying and discussing the latest philosophical ideas. However, these ideas were not accepted on the same level. The very fact that Comte's doctrine of the "Law of the Three Stages"—the Theological, the Metaphysical and the Positivistic—was the one which appealed to Brazilian intellectuals reveals more about the specific characteristics of their political and ideological anxieties than about the nature of positivism itself. I believe that, even more important than what positivism meant in an international context was the way the Brazilian intelligentsia appropriated the doctrine as a means to justify its need to articulate the formation of the idea of Brazil. Since in this doctrine the "Positivistic Stage" is considered the most advanced state the human mind can achieve, the intellectuals' preference for Comte's philosophy disclosed their ideological ambitions within Brazilian society.

Of course the fact that some of these intellectuals later began producing literary works termed naturalist might lead to the assumption that positivist and naturalist ideas were equally accepted. They were not. In "As idéias fora de lugar," Roberto Schwarz has a classic discussion of the extremely complex dynamics governing the adoption of foreign ideas and philosophies in Brazil. He states that

> Throughout its social reproduction, Brazil tirelessly instates and reinstates European ideas, always in an inappropriate manner. It is in this capacity that they will be matter and problem for literature. The writer might not know this—he does not even need to—to use them. But [the writer] only reaches a profound resonance . . . if he feels, registers and unfolds—or avoids—the off-centeredness and the dissonance in them. (24)

The adoption by the Brazilian intelligentsia of positivist ideas ran parallel to the adoption of naturalist aesthetics in literature during the 1870's, and the discussion of both took place more or less concurrently. Merquior writes that positivism prepared the way for naturalism: "the positivistic essay prepared the soil for the flowering of the naturalist aesthetics; however, the implantation [of naturalism] was primarily caused by the influence of Eça de Queirós's *O primo Basílio* and of Zola's work, especially the program of *The Experimental Novel* (1880)" (*De Anchieta a Euclides* 113). In 1883, Sílvio Romero wrote: "It is necessary to found a nationality conscious of its merits and faults, of its force and its weakness, and not just obtain a pastiche, a mimicking of Judas . . . which only serves to shame us at the foreigners' eyes. . . ." For such state of affairs, there is only one solution, "we should dive into the life-giving current of the naturalistic and monistic ideas which are transforming the old world ("Ensaios de crítica parlamentar" 15). However, dissonances in the steady course of mutual adoption led even Sílvio Romero—at once a positivist and ardent defender of naturalism since its inception—to criticize the ways Brazilian writers consolidated the elements of what became an intellectual program. In 1888, writing about Júlio Ribeiro's *A carne*, Raul Pompéia's *O ateneu*, Horácio de Carvalho's *O cromo*, Marques de Carvalho's *Hortência* and Aluísio Azevedo's *O mulato*, Romero called the novels "pseudo-scientific blustering"—*fanfarrices pseudo-científicas*—which lacked "invention, and, since these are naturalist novels, this means lack of direct, firm and personal observation" (*História da literatura brasileira* v).

How may we explain these dissonances between the philosophy which writers and critics said to embrace and the reception of the novels produced by these writers who claimed to have written them as practical demonstrations of the philosophy? These dissonances, I think, can be bluntly characterized: positivism, received as the very incarnation of the most advanced form of human thought, was virtually above criticism, whereas what became naturalist aesthetics required discussion, not to say criticism, because it had to be implemented in specifically Brazilian ways, in order to portray Brazilian characters or represent Brazilian social conditions. Positivism, in other words, can be understood as the premier late nineteenth century example of how, as Schwarz remarks, an originally European vocabulary was used by Brazilian writers as if a different syntax was not therefore made possible, whereas naturalism, on the other hand, was understood from the very outset as something which could only come into existence on the basis of Brazilian difference ("As idéias fora do lugar" 25)

To state the obvious distinction: positivism was an intellectual program, whereas naturalism was an aesthetic practice. The two were not so much different in how each was understood as different in how each was subsequently expressed in political terms. In my reading, the program was eventually subject to the highly formalized and centrist possession of the military. In contrast, no one such group took possession of naturalism, whose evolving "model" was instead discussed and assimilated by the Brazilian intelligentsia through several schools, and, moreover, was not the exclusive property of men of letters. For the non-military intellectuals, nonetheless, two of these schools—the French and the German—were of basic importance for how positivism became more "resonant" (in Schwarz's sense) within the diffusion of naturalist aesthetics among the generation of young writers who came of age in the concluding decades of the nineteenth century. Each of these schools needs to be examined in some detail.

The first among them is the "Academia Francesa" (French Academy), which was formed in Fortaleza, Ceará, and, although it lasted only three years—1872-75—it "would represent the first of a series of local movements which developed by the first years of the republic" (Sodré, *O naturalismo no Brasil* 163). These movements denounced the existence of a differentiated cultural (and economic) area of the Northeast, characterized by a relatively autonomous life based on the provincial small and medium properties. It is always difficult to trace the consequences of ex-centric movements, but according to Nelson Werneck Sodré, the movement of the French School left as its heirs two other schools, the "Gabinete Cearense de Leitura"—whose members took a more conservative position—and the "Clube Literário" in 1886. The members of the "Clube Literário," promoted, in literature, "the introduction of the naturalist methods, which corresponded to the reaction of the petite bourgeoisie against the alienation of romanticism and represented the access of more ample levels [of the population] to scientific knowledge, till then reserved to the elites (*O naturalismo no Brasil* 165).

Although the movement was short-lived, it caused the appearance of several literary magazines, and it was responsible for the publication of the first novel by Manoel de Oliveira Paiva, *A afilhada* (serialized in the newspaper *O libertador* from February 6 to April 29, 1889), and of Rodolfo Teófilo's *A fome*, published in 1890. In 1892, the "Spiritual Bakery"—*Padaria Espiritual*—started its meetings in Fortaleza, Ceará. Among its members was Adolfo Caminha, who authored *Bom-Crioulo* in 1893.

The "German School," founded in Recife by Tobias Barreto[15] in 1868, constituted, in Sodré's words, the most powerful of these movements and the one that influenced the whole country in several ways (*O naturalismo no Brasil* 165). Developed under the auspices of the Law School of Recife, the "German School," also called "Recife School," included, among others, the jurist Clóvis Bevilaqua, the philosopher Artur Orlando, and the literary critic Sílvio Romero. About the activities of the school, Sílvio Romero wrote: "it has not only a scientific spirit, but a spirit of struggle and of conquest" (qtd. in Sodré, *O naturalismo no Brasil* 165). Intellectual militancy, according to Sodré, was necessary, due to the "existence of two nations which [did] not know each other, separated in space and even more in time: on one side, the rural workers, dependent upon the patronage of landowners, and on the other side, the wealthy ruling minority" (*O naturalismo no Brasil* 165-66).

Some idea of art for art's sake was obviously beside the point for these intellectuals, and some other, more properly positivistic idea of art for science's sake was too abstract. Theirs was the moment in which the distinct, multiple realities which composed Brazil had to be represented, and the representation had to be made full and complete through art.[16] The new ideas, united under the

---

[15]Tobias Barreto graduated from Law School in 1869, and, although he took a schoolmaster's post in the interior of the state of Pernambuco, he continued to come to Recife regularly to lead the group of young graduates in their discussions of, especially, German materialist philosophy.

[16]Such concerns were very much in Andrés Bello's mind during his speech for the inauguration of the University of Chile in 1842. When he explains the role of Philosophy and Letters among the different disciplines in the university, he says: "That literary department which possesses a peculiar and eminent quality to polish the customs, which refines the language, making it the faithful, beau-

general distinction of positivism, consolidated themselves among these intellectuals as a highly rationalist philosophy that contended with the conservative authority of the Church (and of the monarchy, which was officially Catholic) and that promoted the claims of intellectuals to an idea of Progress coterminous with the new republican state.

Veríssimo's celebration of the sheer good of "curiosities," however, belied the presence of how any curiosity has profound political consequences, and ignored any possibility that either the curiosity or the consequence was in fact already being disputed by groups (other than monarchists, presumably) who were already excluded from his collective "our." Positivism had no vision of such groups, much less of how its progressive intellectual program might be put to specific nationalistic uses. Sérgio Buarque de Hollanda writes that Brazilian positivists had a "secret horror of our national reality." For Buarque de Hollanda, these positivists, who once formed the aristocracy of the Brazilian intelligentsia and became the favorite counselors for some governors, "were not positive" in the Comtean sense. Rather, they "lived narcotized by a stubborn belief in the truth of their principles and by the certainty that the future would judge them and their contemporaries, according to the position they adopted individually and

---

tiful, diaphanous vehicle of the ideas. . .; which, by the contemplation of the ideal beauty and its reflections in the works of genius, purifies the taste and conciliates the unprescribable rights of reason with the daring flights of fantasy; which, at the same time it initiates the soul in serious studies—necessary auxiliaries of the beautiful literature and indispensable preparation for all sciences [and] for all careers in life—forms the first discipline of the intellectual and moral being; exposes the eternal laws of intelligence in order to lead and affirm its steps, and develops the profound folds of the heart to keep it from fatal deviations, to establish on solid basis the rights and duties of man" ("Discurso pronunciado en la instalación de la Universidad de Chile," *Obras Completas* 314).

Commenting on this passage, Julio Ramos writes that the "letters" did not constitute a privatized activity: "the letters *polish* language and submit the deviations of fantasy . . . to the regularity of reason. Therefore, the letters provide the necessary conditions for the application of the law" (*Desencuentros de la modernidad en América Latina* 42). Ramos also observes how, already in 1873, for Eugenio María Hostos, posterior to Bello and Sarmiento, there is a more advanced degree of rationalization of the pedagogic discourse: "in Hostos's discourse [we no longer see] the operation of a notion of the Belles Lettres or of the 'saber decir' as a device for the authorization of teaching. Rationalization, in this later, positivist, period, displaces the letters from its central role in education" (43).

collectively, in relation to these principles" (*Raízes do Brasil* 120). It is easy to see, then, that an intellectual project unaware of how the cultural production which follows from it is already creating a space for excluded energies to occupy cannot reasonably be expected to know who such energies, or such groups, may be, or even how they might be represented as portions of a nation's subjectivity.

One of these excluded groups, however, was not the military. Indeed, the impact of Comtean positivism on Brazilian military schools provides an interesting case study in how a specific social group becomes transformed and enabled by an intellectual formation acting in concert with historical events. Aquiles Cortes Guimarães remarks that the military schools were the principal focus for the study and dissemination of positivism, perhaps because of two basic reasons: the necessity for extensive use of mathematic language in the didactic-pedagogic structure of the formation of a military officer; and the idea of order as a fundamental component of the society imagined by Auguste Comte (Guimarães, "O espírito do positivismo na cultura brasileira" 27). The young military men, whose studies consisted of official courses in an official institution, a specialized military academy, immediately set themselves apart from the members of other "schools." Moreover, because the military institution was already based on discipline, it was a most appropriate atmosphere for the application of the principles of order and hierarchy, themselves congenial with the positivistic doctrine. Therefore, the military men enjoyed some advantages which the civilian intellectuals, at once located in several schools and divided among themselves, did not have.

Veríssimo mentions the war against Paraguay as a moment in the history of national feeling. The war might be mentioned even more crucially as a moment in its hegemonic formation. The Brazilian military, which had always been considered low in the hierarchy of the imperial society, acquired considerable social and political authority after the war against Paraguay. Predictably, the higher-ranking officers, given their due honors, assured their loyalty to the Emperor and the established order. By comparison, the younger officers, like Euclides da Cunha, after their (first) contact with other Latin American soldiers during the Paraguay campaign, learned, first, a different concept of their historic role, and second, that the Brazilian monarchy constituted an "exotic plant" in the American soil. Arthur Cezar Ferreira Reis writes that the republican feeling, already manifest in Brazilian history in the Mineiro "inconfidência," and in the other several conspiracies—in 1797, in 1794, in 1817—"appears again in 1870 when, leaving the monarchic parties of the time . . . disillusioned with the system, not believing in the continuity of the regime," some Brazilians started considering the republican solution, "which would integrate us better in the continental life and would free us from the denomination of exotic, nonauthentic strangers to the community of American nations" (*Aspectos da formação brasileira*" 214). In 1870, in the Manifest of Rio de Janeiro, these men took the motto "We are from America and we want to be Americans"—*Somos da América e queremos ser americanos* (214). José Maria Bello observes that "the transference of military studies from the central school to a specialized academy also contributed noticeably to the development of pride. The philosophy of Comte thus found among the young military men the best soil for the germination of a spirit of independence, which is always so close to a spirit of defiance" (*A History of Modern Brazil* 42). This spirit of independence formed itself as an act of defiance against both the ideology represented by the monarchic regime and against the older military officers, believed by the younger officers to have been coopted by the honors given to them by the Emperor.

Furthermore, there is a sense in which the younger officers' intellectual training provided the weapons for them to leave the confines of the military school and subsequently participate actively in the government of the country. This new military group, by virtue of its newly acquired status, eventually came to insinuate itself in the space traditionally reserved for intellectuals in society. Indeed, the very existence of civilian intellectuals as a group was dependent upon factors outside a strictly intellectual set of circumstances—factors, moreover, which qualified its potential class strength at precisely the moment when that of the military was in the ascendant.

Intellectuals were heavily dependent on public jobs and on governmental subsidy. Illiterates composed 84% of the Brazilian population in 1890.[17] To state a perhaps obvious point, literature as a profession was virtually impossible[18] for most who were literate. Renato Ortiz states that

> [O] escritor não podia "viver de literatura", o que o levava a exercer funções no magistério e nos cargos públicos. É conhecido o fato de que no Brasil o desenvolvimento da literatura se encontra estreitamente

---

[17]For a detailed discussion on the autonomy of Brazilian literati see Ortiz, *A moderna tradição brasileira* 27-30. For the same subject in Spanish America, see Julio Ramos, *Desencuentros de la modernidad* 82-111.

[18]According to several analyses, as late as 1930 the production and commercialization of books in Brazil was practically non-existent. See Laurence Hallewell, *O livro no Brasil*; and Olímpio de Souza Andrade, *O livro brasileiro*.

> ligado à burocracia do Estado. Dentro deste panorama, o relacionamento de nossos críticos e intelectuais com uma esfera de produção de massa, como o jornal, tinha que ser específico. (*A moderna tradição brasileira* 28)[19]

Sergius Gonzaga gives us a brief summary of the situation: successful romantic writers like Joaquim Manuel de Macedo (1820-82), José de Alencar (1829-77), Bernardo Guimarães (1825-84) worked either as teachers, public officials, or newspapermen. Joaquim Maria Machado de Assis (1839-1908) himself, who started as a proof-reader at the Tipografia Nacional, in 1880 became "oficial-de-gabinete" of the Ministry of Agriculture, and later was nominated General Director of the Ministry of Transportation. Among the naturalists, the situation was very similar: Aluísio Azevedo (1857-1913) worked as a cartoonist for several newspapers until he obtained a position as a diplomat (*Manual de literatura brasileira* 63-96). Claude Hulet writes that Júlio Ribeiro (1845-90) worked as a teacher in the State of São Paulo; Adolfo Caminha (1867-97), after leaving the Navy due to personal problems, worked in the Interior Department of Ceará and in the Federal Treasury of Rio de Janeiro; and Manuel de Oliveira Paiva (1861-92) worked for the newspaper *O libertador* and for the literary magazine *A quinzena*, both in Fortaleza. Sílvio Romero (1851-1914) and José Veríssimo (1857-1916) also worked in teaching and journalism (*Brazilian Literature* 31, 40, 140).

Of course the fact that these writers and intellectuals worked for public offices, combined with the fact that their prospective audience was still very limited, proves Ortiz's point: Brazilian writers of the nineteenth century could not live off their literary creations and essays.[20] Their best way to achieve some sort of readership was through the newspapers. This explains why Olavo Bilac (1865-1918), one of the most published Brazilian poets of all times, remarked that "the newspaper is a blessing for all Brazilian writers. It is really the only

---

[19][T]te writer could not "live off literature," and this led him to work as a teacher or as a public officer. It is a well known fact that in Brazil the development of literature is closely tied to State bureaucracy. Within this landscape, the relationship of our critics and intellectuals with a sphere of mass production, like the newspaper, had to be specific.

[20]Of course I am aware that the situation has not changed either in Brazil or any other country. In present-day Brazil, the only writer who can boast to live solely on the sale of his books is Jorge Amado.

way the writer has to make himself read" (Ortiz 28). Furthermore, in late nineteenth century Brazilian culture, the writers, their group strength already dependent upon their alliance with extra-literary agencies (schools, governmental jobs, newspapers), found themselves further weakened by internal dissension among themselves. The fight between José Veríssimo and Sílvio Romero (to be discussed momentarily in more detail) demonstrated that the Brazilian intelligentsia was far from agreeing on one approach to best represent both themselves and the country. Very much in contrast, no such representational burden was either borne or expected on the part of the military. The study of the several doctrines which took the general name of positivism did not, at any single moment, unite intellectuals as a cohesive and harmonious group, and it is at least arguable, on the other hand, that positivism was one clear factor responsible for making the ascendant young military men so cohesive.

Indeed, although the development of both groups was basically simultaneous, the very systematization which the military schools boasted was more suited to the nature of positivistic ideas under Brazilian scrutiny: determinism, survival of the fittest, rationality, and, inevitably, republicanism. Historian Arthur Cezar Ferreira Reis (not coincidentally a military man himself), writing in 1982, stresses the fact that "the civilians of the republican party were not expressions of the intellectuality at the service of the kind of reforms which were preached at the Military School. They did not have any echo in the conscience of the younger generations who attended the educational institution of the Empire. They were voices without any resonance" (*Aspectos da formação brasileira* 221).

Reis seems to be echoing what both José Veríssimo and Sílvio Romero wrote about the condition of the writer. Veríssimo says: "the writers, in fact without any communion with their people, their nation, are forced to also live out of it spiritually." And, in another instance: "[As far as books are concerned] I believe that here we have the liberty to say whatever we want, because the book, rarely read, has no influence in our midst. The newspaper is something different; however, except in exceptional circumstances, even [in the newspaper] the spiritual liberty is great. . . . Indoctrinary dissertations go absolutely unnoticed. . . ." ("Das condições da produção literária no Brasil" 81, 79). Romero: ". . .who among us writes and who among us reads? [Our readers] certainly are not farmers, cattle ranchers, industrialists, politicians, or even administrators. Only the academic classes and some public workers who came from these classes [read us]. This is the general rule" (*História da literatura brasileira* 36). The issue, then, is the *efficacy* of the literati. On this point, recalling João Alexandre Barbosa's expression "the tradition of the impasse"—"*a tradição do impasse*"—Costa Lima comments that this "tradition" does not mark José Veríssimo alone, but that it goes beyond the socio-political orbit and lives on in the efficacy of these critics' postulations as literary critics. (42)

Indeed, the intellectuals lacked a unified ideological agenda, and did not have much power in society. To sum up, they lacked a central, coherent intellectual program,[21] came from the provinces, and, at the same time, professed to believe in the same "evolutionary" progressivism while attacking each other constantly on the basis of "ignorance," "arrogance," and other sins, including, somewhat ironically, regional origin. Their very idea of discursive authority had been challenged by their own historical circumstances. At one point Veríssimo stated that Tobias Barreto's influence was not as great as his disciple—and Veríssimo's rival—Sílvio Romero maintained: "Only somebody who completely ignores the condition of our intellectual life will admit the influence of a writer—no matter how genial we suppose him to be—whose activity is performed sporadically and fragmentarily in thin pamphlets and short-lived periodicals in a city *of the provinces*" (Veríssimo, "O modernismo" 173, my emphasis). For Veríssimo, it was through his students in Recife that Barreto became known in Brazil.[22]

---

[21]In "O método crítico de Sílvio Romero," in *Teoria literária e literatura comparada*, Antônio Cândido states that the intellectuals embraced the study of the new philosophical ideas as a struggle "in favor of a scientific mentality and of an intellectual orientation free from the colonial formalism and from the romantic belletrism" (125). However, since these intellectuals only had a clear idea of what they were against—the colonial formalism and the romantic belletrism—it was very difficult for them to arrive at a common denominator about what they were for. What happened, instead, is that they used those negative concepts as epithets against their rivals, even when the rivals theoretically professed to believe in similar things: "romantic" became a word associated with not only old fashioned, but also reactionary and pro-monarchy.

[22]José Veríssimo argued that Tobias Barreto not only was not original in his ideas, but also was not a real scholar, since his inspiration was more poetic than scientific. According to Veríssimo, not even Barreto's arguments in favor of a German culture influenced Brazilian intellectuals; rather, the interest in German culture and philosophy was the product of the movement developed by Teófilo Braga, Adolfo Coelho, Joaquim de Vasconcelos, Antero de Quental, Luciano Cordeiro, in Coimbra, Portugal, which influenced Brazilian intellectuals. He also insists that the Recife school was a "pseudo school" whose students-disciples were mesmerized by the master's speeches and by his bohemian habits, and did not care to search in depth about his teachings. Veríssimo sorts out of this group only Sílvio Romero and Graça Aranha ("O modernismo" 169-77).

But such a claim only disputed the master's own authority, and so a virulent reaction on the part of Sílvio Romero ensued, with the two intellectuals waging a long fight in the press of Rio de Janeiro.[23] In fact, what we might call a first "condition" of "intellectual life" was never agreed upon by the intellectuals, and the dispute illustrates the problem quite well. They never agreed that their own position as intellectuals was implicitly at stake in the new republican era, and so they were never able to contend with aesthetic critiques of this era which proposed the acknowledgment of excluded, decentered energies that emanated from pamphlets and provinces, both of which challenged traditional forms of authority and how it was transmitted.

On this last point, consider a statement from the impeccable literary critic Romero, who, in 1888, as soon as Veríssimo attacked the Recife school, publicly defended it and affirmed that the group of the Recife school "understood the extreme enfeeblement and the inevitable death of romanticism and [then] spread the seeds of another literary formula for poetry, novel, for art in general" (*Retrospecto literário, história da literatura brasileira* 259). The "death of romanticism" was of course not a strictly aesthetic question. From a perspective which comprehends the discourse of aesthetics as of a piece with Brazilian intellectual history generally, and military schools more specifically, the "death" of a literary "movement" must, I think, be read as the death of the political regime which came to being at the time romanticism appeared: that is, the Brazilian monarchy. What Romero had at stake in the death of romanticism was his own political fate. In my reading of the dispute, Romero acted as a member of a whole group of intellectuals made possible by adherence to everything which went under the name of positivism.[24] Romero, I think, only fitfully aware that the civilian intel-

---

[23]Part of the articles documenting this fight has been collected by Antônio Cândido in *O método crítico de Sílvio Romero*, and by João Alexandre Barbosa, *José Veríssimo, teoria, crítica e história literária.*

[24]Elsewhere in Latin American a similar anxiety on the part of the literates was being manifest. Writing about Eugenio María de Hostos, the founder of the Escuela Normal de la República Dominicana, Julio Ramos points out that "until the decade of the eighties, the change in the place of the letters in education began to be effective . . . at the moment positivism began to be the ruling ideology for education in many zones of the continent. Hostos insisted on the rationalization of pedagogy, attacking both the vestiges of religious education and the encyclopedist *saber decir*" (*Desencuentros de la modernidad* 52). Hostos himself, in the 1873 prologue to the second edition to his *La peregrinación de Bayoán*

lectuals were in danger of losing power to others such as the military,[25] rather inevitably declared the death of a movement which was associated with the monarchy, now considered outdated and ideologically embarrassing.

In sum, the new literary practice, naturalism, was nothing if not the product of a highly contested, embattled political atmosphere. It is far too simple to say that intellectuals sponsored naturalist aesthetics. At stake was ultimately the "intercontextual horizon," in LaCapra's sense, of the republican nation's imaginary of itself. There were disputes and divisions everywhere: among the young military both against their older officials and the monarchy; among the intellectuals against each other and against the monarchy, and, more subtly, the civilian intellectuals against the military who were threatening their intellectual authority.

II

We will understand only the local intricacies of these disputes unless we see that an articulation of the national idea was being expressed through each of them, as well as a struggle for hegemony on the part of various groups, levels, and constituencies over who could best imagine this idea. I have been emphasiz-

---

(first published in 1863), states: "I saw that the conquest of a literary name is the conquest of a power. The power I needed to serve my forgotten, vexed, ridiculed country immediately. The public judgment . . . was what I needed to authorize my entry in active life, in the difficult propaganda, in the hard struggle which I desired to undertake" (qtd. in Julio Ramos 53).

[25]It is interesting to observe how, in other Latin American countries, this battle was fought in terms of a formalized, rational education versus literature. In 1873 Eugenio María de Hostos wrote: "There are in the world far too many artists of the word, far too many worshippers of form, far too many empty spirits who can only obey the law of proportions; and I wouldn't want to be one of these many talkers (*habladores*) who, at the same time they fill with sonorous words the space where they move, are radically incapable of realizing the thing the world needs most: logical men." (As qtd. in Julio Ramos, "Fragmentación de la república de las letras" 53). For Julio Ramos, during the 1880s "'the logical man' will dominate education, which will also become modernized and will replace the family in the public works, and will oppose itself both to the Church—which still remembered its old dominion over knowledge (*el saber*)—and to the encyclopedism of the illuminist men of letters (*letrados iluministas*)" (56).

ing the struggle rather than the agreement because it is of the utmost importance to my discussion that each of the naturalist texts I consider be seen as a site for irresolution, confusion, questioning, and demystifying. These texts do not constitute a unified front against a common and clear "enemy"; rather, they are a site of contradictions both among themselves and within themselves. Brazilian naturalism was not merely the "product" of late nineteenth century Brazilian history. It was an active participant in this history, especially with respect to who controlled its representation and what interests were at stake in the control.

Let me give a fuller characterization of how problematic this term was. Both as an aesthetic practice and an ideological choice, naturalism of course did not originate in Brazil. Its beginnings in Europe, mainly in France and Germany, have been very well documented in many literary histories. Hulet provides us with a standard characterization:

> naturalism is based on a mechanistic view of the world. It is deterministic in the sense that man is molded and conditioned by his environment. The individual, in this view, is incapable of triumph when the circumstances of his surroundings and heredity oppose his success and aims. But man is not to blame. He is a prisoner. And environment simply reduces man to the level of an animal among animals. In this condition his actions can be explained biologically and through the study of his surroundings. (*Brazilian Literature* 2)

Of course, what Hulet presents here is a simplified explanation of the tenets of naturalism meant to introduce the subject in a survey book. Other writers have discussed the subject under more complex points of view. Lee Clark Mitchell, for example, writes that

> the naturalists' most radical innovation was in their perspective, not their material, and thereby entailed far more than a simple embrace of stupider characters, or more squalid subjects, or less optimistic plots than had been found before in fiction. Such commonplaces of literary history ignore the extreme reversals of a deterministic logic, suggesting that naturalism was little more than a tedious (and awkward) rehearsal of possibilities already mapped out by realist authors. Nothing could be less true of the remarkable variety evinced by naturalist writers from their unusual premise—a variety that belies any single set of principles, thematic, structural, or stylistic. (*Determined Fictions* xvi-xvii)

What interests me especially on this point is the fact that a specific brand of naturalism, the one developed by Émile Zola, was adopted by Brazilian writers. Again, and so unlike positivism, the discourse of naturalism is inseparable from the discourse of adoption—and therefore difference and dissonance. José Guilherme Merquior, for example, maintains that "it was the naturalist novel after Zola—which exchanged Flaubert's estheticist objectivity for the analysis of scientific pretentions—which constituted, among us, the first weighty manifestation of a post-romantic style (*De Anchieta a Euclides* 108-9). Also, the preference for Zola, according to Flora Süssekind, reflects "the preference. . . for any thought which helps establish an ensemble of identities, laws and similarities" (*Tal Brasil, qual romance?* 53). This preference, still according to Süssekind, is also reflected in the adoption of Comte and Spencer instead of Marx (52). Nevertheless, some questions remain as to the reason for these choices. For the sake of clarification, let me consider Zola's method for a moment.

The work which inspired Zola's seminal *Le Roman expérimental*, was Claude Bernard's *Introduction à la médicine expérimentale*. Zola started by quoting from a passage of Bernard's book, and then applied Bernard's text to his own purposes:

> All things hang together; it is necessary to start from the determinism of inanimate bodies in order to arrive at the determinism of living beings; and since savants like Claude Bernard demonstrate now that fixed laws govern the human body, we can easily proclaim . . . the hour in which the laws of thought and passion will be formulated in their turn. A like determinism will govern stones of the roadway and the brain of man. (*The Experimental Novel* 17)

Following Bernard's prescriptions that the physiologist use the scientific method, Zola determined that the novelist should do the same through observation and experimentation. The method requires that the novelist should seek out and record his data, then set "his characters going in a certain story so as to show that the succession of facts will be such as the requirements of the determination of the phenomena under examination call for. . ." (8).

Of course, we may conclude that Zola seemed unaware of the basically unscientific characteristic of his method. Perry Westbrook writes that "[f]ar from experimenting, [Zola] adopts an a priori approach, interpreting his observations by "laws" arrived at by others in other sciences" (*Free Will and Determinism* 91). We recall again Zola's method, in his own words:

> In fact, the whole operation [of writing a novel] consists in taking facts in nature, then in studying the mechanism of these facts, acting upon them, by the modification of circumstances and surroundings, without deviating from the laws of nature. Finally, you possess knowledge of man, scientific knowledge of him, in both his social and individual relations. (*The Experimental Novel* 9)

This method, quite obviously, maintains that man is determined by both "the facts of nature"—heredity—and by the "circumstances and surroundings." Man cannot change his fate or even his most intimate thoughts; he is caught in a world "in which the distinction between good and evil—dependent as it is on the existence of moral agents endowed with freedom of choice—no longer obtains" (Westbrook 94). However, this remorselessly deterministic view of life is in rampant contradiction with Zola's belief that, once the causes determining human behavior are discovered, "we can act upon them and modify them in accordance with the laws of nature . . . in such a way as to develop the good and reject the bad, from the point of view of their utility to man" (*The Experimental Novel* 31). As pointed out by Westbrook, Zola "excludes from ironclad determinism the mental processes of scientists like himself and Bernard" (94). Thus, scientists like Bernard, or artists like himself, are—or should be—according to Zola, above the fate destined to common creatures. Artists and scientists can *act upon* nature, whereas the other beings can only suffer nature's laws.

For the incipient Brazilian naturalist movement, whose members were "strongly Republican, anti-clerical, anti-slavery, and held a generally optimistic view concerning the development of society and the progress of mankind" (Hulet 3), the basic beliefs of naturalism posed a serious paradox. How could they maintain an optimistic view concerning society at the same time they subscribed to Zola's deterministic, mechanicist view of individual human beings? In Brazil, naturalist practice counted for far more in real social terms. Positivism, in contrast, counted for little more than a "humanist" or progressive way to resolve the paradox in strictly intellectual terms.[26]

---

[26]Indeed, as Sérgio Buarque de Hollanda remarks, for the positivists, "the world would fatally accept [the positivist ideas] just because they were rational, just because their perfection could not be doubted and [therefore] they necessarily imposed itself to all men of good will and good sense" (*Raízes do Brasil* 118-19).

It is of course a commonplace that naturalism took "too long" to get established in Brazil. Another problem with naturalism is that it had to negotiate from a marginal social space both with romanticism and with realism, the latter appearing at approximately the same time and expressing something of similarly ascendant bourgeois interests. It is possible to argue, in fact, that naturalism never "became established" at all in the same sense as either romanticism or realism; certainly, naturalism has never had any writer as acclaimed as the romantic José de Alencar, or the realist Machado de Assis. As a literary practice, naturalism was never formalized by the literary intellectuals because the exact social formations from which it sprang and the class hierarchies it proposed were never clear. Naturalism took too long to get established—if we want to continue the commonplace—becauseit has never been easy to understand how the familiar grounds about what it means for a "movement" to be "established" were confirmed by naturalism itself.

Süssekind is right when she says that "perhaps what is lacking in most analyses made to date about naturalism is precisely the understanding of the principle of transformation which determines the 'importation' of ideas" (*Tal Brasil, qual romance?* 34). The character of embattlement which enables the importation of ideas into Brazil was never more apparent than in Sílvio Romero's attack on naturalism in 1882: "Naturalism, especially in its empiric manifestation, until now has only counted, in poetry, novel and drama, some minimal, pitiful simpletons. The glory of invention of the doctrine does not belong to them: it belongs to foreigners. To them is left the little glory of imitation, and even that is so clumsy, so unskillful, that it causes pity" (*História da literatura brasileira* 34). Veríssimo also expressed a similar criticism against the movement: "even closer than our romanticism followed the French (romanticism), the *indigenous* (*indígena*) naturalism mimicked the naturalism of the same origin, modeling itself almost exclusively on Émile Zola and his Portuguese disciple Eça de Queirós" (*História da literatura brasileira* 294, my emphasis).

Süssekind contends that "some time later, this radicalization is lessened by Veríssimo himself, when he stresses at least one positive point in the naturalist fashion" (*Tal Brasil, qual romance?* 51). For Veríssimo, naturalism "brought to our fiction a more just feeling of reality, a more perfect art in its figuration; more human interest, a more clear intelligence of the social phenomena and of the individual soul; a clearer expression; in sum, a less defective representation of our life, which it intended to define" (*História da literatura brasileira* 295-96).

However, in spite of Veríssimo's concession, the habit of referring to it in negative terms has continued. Later in this century Merquior, for example, writes that "naturalism, although benefiting from the *caboclo* scientificism, was not its simple derivative: like scientificism itself, it was, before anything else, a transoceanic *plagiarism*" (*De Anchieta a Euclides* 114, my emphasis). I believe that, at this point, some revision of this consistent presentation of naturalist aesthetic origins is necessary. We may begin by examining the terminology used by the critics to refer to naturalism.

It is interesting to observe that Merquior also uses a racial term, "caboclo," where in the same circumstances Veríssimo uses the term "indigenous." What seems to be at stake here is not only the fact that there was importation, but that there was an *imperfect* importation. Would a perfect importation be another name for what already existed? The troubling uncertainty about exactly what was present in Brazil before naturalism is again disclosed by the word "plagiarism," which provides an extra strain for Merquior's thought. It seems to me this is yet another instance of Schwarz's fateful principle of "dissonance." "Plagiarism," after all, means "the wrongful appropriation or purloining, and publication as one's own, of the ideas, or the expression of ideas (literary, artistic, musical, mechanical, etc.) of another" (*The Oxford English Dictionary*). If naturalist writers, as well as their critics, always maintained that the movement originated in Europe (Júlio Ribeiro, for example, even wrote a very flattering dedication to Zola on the first pages of his novel *A carne*), there is no sense in saying that there was "plagiarism." There was, instead, imitation of an artistic formula developed in Europe; this formula had to be adopted (or adapted?) by the "indígenas" and the "caboclos," because, being "indígenas" and "caboclos," the writers could not imitate "as Europeans."

Süssekind, writing about these same two passages, concludes that

> in [Merquior's] 1979 text, as well in [Veríssimo's] 1882 text, the rejection of naturalist aesthetics is justified because it is not [the aesthetics] which is rejected, but the whole dependent character of our culture. It is "plagiarism," "imitation," which is rejected, and not naturalist aesthetics. (*Tal Brasil, qual romance?* 53)

This is an argument of some delicacy. Süssekind misleads in at least one serious respect. Given the very real character of cultural dependency, there simply was no way of adopting a naturalist aesthetic—or, for that matter, of any aesthetics—without exposing this dependency. It seems that the Brazilian intelligentsia, of the nineteenth (and the twentieth) century, nursed almost exclusively on the cultural milk produced in Europe, at a certain point turned against the digestion of this milk by the "indigenous" and "caboclo" organism. The fault, therefore, lies not in the milk itself, but in the inappropriate ways the body has fed on it. I must trust my own position, on the other hand, is clear: nourishment is a far more devious affair, and understanding how it operates is not helped by a naively held notion of originality, whereby what is prior can be kept separate from what comes after.[27]

One other point which might help us understand intricacies in the implantation of the naturalist aesthetic is the matter of the time it took for Brazilian writers to produce anything "naturalist." Lúcia Miguel Pereira's standard history of Brazilian narrative in the later nineteenth century is very informative on this point. Comparing the considerably shorter time it took for the adoption of romanticism from the European model, Pereira suggests several reasons for the delay in the development of naturalist ideas in Brazil. Contrasting Veríssimo and Romero, she concludes that

> a melhor prova de que o naturalismo nos foi imposto pela moda está em ter sido tão mal assimilado. Praticaram-no sempre como quem executa uma receita os nossos romancistas, que, no espírito, continuavam românticos; não há disso prova mais expressiva do que *O mulato*, que representou a vitória da nova escola, tendo entretanto apenas disfarçado com cenas realistas o seu romantismo. (*Prosa de ficção* 122)[28]

---

[27]Julio Ramos has a very interesting discussion about the importation of ideas and aesthetic practices in "Límites de la autonomía: periodismo y literatura," *Desencuentros de la modernidad* 82-111. He asks: "Wouldn't it be possible to think of the (European) origin, the referent displaced by the (Latin American) parodic representation as a place always crossed by contradictions, where literature, for instance, since its emergence, was not regulated by an institutional homogeneity, but by a critical impulse of 'truth' and 'discipline'?" (82). Ramos then proceeds to question the possibility that, even in Europe (in France, more specifically), this "purity" ever existed. For Ramos, fragmentation can be read even in *Flores del mal* as a fundamental fissure on the surface of a "pure," institutionalized subject (82). However, even considering that the European subject is itself heterogeneous, and that each North carries the marks of its South, Ramos insists that there is still the problem of the fundamental "estrangement" of Latin American literature (83).

[28][T]he best proof that Naturalism was imposed by fashion is that it was so poorly assimilated. Our writers always practiced it as someone who follows a recipe; however; they were still romantics in spirit. The most expressive proof of this is *O mulato*, the novel which represented the victory of the new school,

It is quite apparent here that something called "naturalism," far from being explained, is actually being processed through romanticism and realism. What Pereira calls the "poor assimilation" of naturalism is what I would like to relocate as the problem of its lack of political sponsorship. It is a fact of Brazilian literary history that critics have consistently repudiated naturalism. Its very subjects are considered unworthy of representation, and its representation challenges canonical principles of representation so profoundly that naturalist aims have to be rendered unrepresentable—servile—all over again. I would remark that it is no accident so many naturalist texts figure forth the terms of this very conflict; *O mulato* is, for example, precisely structured around a mulatto's challenge to the landed Creole elite, that is, around the question of "assimilation."

Pereira also opposes Sílvio Romero's understanding of naturalism as "a product of a Northern movement." After stating that she does not accept Romero's idea, Pereira continues that "Northerners, especially Northeasterners, more extroverted and therefore more apt to observe, act usually more in the realist sense, whereas the contributions which come from the Centre and from the South are more marked by interiorization and idealism" (*Prosa de ficção* 123).

I believe that the operative distinction on this crucial point is "center" versus "ex-centric" rather than "northerners" versus "southerners." Pereira, from the secure vantage of the mid-twentieth century, is continuing a hegemonic discourse about the "national essence" which was not hegemonic during the period under consideration, although there were already groups in existence whose enunciation of this essence possessed hegemonic force. Indeed, as I have emphasized, what should be the constituent elements of such an essence, or whether there was any such thing, remained precisely the political issues which animated any sort of discourse at all in Brazil during the decades immediately preceding and following the end of the monarchy. Rio was the capital. The national military school was established there. The need to appropriate both new European philosophy and mathematics emanated from there, and all groups with any pretensions to political power contemplated the idea of the republic as the ultimate goal of their efforts. However, intellectuals such as Veríssimo and Romero, themselves not originally from the capital, were very uncomfortable with the existence of writers from the "sertão" (backlands) whose necessarily de-centered artistic gaze threatened to disrupt a potential representation of the country as a whole.

One strategy became to refer to them as lacking in capacity to represent the country. Veríssimo, for example, did not spare anybody in Brazilian literature

---

and which just disguised its romanticism with some realist scenes.

when he stated that "there is an observation which anybody who studies the facts of our literary evolution cannot miss: the lack of a national feeling, of a national temperament, I would add, in the works (and therefore in the authors) even the most notable of our literature" (*Teoria, crítica e história literária* 196-97). Although he intended to criticize all Brazilian writers in general, the main focus of Veríssimo's accusation of lack of national feeling fell on the naturalists, because they were the main point of his discussion in the essay. Another strategy was to counterpose Machado de Assis against the naturalists as either a distinguished exemplar of the "romantic" or a refined one of the "realist." The case against what then could be known as "naturalism" conceded Machado a more honorable place, preserved the ideological space for what was aesthetically "honorable," and, most crucial of all, ratified Machado's "art" as something which transcended Brazilian frontiers. Pereira, for instance, repeats this operation in her comparison between Machado and the naturalists (*Prosa de ficção* 17-32). However, not all critics praised Machado de Assis. Consider Sílvio Romero's wrath at critics who presumed to term Machado a naturalist. First he attacks what he calls "the so-called directors of Brazilian intelligentsia," who "do not even have a clear notion of the schools and literary individualities of the country." To better exemplify his point, Romero says that [the critics'] "indigence of criterion is so great that they take the most prominent specimens of a decrepit romanticism . . . Mr Machado de Assis & Mr Luís Delfino and place them among the *naturalists*. Now, [to have] Machado & Delfino, two *sobriquets* of romantic taails [*sic*: *cauda romântica*], two unclassified bastards, named as reformers . . . it is too much!" (*Teoria, crítica e história literária* 100).[29]

Two points about Romero's invective against Machado: the accusation of ignorance against those who "lack study," and the definition of romanticism as "decrepit" as over against naturalism. Of course, it is obvious that Romero does not like Machado, much less Delfino. However, more than his personal dislikes, what this passage discloses is the fact that, at the time the new literary aesthetics was being introduced in Brazil, the intellectuals represented by Romero, whose

[29]Such epithets applied to Machado de Assis should not alarm us, when we remember that, as Luiz Costa Lima says, Machado was Romero's favorite victim. One contemporary of Romero, Lafaiete Rodrigues, writing under the pseudonym of Labiento, says: "The first logical necessity that Mr. Romero feels when he starts his study is to attack Machado de Assis, and to say to which school he belongs. Is he a classic, a romantic, a naturalist?" (qtd. in "A crítica literária na cultura brasileira no século XIX" 39).

job it was to mediate, did not in fact know what naturalism was, or only did, once again, by proclaiming its difference from romantic and realist fiction.

There is a final development that follows from this proclamation: naturalism is read out of contention in the stakes for national representation. Veríssimo, comparing romanticism to naturalism, conceded that romanticism was decadent, "worn out by a usage of half a century, and disoriented by the conviction that with Indigenism it erred in its direction." Naturalism, however, was not the solution because "unfortunately . . . it was, in a much higher degree than romanticism, inattentive to the Brazilian spirit. Besides being poor in writers and works, this naturalism is the least national of our literary schools, and none of its books gives us the sense of our society and our civilization" (*José Veríssimo; Teoria, crítica e história literária* 208).

These are Veríssimo's topoi of the *criterion.* The main problem in naturalism, therefore, was that it could not represent the Brazilian spirit. Such a statement obviously means that there was a "Brazilian spirit" which not only existed but was clear for anyone to see. Moreover, the naturalists' failure to attend to this spirit constituted a fault even greater than those committed by romanticism. What Veríssimo claimed to be "our society," and "our civilization" that was absent in naturalist books, was the "society" and the "civilization" of the high bourgeoisie of the court. Since the most significant writers of the naturalist school were all from places other than the capital, it is no wonder that they could not portray this "society" and this "civilization." Veríssimo deemed an entire ideological succession to be *the* Brazilian one. For the scorned naturalist writers, on the other hand, I believe the very idea of the capital of Rio de Janeiro was in itself vitiated either by the aristocratic ideals of the monarchic elites, or by the military positivism which favored the new republican regime.

Naturalism in Brazil constituted a rebuke to all totalizing schemes, even as it was itself the product of the centralizing energies of nationalistic ideology. We can detect a similar instance of how the peculiarities of naturalist practice become lost in a certain comprehension of a national idea if we turn to Georg Lukács's well known essay dealing with the phenomenon of naturalism in a larger European setting. Lukács argues that its method of observation developed "as part of an attempt to make literature scientific, to transform it into an applied natural science, into sociology." "But," he adverts, "investigation of social phenomena through observation and their representation in description bring such paltry and schematic results that these modes of composition easily slip into their polar opposite—complete subjectivism" (*Writer and Critic* 140). If we compare Lukács's stricture with Veríssimo's study of the faults of Brazilian naturalists, it seems to me that, for the latter, these faults could be summarized as their not being "subjective" enough, whereas, for Lukács, they would undoubtedly be considered "too subjective." The "subjective," for Veríssimo, would be a function of the center, of the centrist instance which dictated what should be considered authentically "Brazilian." What if, however, subjectivity is a function of the ex-centric? In his discussion, Lukács clearly presumes a national formation already in place; therefore, it is applicable to a European milieu, where the battles for and about nationhood were already centuries old when Brazil—and Latin America—started theirs. The ex-centricity of Brazilian naturalism, instead, was something I want to offer as a vehicle for simultaneously contributing to the emerging national idea *and* for staging the interaction of energies which were about to be—or in danger of being—excluded. The politically empowered, positivistic idea of "Order and Progress," because it was a utopian ideological construct, simply eliminated the "people." Naturalism, by attempting to enable the idea of the nation as an entity composed of different people, rewrote the idea of nation from the periphery.

What the professoriate of the time seems to have missed in its reception of these novels is the very intricate and powerful reading in them of the social, historical, and even linguistic situation Brazil was undergoing. Süssekind's recent criticism on the movement provides an interesting development. Although her discussion is aware of how the naturalist text registers political turmoil, she is persuaded that these "apparent differences and divisions in the historical scene are erased in the studies of temperament in the most successful novels of the time" (*Tal Brasil, qual romance?* 173), and that there is a "conservative leap"—*salto conservador*—(93) in Brazilian naturalism when it calls attention especially "to its ideological compromise with nationality, with the rediscovering of the 'nation' of divisions and fractures" (93). Furthermore, Süssekind insists, this compromise "equally associates itself with a blind obedience, with an aesthetics of objectivity, of analogy, of identity, and with a constant appeal to whatever might have the label of 'scientific' or 'national'" (93). In other words, what Süssekind does is to serve up a virtually unrevised version for Brazil of Lukács's famous critique of naturalism as the form of prose narrative which enunciates the imperialist period of capitalism. At the same time she misses the way naturalist writers depict conflict of any sort, the manner they focus on the matter of linguistic appropriateness for the representation of struggle, or the means through which the volatility of gender or race is represented. In short, Süssekind misses everything in naturalism that enables an ideology to be understood as either divided against itself or competing with others.

There is no question that naturalist texts are not free of scientism or positivism. It would be surprising if this were not so. In my own view, what naturalism assimilates is the very source of its power, which would indeed be "conservative" if the matter of some supervening national idea was merely the result in it of regional reactionism. I do not think that this assimilation, however, is the product of an ideological structure; indeed, it may well be better understood, on the contrary, as a reaction against one.[30]

Süssekind, and her mentor, Lukács, would of course not have this be so. At one point, Lukács states the following: "Without an ideology a writer can neither narrate nor construct a comprehensive, well-organized and multi-faceted epic composition. Observation and description are mere substitutes for a conception of order in life" (*Writer and Critic* 143). In fact the matter of some "political agenda" in naturalism is elusive. The novels do not depict class struggle or economic dislocation in any univocal way. The texts seem at times baffled and overwhelmed by ideological pulsions. Although it is clear that hegemony can also be built on the absorption of contradictions, the naturalist novels I analyze in this work do not constitute the basis for a hegemonic instance which would encompass all the different ideological positions which the novels represent. On the contrary, the very fact that these works of fiction have been deemed inferior in traditional Brazilian literary histories—with the exception of Azevedo's *O cortiço*—already demonstrates their basic recalcitrance in the traditional narratives about Brazilian literature, or Brazilian literature as narrative.

The texts I analyze—*O mulato*, *O cortiço*, *A carne*, *Bom-Crioulo* and *Dona Guidinha do Poço*—allow us to describe the means by which the operation of political coding for Brazil was consolidated both immediately before the fall of the monarchy and during the first decades of the republican era. More precisely,

---

[30]Writing about North American naturalists, Walter Benn Michaels makes an interesting distinction which can be useful for our understanding of the complex matter of the ideological structure behind Brazilian naturalist texts. Michaels writes that he felt the need "to transform an argument about the effective relation of certain literary texts to American capitalism into an investigation of the position of those texts within a system of representation that, producing objects of approval and disapproval both, is more important than any attitude one might imagine oneself to have toward it" (*The Gold Standard and the Logic of Naturalism* 19). For the Brazilian naturalists, the visibility their texts brought to their subjects, and even the discussion of their appropriateness for literature, were already effective. Approval by the bourgeoisie was beyond reach. Disapproval, although inevitable, was at least a sign that the texts existed. At that moment, this acknowledgment was, perhaps, the most that the naturalist writers could hope for.

these texts discuss the positionality of blacks, women and homosexuals—or race, gender, and class—insofar as these categories embody history and ideology. Hence, they dramatize what Fredric Jameson calls "an *interference* between levels . . . a subversion of one level by another" which emerges "only when the appearance of formal unification is unmasked as a failure or an ideological mirage" (*The Political Unconscious* 56). The success or failure of such "mirages" is not a part of my argument. *Interference* and *subversion,* however, are, because it is one of the most profound ironies of Brazilian history at the end of the last century that just at the time regional, racial, and sexual differences became, we might say, "formally" unified, a literary practice emerged that challenged the completeness of a national form insofar as it could *only* be comprised of a bourgeois, white, heterosexual subject.

1. *O MULATO*, OR, "O SANGUE GRITAVA-LHE"

By the time Aluísio Azevedo published *O mulato*, he was not a novice writer. He had previously published *Uma lágrima de mulher*, in 1880, and worked as a cartoonist for newspapers such as *O mequetrefe*, *O figaro* and *Zig-Zag*. What distinguishes *O mulato* from his previous work is the fact that in this novel Azevedo seems to have adopted naturalism. For Massaud Moisés the naturalism of *O mulato* is "a balanced naturalism," because in this novel, as well as in the others of the trilogy which made Azevedo famous—*O cortiço* and *Casa de pensão*—he "produced the best of his talent" (*Realismo* 37). Although these three novels do not "obey a consciously structured plan," they have "similar characteristics which allow the supposition of a subterranean connection" (38). Moisés continues:

> Como adepto do Naturalismo, [Azevedo] partiu de bases científicas para analizar uma sociedade considerada decadente, a sociedade burguesa, romântica, brasileira, da segunda metade do século XIX, composta de doentes dos sentidos, sujeitos a imperativos do sangue e do "meio" e a convenções hipócritas. Do quadro social, o romantista escolheu, entre pessimista e revoltado, três chagas e lancetou-as, como um clínico impassível, o problema do mulato, o cortiço e a casa de pensão. (38)[1]

At the time of its publication, *O mulato* was immediately acclaimed by the reading public, but received mixed reviews from literary critics. Writing about the novel, Araripe Júnior stated:

---

[1]As a practicioner of naturalism, [Azevedo] took hold of scientific bases to analyze a society considered decadent, bourgeois, romantic, Brazilian, of the second half of the nineteenth century, [a society] composed of people with diseases of the senses, subject to the demands of the blood and of the 'environment' and to hypocritical conventions. From the social picture, the pessimist and revolted novelist chose three blisters and punctured them, as an impassive physician[:] the problem of the mulatto, the tenement house and the boarding house.

> Ali há páginas tão suaves, tão doces, tão cheias da claridade rosicler, alencariana, que sou levado a crer que o mergulho dado pelo poeta nas águas encapeladas do Estige da nova escola foi apenas à superfície... O novo romancista apresentou-se francamente como é; no período de transição, de lutas, de vacilações. O seu livro, em que se encontra cenas admiráveis, pode-se dizer a crisálida de uma obra realista. Nem lagarta, nem borboleta. (*Obra crítica* 176)[2]

The fact that Araripe Júnior considered the novel a transitional work, struggling to find its way to a new aesthetics is in itself no surprise. Transitional characteristics are the fate of all writers working at a time when an older literary regime is giving way to a new one. What is surprising and extremely fitting for the purposes of my discussion of this novel are the terms Araripe Júnior used for these characteristics—chrysalis, caterpillar, butterfly—all relating to the natural world within an inexorable sequence; that is, a butterfly has to pass through the stages of caterpillar and chrysalis before it reaches its most developed stage and can fly. If as a novel *O mulato* is compared to a chrysalis, what would make a novel a butterfly?

Wilson Martins relates that Aderbal de Carvalho, in a book published in 1894, links *O mulato* to the "struggle against the priests" of the Catholic newspaper *A Civilização*. This struggle, according to Carvalho, was a polemic between Tobias Barreto (and his followers), against the priests (qtd. in *A crítica literária no Brasil* 296). For Massaud Moisés, *O mulato*, "although inscribed within a heated polemic between Freemasons and the Clergy, still shows the effects of the romantic contagion" (*Realismo* 39). Daphne Patai and Murray Graeme MacNicoll write that *O mulato* "is a young man's novel, full of passion, venom, and caricature": "its themes are the corruption of the church, the evils of slavery and racism, the malice, savagery, and political ignorance of provincial life—but also love and desire, the search for one's past, the consequences of a personal and cultural amnesia, the struggle between individual and society" (Introduction 7).

---

[2][In the book] there are pages so tender, so sweet, so full of a rosy, Alencarian light, that I am led to believe that our writer's diving in the stormy waters of the Stygian river of the new school stopped on the surface. . . . The new writer presented himself as he is—in a period of transition, struggles, vacillations. His book, in which one finds admirable scenes, can be considered a chrysalis of a realist work: neither a caterpillar, nor a butterfly.

Indeed, *O mulato*, traditionally accorded the title of the first Brazilian naturalist novel,[3] is a work that reveals that its author did not completely succeed in reaching the depths of the new aesthetics in his attempts to produce a novel. Nevertheless, the novel displays several anxieties about the specific conditions of the country, and several undeveloped characteristics of the young writer Aluísio Azevedo. The novel, he says in his preface to the third edition, was well received by the press in the capital of the empire, in the provinces of the North and the South. Of the critical reception, he says that

> Amparou-me a generosidade de Joaquim Serra, Sílvio Romero, Araripe Júnior, Valentim Magalhães, Lúcio de Mendonça, Capistrano de Abreu, Raul Pompéia, Urbano Duarte, José do Patrocínio, Clóvis Bevilaqua, Tobias Barreto, Adelino Fontoura, Sá Viana, Koseritz e outros muitos escritores de nome brilhante, cuja fulguração, refletindo sobre a minha pobre obra, deu-me um prestígio que nela estava bem longe de ambicionar. Mais de cem artigos se agruparam logo em torno de *O mulato*, e só o Maranhão, a minha província, não deu palavra! (10)[4]

---

[3]José Veríssimo disputes this notion and says that his *Cenas da vida amazônica*, published in 1886 is the first naturalist book published in Brazil (*Teoria, crítica e história literária* 180). Other critics prefer to give to other writers the honor to have written the first naturalist novel. Lúcia Miguel Pereira discusses the subject at length in *Prosa de ficção (de 1870 a 1920)* 119-74. Nelson Werneck Sodré says that Inglês de Souza's *O coronel Sangrado*, published in 1877, or even *O cacaulista*, by the same Inglês de Souza, published in 1876, "reveal the intention and the control of naturalist techniques and processes which Aluísio does not have in his famous book" (*O naturalismo no Brasil* 175). However, Sodré says that the "public consensus" considers *O mulato* the first naturalist novel written in Brazil.

[4]I was supported by the generosity of Joaquim Serra, Sílvio Romero, Araripe Júnior, Valentim Magalhães, Lúcio de Mendonça, Capistrano de Abreu, Raul Pompéia, Urbano Duarte, José do Patrocínio, Clóvis Bevilaqua, Tobias Barreto, Adelino Fontoura, Sá Viana, Koseritz and other brilliant writers whose brilliancy, reflecting itself on my poor work, gave me a prestige which I was far from coveting. More than a hundred articles were soon grouped around *O mulato*, and only Maranhão, my province, did not say a word!

Azevedo's mentioning of these names accomplishes two things: first it shows his acquaintance with the most famous men of his time, and second, the sheer *quantity* of names of people in favor of his work is played against the sheer *lack* of names from his native province, Maranhão. It is true that in the next paragraph he decides not only to mention but to quote in toto the opinion of Euclides Faria of Maranhão, who, in the magazine *A Civilização* of July 23, 1881, suggests that the young writer give up literature and "go plant potatoes" (10) because "agriculture makes the individuals happy and the nations rich! to the sickle! to the hoe! *Res non verba*" (10). It is interesting to notice that in a magazine called *Civilization*, a reviewer exhorts a writer to go back to agriculture, because there his talent would have more application and utility. The paradox in this urging derives from the fact that, it seems, agriculture—the direct dealing with the natural world—is the cure for the evils of a man who deals with the intellectual world. Azevedo's greatest sin, this article seems to say, is that Azevedo leads the "vagabond life of silly scribblings" (10) of a person who "does not believe in Metaphysics and does not respect religion" (10). The disbelief in Metaphysics and the disrespect towards religion were serious enough for Faria to condemn Azevedo to agriculture. Curiously, the split between the Metaphysical—or the cultural, and agriculture—or the natural—is an important component of the novel itself. In fact, nature and culture constitute a battleground on which the story of the mulatto son of a white farmer and a black slave will be fought.

The story consists of the following: Raimundo—who doesn't know he is a mulatto— after graduating in Law in Coimbra, arrives in São Luís and stays at the house of his uncle Joaquim Pescada. He intends to sell his properties and establish himself in Rio de Janeiro, but two factors prevent him from doing so. First, he falls in love with his cousin Ana Rosa, and second, he is denied his proposal of marriage to her due to his racial origin. Besides, Joaquim Pescada has already made plans to marry Ana Rosa to Dias, a Portuguese clerk who works in his commercial establishment. Through his uncle, Raimundo finds out that his mother is a black madwoman, a former slave, and that his father, José do Eito, was murdered in mysterious conditions. These conditions are clarified in some flashbacks through which we learn that José do Eito's murderer was the priest Diogo. Raimundo decides to leave São Luís immediately after he learns about his racially mixed origins, but he is prevented by Ana Rosa, who attracts him to her room and locks the door. Afterwards, Raimundo leaves his uncle's house and goes to live alone in a little house. Later, when Ana Rosa discovers her pregnancy, she and Raimundo decide to elope together. On the night of the elopement, Raimundo is killed by the clerk Dias, who is white, Portuguese, and has the protection of the priest Diogo. Ana Rosa has a miscarriage. The story then leaps to five years after Raimundo's death. Ana Rosa is happily married to Dias and has three children by him. An important point in the story is that, although a mulatto offspring—Raimundo—was produced through the union of a white man and a slave, further racial miscegenation was prevented with Ana Rosa's miscarriage and the murder of Raimundo. That is, both nature and society checked Raimundo's black blood from entering into Ana Rosa's white blood.

Of course concerns about such miscegenation processes were very much on the mind of the scientists of the time the novel was written. Since the eighteenth century they were busy studying what they believed to be a potentially destructive "degeneracy" caused by racial mingling. From an initial preoccupation with defining a typology of the human species, to the assertion of the inferiority and degeneracy of certain races, this science had developed into racial biology. The nineteenth century saw the appearance of a great interest in science, or in scientific empiricism, the popularization of evolutionary biology, and the development of clinical medicine. Stuart C. Gilman writes that by the middle of the nineteenth century

> science became such a dominant cultural idea that it rivaled religion in its explanatory power. Clinical medicine attached science and scientific measurement to the role of "healer," and this ultimately led to an unquestioned legitimacy for physicians. Ironically, this also helped to illuminate the role of the medical community in scientific racism. ("Political Theory and Degeneration" 168)

Nancy Stepan writes that around the same period, "Racial biology . . . was a science of boundaries between groups and the degenerations that threatened when those boundaries were transgressed."[5] Theories ranging from Van Evries's "prop-

---

[5]She continues, about the situation in the United States: "As slavery was abolished and the role of freed blacks became a political and social issue, as industrialization brought about new social mobility and class tensions, and new anxieties about the 'proper' place of different class, national, and ethnic groups in society, racial biology provided a model for the analysis of the distances that were 'natural' between human groups" ("Biological Degeneration: Races and Proper Places" 98). In Brazil, although slavery was completely abolished only in 1888, the great number of mulattoes in society, and their success in some social and intellectual areas was a cause of dismay—or disgust—to some. See for example the case of Sílvio Romero's repeated attacks on Machado de Assis. The clearest example of these attacks appears in his 1897 *Machado de Assis; estudo*

er places" for races, to Nott and Gliddon's ideas on deterioration of races taken to places "unnatural" to them, culminated with the concern about racial mixing and degeneracy (Stepan 100, 101). When the initial idea that the different races belonged to different species and do not produce fertile offspring was refuted by the existence of a great number of fertile mulattoes, scientists turned to the theory of the deterioration of the white race and the dangers of "hybridization."[6] For polygenist Nott, the mulatto was a "hybrid," which was "a degenerate, unnatural offspring, doomed by nature to work out its own destruction" (qtd. in Stepan 107). Behind all these "scientific" statements was, obviously, the fear of the presence, in society, of that element which, according to Davenport, "would combine the intellectual inadequacy of the black with the ambition of the white, which would make him 'unhappy to himself and a nuisance to others'" (qtd. in Stepan 111). In the case of Aluísio Azevedo's *O mulato*, Raimundo's existence and his intellectual development into a graduate from Coimbra, proves that, in fact, mulattoes were viable, healthy and intelligent. It is up to the society of São Luís to see that further "degeneration" is checked right there. But, we must not forget, the São Luís society is not a unitary, univocal entity, and not all members of the society have the same amount of power. Raimundo's fate is inevitably

---

comparativo da literatura brasileira, in which he writes that Gonçalves Dias (one of Brazil's first romantic poets) was a "physical and moral mestiço," and that Machado de Assis was "a typical Brazilian, a clear model of this American subrace which constitutes the differential type of our ethnography, and all his work does not deny either his physiology or the psychological peculiarity that originates from it." Further ahead, in order to make his point even more insulting, he writes: "I don't know for sure if he is a Germanic to any degree; I don't know if in North America, when the mixed bloods (*mestiços*) speak of themselves, they say: we the Saxons. . . . Here in Brazil the greatest proof, the greatest characteristic of their humor is when they say: we the Latins!—It's unbelieavable!" (qtd. in Wilson Martins *A crítica literária no Brasil* I, 274, 315).

[6]According to Nancy Stepan, "attacks on racial typology and the theme of racial hybrid degeneracy began in a piecemeal fashion, starting early in the twentieth century. . ." (115). She then mentions the American physical and cultural anthropologist Franz Boas, who "asserted that the antipathy to race crossings was not biological but social in origin, and that biologically speaking, crosses were not inferior" (115). However, it was only in 1950, with the first *UNESCO Statement on Race*, that biologists for the first time rejected publicly the "well-worn themes of cosmopolitan races and 'hybrid degeneration'" ("Biological Degeneration: Races and Proper Places" 115).

decided through the negotiation among all levels of power and among the individuals who handle it.

A *Brazilian* Tragedy?

O mulato has been characterized since its first publication as being a "romantic plot" spiced up with some rough descriptions of carnal love. When one reads the novel, however, one sees as some of the "spiciest moments" a young woman, Ana Rosa, reading an anatomy book in which the drawings of the moment of childbirth and of "the act of fecundation" (75) are depicted, and later, at the end of the novel, Ana Rosa herself faints and blood streams down her skirts, staining her feet. In the place she falls, there is an enormous red puddle—she has had a miscarriage (186). Early on, other "several miscarriages" are also mentioned. Important as this explicitness about the female body might be when compared to sugared romantic plots and descriptions, the framework inside which the novel was conceived lies not in romanticism, as critic Araripe Júnior says, but in Greek tragedy.[7]

It is important to notice that Ana Rosa, in order to discover the depths of her "female" nature, has to ground this discovery in a book—a book of nature, an anatomy book—thus showing that even at this level, the very awareness of nature has to be mediated through a cultural artifact. What is under discussion is the matter of the origin of nature, and the processes through which a human being can be originated. Raimundo, the mulatto, is the son of a white farmer and of a slave. Although he is freed together with his mother during his baptism, and is later educated in Europe, Raimundo inadvertedly carries with him the stain of his origins. These origins are based on his father's double sin: the bearing of a child of mixed race and the freeing of this child. A third sin can be the educating of this child in Europe, where he studies law and becomes an "illustrious" man, unaware of his humble beginnings.

---

[7]Machado de Assis's third novel, Helena, published in 1876, can also be considered part of this tradition. In *Helena*, as in *O mulato*, the title character is innocently involved in the sins of her parents and pseudo-stepfather, and pays for these sins with her life. In *Helena*, however, what is at stake is not racial but potentially disturbing class miscegenation. For insightful readings of this novel, see Helen Caldwell, *Machado de Assis, the Brazilian Master and His Novels*; Lúcia Miguel Pereira, *Machado de Assis, estudo crítico e biográfico*.

These original sins, over which Raimundo has no control, ground other errors: his return to São Luís, his proximity and consequent attraction to his cousin Ana Rosa, and finally, his getting her pregnant. The sequence of events was determined before Raimundo's story begins, and he is but a victim of destiny. The matter of origins, the working out of these beginnings, which are so important for the framing of the book, are themselves grounded on a previous cultural form. The sequence of errors starts long before Raimundo's birth. His father made his fortune smuggling slaves into Brazil. In itself, this profession already reveals disrespect for the established laws of the country, which, at that time, had complied with international demands for the end of slave importation.[8] Besides being a smuggler, José do Eito was also hated by his own slaves, who turned against him and did not kill him only because one of his youngest slaves, a mulatto girl called Domingas, helped him escape from Pará to Maranhão. As expected, Domingas becomes his lover, and, after several miscarriages (36), gives birth to Raimundo. The boy's beginnings are, therefore, enmeshed in a complicated plot of crime, cruelty, escape and, ultimately, preceded by "several miscarriages." The fact that Domingas becomes José do Eito's lover does not merit one single comment from the author; after all, José is the white man and the owner; she is the black woman and the slave. In a way, their relationship is expected. The solemn freeing of both mother and son during the ceremony of the child's baptism doesn't merit further comments because such practice was fairly common (Schwartz).

The similarities between *O mulato* and *Oedipus* are very strong. What is distinctive in this case is both the role racial determinism plays and the outcome of the tragedy. Unlike Oedipus' story, however, here it is not the mother but the cousin who becomes the unwilling agent who will take the universe back to the old order. Although the marriage between cousins does not constitute incest (at least in Brazilian law), this idea is suggested by the fact that Raimundo, coming from the farm where he was born to a black slave, is cared for by Ana Rosa's mother who gives him the "tender shelter of her motherly wings" (39). Raimundo

---

[8]The first emperor, D. Pedro I, was against slavery, and in 1826 he signed a British-Brazilian treaty on the slave trade. The final ratification of the treaty took place in London in March 1827. However, although this document gave the British navy the power to search and seize any Brazilian-flag vessels suspected of carrying slaves, the complete cessation of the trade only happened in 1850, under D. Pedro II, with the Queiroz Law (Bushnell and MaCaulay, 179). For more details on the complex issue of slave trade in Brazil, see also Robert Conrad, "Neither Slave nor Free: The *Emancipados* of Brazil."

is then given "the premises of her maternity" (39). When Ana Rosa is born, Raimundo is called "the other son"; his acceptance as a child of the family is then complete, and he forgets his black mother (39). On the farm, where he lived among the slaves and was treated as an animal, Raimundo was an animal. His arrival in São Luís, and the care Mariana gives him transform him: "from an ugly to a strong, healthy and beautiful child" (39). His recovery and his transformation are a good omen for the family, because soon Ana Rosa is born. It seems that his "nature" evolved from a previous one to prepare for the birth of his cousin. When, as an adult, Raimundo comes back from Europe, it is this white cousin who attracts him. He cannot be attracted to his own mother because she is marked both by her color and by her madness, and any closer proximity to her would disclose the basis of the father's sin. He is instead attracted to a cousin who once was in the place of a sister.

In the development of Raimundo and Ana Rosa's affair, the text also has to make some adjustments which fit this particular kind of tragedy. The cousins cannot marry not because that would constitute incest of the sort Oedipus committed by marrying his mother. Rather, they cannot marry because that would involve the proliferation of the undifferentiation Raimundo is a living proof of: neither white nor black. It is no surprise, therefore, that when Ana Rosa begins feeling the movements of the fetus in her body, she writes Raimundo a letter asking him to come back to her as soon as possible, to reassure her that they are not "two monsters" (169). The character of this monstrosity[9] derives both from the fact that they have challenged the morality of their time by having sex before marriage and, especially, from the fact that they come from different racial origins, since their race is the main factor in the opposition against their mar-

---

[9]René Girard says that "the marriage of beneficent and maleficent constitutes, of course, the original and fundamental monstrosity, the superhuman creature's absorption of the difference between 'good' and 'bad' difference, that basic difference that dominates all the others" (*Violence and the Sacred* 251). In this case, Raimundo's and Ana Rosa's monstrosity stems from the fact that, by conceiving a child, they are collaborating in the process of racial undifferentiation. Their child will carry both the mother's "white blood" and the father's "black blood." Terry Caesar argues that "monsters are monsters precisely because they are undifferentiated—that is, combinations of various human beings, such as a man and a beast—and for this reason they evoke both awe and dread" ("Beasts Vaulting among the Earthworks" 158). "Awe and dread" would certainly accompany Ana Rosa and Raimundo's child, if it were born.

riage. What is at stake here is the danger of what their relationship can bring for the racial contamination of São Luís's elite.

Raimundo goes through life without knowing his origin and only learns it when it is already too late. Like Oedipus, he was also sent away from his place of birth in infancy. Like Oedipus, too, he comes back a wise man. Only, in his case, Raimundo's knowledge—the law studies he undertook in Coimbra—will not help him learn the truth about his birth: he needs his uncle, José Pescada, to tell him that the mad black woman is his mother.[10] The Sphinx is represented by Amância, an old witchlike woman who once presents him with a mirror and says, "now, look at yourself!" (131). The riddle posed by Amância, like the riddle posed by the Sphinx to Oedipus, refers to the inescapability of genetic laws—Sphinx: man comes from baby (walks on four legs) to adulthood (two legs), to old age (three legs); Amância: a man who comes from one black parent, no matter how white he looks, will still be black. This is so evident a truth for Amância that she believes a mere mirror can show it.

When, after Raimundo's birth, his father marries Quitéria Inocência de Freitas Santiago, "widow, Brazilian, rich, full of religious and racial scruples, for whom a slave was not a man and the fact of not being white constituted a crime in itself" (37), he commits his biggest mistake. Quitéria soon discovers his liaison with Domingas, and almost kills her and the child during one of José's absences from the farm. What follows—Quitéria's departure from the farm, José's later finding her in "intimate conversation" with the priest, and José's killing of the wife—is all of a piece with the feeling of inescapability which will later doom Raimundo to a violent death. A white woman—Quitéria—is killed so that he could live; later on, he will be killed so that a white woman—Ana Rosa—can marry a white man and the unmixed society can continue its claim to purity: one "nature"—black—will be prevented from collapsing into the white "nature."

As the text shows, it is not culture which determines the keeping of mulattoes apart from the white society, since Raimundo does study and acquires a degree in law which enables him to be granted admiration and respect. The keeping of the "black" nature from the "white" nature is trusted to women. What

---

[10]If Raimundo studied law anywhere else, his degree would not be accorded the status a Coimbra degree gives him. When Raimundo arrives in São Luís, he should be automatically given the status of intellectual, since only the best sons of the richest Brazilian families had the chance to undertake law in Coimbra. What happens, instead, is that Raimundo is brought down to the sheer reality of his "nature"—his mixed blood.

is in question is that which constitutes the "nature" of women and distinguishes it from a male "nature" in *O mulato*.

Erratic Desires

The gallery of women portrayed in *O mulato* have in common either chronic or sporadic crises of hysteria[11], and the story itself develops in distinct directions due to these crises. The register of female psychology is always predicated upon the possibility that it can take a life of its own and derail completely.

This hysteria comes disguised as a general "nervousness," or madness. Quitéria, José's white wife, is first described as a "beast" in whose hands several slaves died under torture, hunger, or thirst. During the torture of Domingas she stands, "horrible, drunk with rage, laughing, yelling obscenities, howling in spasms of fury" (37). Domingas, at this moment, "almost dead, moaned, lying on the ground. The disarray of her words and of her gestures already denounced symptoms of madness" (37). Quitéria's action becomes the reason for the development of the rest of the story. It is interesting that it is not the fact of Quitéria's constant cruelty to her slaves in general which determines her murder; rather, it is her cruelty to Domingas and to her mulatto child, and, especially, the specific kind of cruelty, which constitute an unforgivable crime. We are not spared details of the torture:

> Estendida por terra, com os pés no tronco, cabeça raspada e mãos amarradas para trás, permanecia Domingas, completamente nua e com as partes genitais queimadas a ferro em brasa. Ao lado, o filhinho de três anos, gritava como um possesso, tentando abraçá-la, e, de cada vez que

---

[11]Here I am referring to hysteria as it was understood by the ancient Greeks and, also, to the common understanding of the disease, even nowadays. According to Charles Rycroft, "the notion of hysteria derives from the ancient Greeks, who applied the term solely to diseases of women, which were explained as being due to malfunctioning of the UTERUS (hysteron). According to one theory, the uterus is a mobile organ capable of moving about the body and pressing on other organs; according to another, sexual abstinence leads to 'starvation of the womb' or to retention of unused animal spirits which passed out of the uterus leading to disturbance in other organs" (*A Critical Dictionary of Psychoanalysis* 64).

> ele se aproximava da mãe, dois negros, à ordem de Quitéria, desviavam o relho das costas da escrava para dardejá-lo contra a criança. (37)[12]

By burning Dominga's genital parts and shaving her hair, Quitéria is maiming her for the functions of a female, and ultimately usurping the man's prerogative to use a female slave sexually. By ordering the whipping of the husband's son she is also taking his place both as a father and as the owner. Quitéria's brand of hysteria, then, constitutes a reversal of gender roles.

Ana Rosa's hysteria leads to her obtaining what she wants, even when her wishes go against her father's. At first, her crises are erratic, and range from a "violent and nervous satisfaction" (20) when she learns about a new trolley line to Cutim, to nervous attacks after dance parties. These crises reveal, according to the doctor, "the need to make the nest" (33), because she is already a twenty-year-old girl. In fact, this need is an old one, which revealed itself when Ana Rosa was fifteen and felt she needed to have

> ...um marido! "O seu", o verdadeiro, o legal! O homem da sua casa, o dono do seu corpo, a quem ela pudesse amar abertamente como amante e obedecer em segredo como escrava. Precisava dar-se e dedicar-se a alguém; sentia absoluta necessidade de pôr em ação a competência, que ela em si reconhecia, para tomar conta de uma casa e educar muitos filhos. (20-21)[13]

In fact, Ana Rosa does not only "need to make the nest"; she needs to have an *owner*, somebody to obey, somebody who can organize her life as both mistress and slave, and, most importantly, somebody who can "fecundate" her. It seems

---

[12]Lying on the ground, with her legs in the trunk, hair shaved and hands tied to her back, there was Domingas, completely naked and with her genital parts burnt with a live iron. At her side, the three-year-old child screamed like a possessed one, trying to embrace her, and, every time he got close to the mother, two Negroes under Quitéria's orders turned the whip from the slave's back to the child's.

[13]. . .a husband! "Her own", the true, the legal one! The man of her house, the owner of her body, whom she could openly love as a mistress and secretly obey as a slave. She needed to give herself and dedicate herself to somebody; she felt absolute necessity to put in action the competence, which she recognized in herself, to take care of a house and educate many children.

that, without a constraint, a boundary, a grounding for her erratic desires, Ana Rosa can only be hysterical. The nature of her being as a woman can only fulfill itself on the condition of being dominated by a man.

The obsessive quality of Ana Rosa's desire will be the material cause of Raimundo's death. It is the fact that she is "in love" with him and unwilling to give him up that finally gives the clerk Dias the courage to kill the mulatto. Once more, Raimundo is prey to a hysterical woman's demands. The difference is that now Ana Rosa wants to perpetrate what Quitéria wanted to avoid: the proliferation of mulattoes.

Besides these two main hysterics, at least two others can be pointed out: D. Maria do Carmo, an extremely nervous woman who "spoke only about diseases and knew medicines for everything" (48), and Ana Rosa's paternal grandmother, D. Maria Bárbara, who was "a fury! A serpent!," and "beat the slaves as a habit and as a pastime" (17). Maria do Carmo's and Maria Bárbara's position as role models to younger women confirm their power both as older women in their family and as authority figures in their society. D. Maria Bárbara tries to convince Ana Rosa of the horror of having anything to do with a "cabra" (another derogatory term for "mulatto"), whereas D. Maria do Carmo keeps a close eye on her marriageable nieces. Both also have in common an extreme attachment to the things of the church, to which they dedicate the best of their time.

Confirming the popular belief that sexual abstinence is the cause of hysteria, all these women are portrayed as not having regular sexual intercourse. Quitéria, José's white wife, was a widow for an indefinite period of time before she married José; the existence of Domingas as José's lover hints at the fact that he was not always available to his wife. Maria do Carmo and Maria Bárbara are widows, and Ana Rosa is a virgin. Ana Rosa's need for sex is acknowledged even by the "enlightened" Raimundo, who, upon seeing her pacing nervously around the house, cautions her father that "that age is very dangerous for single women . . ." (71). The interesting point about Ana Rosa's personal brand of hysteria is that, because she does not have strong religious beliefs to discipline her need for sex, she transposes it to a more socially acceptable need of having babies. When she sees Raimundo's anatomy book,

> todo o seu ser se revolucionou; o sangue gritava-lhe, reclamando o pão do amor; seu organismo inteiro protestava irritado contra a ociosidade... [P]ercebeu que viera ao mundo para ser mãe; concluiu que a própria

> vida lhe impunha, como lei indefectível, a missão sagrada de procriar muitos filhos, sãos, bonitos, alimentados com seu leite... (76)[14]

At this point, it seems that life—as a kind of demanding husband—is imposing itself on her, demanding that she pay tribute for being a woman, and that she use her body the way only a female can use it—for having a baby. Pereira, commenting on this episode, writes that Ana Rosa, "because she did not marry at fifteen, had funny moods, hysteric crises, and felt mutilated. . . . This little girl from the provinces, raised under the gaze of an overpious grandmother, had moments of impudence which were absolutely improbable" (*Prosa de ficção* 186).

However improbable Ana Rosa's crises and nerves might be, they are insisted on because they are fundamental for the development of the plot: it is one of these attacks of audacity which determines the outcome of the story, when she forces Raimundo to stay with her in her bedroom and locks the door. Her scenes of hysteria do, therefore, confirm the notion that all crises came from her "idle womb." When Ana Rosa is last seen in the novel, she is all tenderness towards the husband, the previously despised clerk Dias, whom she now calls Lulu and who now gives her a child a year. By owning her, the husband provides her with a sense of self-ownership; by getting her pregnant every year, he substitutes her erratic desire with a desire for him; by keeping her fecundatory energies within her white "nature," he prevents the appearance of more undifferentiated beings like Raimundo.

The Proliferation of Mulattoes

It is important to take into account the year Azevedo published *O mulato*—1881—to fully appreciate the daring this novel represents in the society of

[14][A]ll her being rebelled; her blood screamed, asking for the bread of love; her whole body protested against idleness. . . . [She] noticed that she had come to the world to be a mother; [she] concluded that life itself imposed on her, as an inexorable law, the sacred mission to bear many children, healthy, beautiful, fed with her milk. . . .

the time.[15] Laws such as the 1871 "Law of the Free Womb" ("Lei do Ventre Livre") and the 1885 law which mandated every slave above 65 should be free, the "Lei do Sexagenário," although already in the political horizon, did not change the fact that Brazil was still a "slavocratic society."[16] The fact is that *there were* black slaves in white Brazil, and the open acknowledgment of the existence of mulattoes demonstrated the collapsing of boundaries supposed to keep white and black apart. *O mulato* is the first Brazilian novel to discuss a male mulatto who is evidently superior to the white population of São Luís, Maranhão, in the North of Brazil. The question, here, is whether the appearance

---

[15]Of course black and mulatto characters had already made their appearances in nineteenth-century Brazilian texts. In José de Alencar's plays *A mãe* and *O demônio familiar*, they appear very prominently. About the black characters in these two plays, Doris Sommer says that "they figure as future, and desired, absences" (*Foundational Fictions* 156). Colin M. Pierson discusses these two plays and says that, in them, Alencar's "lack of outright abolitionist propaganda in either play is due, in part perhaps, to dramaturgic good sense, and most certainly, in part, to his political conservatism. He did not believe in outright emancipation but rather in the gradual integration of the Negro in the mainstream of Brazilian society as a responsible individual and an equal. Alencar believed that the abrupt freeing of the slaves would be a financial disaster for the economy as well as a personal one for the unprepared slaves themselves" ("José de Alencar: Realistic Dialogue and Characterization in the Anti-Slavery Thesis Play" 166). In fact, both the black mother of the first play and the slave of the second are taken away from the dramatic scene in order to make room for other "more deserving" characters, usually light-skinned ones, or, in the case of Alencar's novel *Til* (1872), Negroes are used to provide a contrast with the Indian hero, to the latter's advantage. In Machado de Assis, blacks usually appeared in the text as background figures who ran errands, opened doors, delivered messages, accompanied the ladies, and were always referred to as "um escravo," or "uma escrava." It is only in last novel, *Memorial de Aires* (1908), that Assis discusses the theme of abolition.

[16]One proof of this is the fact that, as J. H. Galloway points out, even after the "Lei do Ventre Livre" was signed, "most owners elected to employ the children of their slaves . . . until the age 21, rather than relinquish them earlier in return for financial compensation." As for the "Sexagenarian Law," it also was not a significant factor in absolute number of freed slaves: in Bahia, by 1887 "only 1,001 slaves had obtained their liberty under this law" ("The Last Years of Slavery" 588).

of an educated *mulato* instead of a *mulata* really implies a different treatment of the matter of people of mixed races.

In *Preconceito de cor e a mulata na literatura brasileira*, Teófilo de Queiroz Júnior analyzes the novels *Memórias de um sargento de milícias*, *O cortiço*, *Gabriela cravo e canela*, *Corpo de baile*, and *A escrava Isaura* and concludes that the literary treatment of the *mulata* denounces "opposition to racial mixing" (122). In his study, Queiroz argues that the *mulata* is always treated as a stereotype, and her appearance in literature serves as a very efficient way to support the general prejudices against her. Basing his studies on works by Gregório de Matos, Bernardo Guimarães, Manoel Antônio de Almeida, Guimarães Rosa and Jorge Amado, Queiroz studies three hundred years of Brazilian literature and recovers the several works in which the figure of the *mulata* has served as a symbol for male lust without the responsibilities of a family. He makes the important distinction between "preconceito de cor" (color prejudice) and "preconceito de marca" (mark prejudice). He offers as an example Amado's treatment of the granddaughter of Rosa de Oxalá, a character in *Tenda dos milagres*: after three generations of mixing with the whites, the granddaughter deserves a more respectful treatment and the name of "morena" (brunette). At the same time, another woman, Ana Mercedes, a *mulata*, is denied "literary and journalistic talent" (107-11). Queiroz is adamant in considering Amado the most outspoken voice for the capacity of the mulattoes and their inevitable ascension in Brazilian society. However, Queiroz asserts that even Amado is contaminated by prejudices. Such is the case when he portrays the marriage to a "very blonde woman" as the apex of the life of the most accomplished of his mulatto characters: "Tadeu Canhoto marries a very blonde girl(!) from a rich and traditional Bahian family after overcoming resistances and imposing himself on the in-laws due to his qualities and his success" (109).

If this is the case in twentieth-century literature, it is no wonder that in a novel of the nineteenth century a mulatto was not accorded the full humanity a white man was, even when the novel is called *O mulato* and proposes to speak against racial prejudice. In 1881, in a society very much aware of being surrounded by a great number of persons of black and mixed race, the matter of keeping racial mixing under control took the character of civil defense. The social economy could not permit the proliferation of beings who would, like Raimundo, take the privileges of the white children. It is no accident that, early in the novel, Ana Rosa is moved to tears when she sees a little Portuguese clerk, Manuelzinho, a ten-year-old child who works in her father's store. Like Raimundo, Manuelzinho was sent to a foreign country and separated from his mother; but, unlike Raimundo, the white Portuguese boy has to work for his livelihood and endure all sorts of hardships; for him, there was no inheritance other than the colour of his skin. It is also no coincidence that Manuelzinho appears in the story shortly after Raimundo's impending arrival is announced. The mulatto has everything money could buy: a good education, travels, luxury, whereas the white child has to suffer whatever the other Portuguese clerks deem necessary for his education: curses and beatings. These two men, Raimundo and Manuelzinho, can be seen as being at different poles of the same spectrum—race—but their conditions of education, or of class, determine their present situation.

Near the end of the novel, when Raimundo already knows of his racial origin, two older men talk about the situation of mulattoes in Brazil:

> "—Que eles têm habilidade, especialmente para a música, isso é inegável!..."
>
> "—Habilidade?...segredou outro, com o mistério de quem revela a coisa mais proibida. Talento! Coitadinhos dos brancos se (essa raça de mulatos) pilha uma pouca de instrução e resolve fazer uma chinfrinada. Então é que vai tudo pelos ares! Felizmente não lhe dão muita canja!" (141)[17]

The occasion for such conversation is Raimundo's recent departure from Manuel Pescada's house. Since nobody knows the reason, everybody offers a conjecture, and some of them refer to the possibility of a theft, or to his impossible love for Ana Rosa. This conversation among the townspeople reveals the racial anxiety which dominates the lives of all characters and makes space for a kind of social authority which ultimately helps shape the outcome of the story.

Present in the conversation are Freitas, a bureaucrat, Amância, an old woman who prides herself in being the granddaughter of a famous general, the widow Eufrasinha, and a number of other unnamed old men. Except for the old men, the other three are always present in other social occasions where Raimundo's story and destiny are discussed behind his back. Although São Luís is referred to as "the city," within hours stories about Raimundo's arrivals, departures, and slightest movements, are on everybody's lips. The ability of gossip to travel at

---

[17]"That they have ability, especially for music, is undeniable! . . ."

"Ability? . . . said the other with the mysterious way of somebody who reveals the most forbidden thing. Talent! Poor whites if (this race of mulattoes) acquires a little bit of education and decides to cause an uproar. Then everything will blow up! Fortunately (the whites) don't give (the mulattoes) much chance!"

such speed is Azevedo's commentary both on the smallness of the city and, especially, on his view of the articulation of the mechanisms by which gossip binds communities together and leads them to act in unison.

In the case of Raimundo, gossip travels fast because his story is always already known. Actually, nothing about Raimundo is news because the São Luís society already knows *his* story: it is an old story; it has happened before; it will happen again. Gossip functions, therefore, as a form of social control, a discursive practice which defines both the community and its participants. This gossip does not operate through clear acts of force: the participants of these conversations never urge anybody to take a specific step, neither do they ever speak their minds to Raimundo. Rather, by diffusing themselves in different occasions, parties and locations, the members of the gossip mill acquire more force because their meetings are circumstantial and their commentaries seem not to have any visible source (Max Gluckman; Jan B. Gordon). The very diffusiveness of this gossip transforms it into a model of social authority: it represents not the opinion of a single individual nor the beliefs of the people of one household; rather, it is the collectivity itself speaking through the mouths of several characters. And what this collectivity has to say is that Raimundo is doomed. Whether he stole money from Manuel Pescada or not is beside the point. What the gossip means is that he *could have stolen it,* therefore, even if he did not steal, he is guilty of something, because *there is* in him the drive to steal.

This form of social control ends up contaminating even the victim of the gossip, Raimundo himself. In the beginning of the story he "boasted having acquired a great worldly experience; he was at ease speaking about any subject; he not only knew how to position himself in a first class room, but also to give a lecture among young men either in a newsroom or in a theater box" (48). When he arrives in São Luís, Raimundo knows what he wants to do: sell his properties, meet the family, and go back to Rio de Janeiro, where he plans to start a career. On the last day of his life, he wanders through the city, "pretending to be in control of himself," "his heart filled with discouragement" (182). And, confirming the gossip about the mullatoes' inherent danger to their society, towards the end, Raimundo wants to take possession of Ana Rosa as

> uma espécie de vingança contra aquela maldita gente que o envilecia e rebaixava; queria amarrá-la ao seu destino, como se a amarrasse a um poste infamante; queria espalhar bem o seu sangue, porque onde ele caísse, deixaria uma nódoa incandescente; precisava, para sofrer menos,

> ver sofrer alguém... Ana Rosa... com um filho nas entranhas... lhe obedeceria como uma escrava! (182)[18]

Of course the implications of such desire on the part of Raimundo reflect the fear expressed by gossip: the overthrow of the established order and the installation of mulattoes in power. What could pass for the desires of a lover in this story assumes the character of a political statement. On several occasions the text calls attention to mulattoes' power hunger and to the metamorphosis they go through in order to achieve not only a better social position but power itself. For these commentaries, again Azevedo uses a minor character, Amância, who describes going to one of the black people's parties (chinfrins) to look for her husband: "And the best is that these impudents do not address each other by their own names; they call each other by their owners' names!" Of a mulatto called Filomeno, she says: "Well, this one was called 'Mr. President!' The others were 'Judges, Doctors, Majors and Colonels!'"(53). The potential disruptiveness of such behavior for the established social order and the very destruction of society can be summed up in the townspeople's dismay at the fact that "here we have already had a president as black as any of those workers who are carrying a barrel of rum!" (141). The consequences for the hegemony of the white society of Portuguese origin are obvious. Since mulattoes could not be prevented from acquiring—and taking great advantage of—education; since women could not be counted on to keep themselves apart from the mulattoes; since even public opinion could not be forceful enough to maintain mulattoes "in their place," which agent or entity could stop the proliferation of mulattoes and prevent the consequent collapsing of boundaries? The whites in *O mulato* are afraid, and this fear was nothing new in Brazil. Emília Viotti da Costa writes that this uneasiness about the existence of so many blacks and half-castes dates back to the time of the Inconfidência Mineira, because, "for the mass of the people, largely blacks and mixed bloods, the revolution for independence was essentially a struggle against the whites and their privileges." She then quotes from the "Autos da devassa da inconfidência" what one of the indicted blacks said: "We will soon throw out of Brazil those whites from Portugal who wish to take over our country" ("The

---

[18][A] kind of revenge against those cursed people who reviled and degraded him; he wanted to tie her to his destiny as if to an infamous post; he wanted to spread his blood because where it fell an incandescent stain would appear; in order to suffer less, he needed to see somebody suffer . . . Ana Rosa . . . with a child in her womb . . . would obey him like a slave!

Political Emancipation of Brazil" 60). Viotti da Costa also remarks that, in 1821, Carneiro de Campos, "a high officeholder in the administration, a councilor, and subsequently deputy, senator, and minister[,] confessed in a letter to a friend that he feared the heterogeneity of the population, composed largely of slaves" (69). "If there were to be a revolution," Viotti da Costa continues, "blacks and mulattos, having the prospect of liberty, would join forces. The horrors of Saint Domingue, where the blacks had revolted and massacred the white population, would be repeated in Brazil" (70). It seems clear, then, that the fear Azevedo portrays in *O mulato* was very much present in the Brazilian society of the time. The point, at the end of the story, is how to keep this tremendous black and mulatto force from taking over and exacting revenge against the whites. More specifically, how to prevent blacks and mulattoes from "spreading their seed" and continuing the proliferation of people with mixed blood?

Deus ex Machina?

The regularizing entity which prevents the distinct "natures" from collapsing into one another is *not* based on culture, since Raimundo, a mulatto, does obtain a degree in law and becomes a gentleman; it is not based on race either, since the fact that Raimundo is a mulatto does not prevent Ana Rosa from falling in love with him. Control is not managed by gender: the undeniable power Ana Rosa's grandmother has is not adequate to dominate the girl and prevent her from approaching (and seducing) her mulatto cousin, and even the father—supposedly the most powerful person in the family—cannot convince her of the undesirability of her union to Raimundo. And finally, control is not in the hands of the elements who constitute the gossip mill; after all, they cannot either prevent anything that happens or change the course of events. The text makes clear that the axis where all the strings are tied, the place from where all power emanates is the priest Diogo—a metonymy for the power of the Church—under whose authority all other powers pale. Throughout the development of the plot of *O mulato* it is clear that it is the priest Diogo who is behind all evils. He engineers the destruction of Raimundo's father and of Raimundo, and he maneuvers to have Ana Rosa marry Dias. It is under the guise of a religious festival that the important members of São Luís society—the ones responsible for the gossip—gather at the farm of Ana Rosa's grandmother. In addition, all powerful women of the story have as a common denominator their extreme attachment to the things of the church. Diogo is, ultimately, the real Sphinx of *O mulato*. He poses the riddle, which is *not* about Raimundo's origin, but about Raimundo's end. Diogo controls the alignment of "natures" in *O mulato*; his is the power which impedes the collapsing of different natures into one another; his is the force which can stop the proliferation of mulattoes and other "monsters" alike. In other words, it is Diogo, or, rather, what Diogo represents, who codifies the flows of desire, recodes them, and sees that no flow is left unattended, undammed, unchanneled, and, especially, unregulated.

However, the text does not say this without the screens provided by the females' hysteria, or by the doctors' prescriptions of marriage for the young ladies, or even by the description of gossip in a small city. Although in the end of the story the universe returns to its original order—mulatto man is punished with death for daring to get involved with white woman, and white man marries white woman—the theme of heredity, so dear to naturalism, is put to question. Good and evil, in *O mulato*, are not dependent upon racial origin or heredity: Raimundo, a mulatto, achieves great intellectual knowledge, despite the fact that his mother is mad; Ana Rosa, although white, is capable of forgetting her former feelings for the clerk Dias and, not only marries him, but seems to totally forget Raimundo and his sacrifice for her. Heredity, in this case, is replaced by historical and social contingency: the mulatto is killed because he dared to love a white woman in a country where slavery existed. The outcome of Raimundo/Ana Rosa's affair, however, does not refer simply to social determinism in general; rather, it points very precisely to a very Brazilian social and historical situation.[19]

The novel, however, has not been seen as a critique on the whole Brazilian society. From Euclides Faria, who in 1881 considered the story an attack on the people of São Luís, to Massaud Moisés, who in 1984 wrote that the murder of Raimundo dramatizes the "only way the middle class of São Luís of Maranhão

---

[19]This subject was of course in the minds of other Latin American writers. A case in point is the mulato Sab, of the novel of the same name, by Cuban writer Gertrudis Gómez de Avellaneda (1814-73). About Sab, Doris Sommer writes that he cannot be a father, despite the fact that he combines the contrasting virtues of disinterested sweetness and energetic dedication: "What Sab lacks is any claim to *legitimacy in the patriarchal symbolic order*, precisely because he has no father and no patronym, because there is no space in his language in which he could occupy the place of the name of the father" (*Foundational Fictions* 119, my emphasis). In Raimundo's case the very fact that his father's name is finally known remits him to the fundamental problem with his existence, an existence engendered in a double bind of illegitimacy: he was born out of wedlock and out of an accepted racial economy.

found to solve the impasse,"[20] the novel has constantly been seen as a commentary about the place where the story happens. In a sense, by insisting on the specific provincial location of the story, as opposed to the social and historical circumstances of the country which enabled such stories to happen, this kind of criticism at once diminishes the range and trivializes the depth of Azevedo's critique. Doris Sommer, discussing the role of women in what she calls "foundational fictions," states that they are a metonymy for the wilderness, and that they constitute "the object of man's desire and thus the source of his guilt as a conqueror" ("Irresistible Romance" 83). Because she stands for the land, woman necessarily has to be husbanded, fecundated, so that, from the union, babies can be born. The populating of the country becomes necessary both as a biological and political project. "Unproductive eroticism," Sommer writes, "is not only immoral; it is unpatriotic and often related to the barbarous prehistory of the American mission and can be represented by 'unnatural' women for whom sensuality is power" (87). Indeed, if in *O mulato* Ana Rosa stands for the land, she has to be married in order to produce the babies necessary for the continuation of the project to populate the country. She does produce a first baby, but this child is the result of her union to a member of the race considered "perennially immature" (in Sommer's words)—a mulatto. The necessary result is, therefore, the death of the child simultaneous with the death of the child's father. To permit this child to live, in literary terms, would be equivalent to permitting the spread of undifferentiation—and, ultimately, of monstrosity—in real terms.[21]

---

[20]In *Realismo*, of 1985, Massaud Moisés rephrases his comment on the novel: "*O mulato* tries to be the picture of the Maranhense bourgeoisie dominated by color prejudice and by religious dogmas. From this point on, the mulatto functions as a counterpoint, or, rather, a scapegoat for a society overcome by an irrational panic when it sees its values of blood threatened" (40).

[21]If we consider the different fate of another fictional baby, Moacir—the child of Indian priestess Iracema and Portuguese warrior Martim, in José de Alencar's *Iracema*—we can see why Moacir survives whereas Raimundo and Ana Rosa's child is not even born. Moacir's mother represents a Brazil that is fecundated by a European father. Such arrangement can be acceptable—or inevitable—in the economy of nation building, because the virgin American land could not help but being inseminated by the European conqueror. Furthermore, the child is taken to Europe by his white father. There, Moacir will presumably be completely whitened and educated. Raimundo and Ana Rosa's child, on the other hand, reverts the economy of fecundation: it would be the result of a white

The appearance of black characters in Brazilian literature can be dated from Gregório de Matos (1623-1696), who tirelessly praised the beauty of the black woman.[22] The union of whites and Indians had already been portrayed in Brazilian literature in José de Alencar's *O guarani* (1857), and *Iracema* (1865), and of a white man and a mulatto woman in Bernardo Guimarães *A escrava Isaura* (1875). However, in that novel the choice of the woman is a white man's prerogative: both Leôncio and Alvaro are white and belong to the landed elite. In *O mulato*, on the other hand, Ana Rosa is disputed by a white Portuguese and a mulatto, and the outcome of the dispute can only be the destruction of the latter so that a family made up by Ana Rosa and Dias can come into being. Ana Rosa's initial love for Raimundo, besides being the emblem of the upsetting of the racial order, also points to her basically subversive character: she wants the power to choose a husband, and her choice threatens her father's plans to make Dias his partner. The family started by Ana Rosa and Dias has both elements in place: the patriarchal husband/father and the submissive wife/mother are white. As pointed out by Sommer, "the interdiction against exercizing power, usually coded as pursuing sexual desire, goes for any mix of Old World habits and the new acquisitiveness, because they threaten reasonable, chaste love and may block the liberal project of commercial development" ("Irresistible Romance" 88). Because at the end of the novel Ana Rosa marries the right (white) man, she can form with him a familial unit which does not upset the racial and commercial balance of society: the children born of this marriage will not be monsters. This marriage also maintains the economy of gender roles which, if permitted to deviate from the established norm, would ultimately provoke the undoing of the whole structure of distribution of power in society.

On a first level, it seems that the tragedy in *O mulato* stems both from the fact that Raimundo was seduced (fell in love is not appropriate) by a white woman, thus upsetting "proper" boundaries of race and gender. However, it cannot be forgotten that the first tragedy, the one which gives existence of all others, is slavery. The foremost first sin, which occurred even before José do Eito's sin of taking a slave for lover and later manumitting both her and their

---

woman's fecundation by a mulatto. It would be, in a sense, as if Europe was fecundated by Africa.

[22]Gregory Rabassa has a very detailed study on the subject. See *O negro na ficção brasileira*. Also of interest is Macedo, *Crônica do negro no Brasil*, and Marotti, *Black Characters in the Brazilian Novel*.

son, is the sin permitted—and encouraged—by the State: the appropriation of human beings for a life of bondage and degradation. Raimundo's death at the hands of his murderers remains as a symbol of the crimes that the State condoned and others—the Church among them—took advantage of under the pretense of the blacks' and mulattoes' immaturity, sensuality, or outright danger to white society.

2. *O CORTIÇO*, OR, "A FEROZ ENGRENAGEM DAQUELA MÁQUINA TERRÍVEL"

In *O cortiço*, sometime after Pombinha has her first menstrual period, Bruno, one of her neighbors in the tenement house, asks her to write a letter for him. This task is part of Pombinha's work in the place, where most people, illiterate, have to rely on her ability with words in order to contact their friends and relatives. Her function as letter writer, accountant for the washerwomen, and reader of newspapers, has made her the darling of the tenement house; everybody likes her; everybody gives her little presents. The request for another letter is nothing special for Pombinha, who, until now, restricts her letter writing to copying almost exactly what the neighbor is dictating.

Up to this point in the story, the text has set the characters in place and delineated the environment, a tenement house in Rio de Janeiro. The tenement house was built by João Romão and former street vendor Bertoleza. The negress is Romão's first victim, because he makes her believe he has bought her off from her owner. From this moment on, she works exclusively for João Romão and helps him start and enlarge the tenement house. Among the tenants who occupy the little houses are: Rita Baiana, Pombinha and her mother, and the Portuguese Jerônimo and his wife. Pombinha leaves the tenement house to get married as soon as she has her menses; she later abandons the husband and becomes a prostitute under the protection of Léonie. Jerônimo abandons his wife for Rita Baiana. João Romão who, since the beginning envies the rich neighbor Miranda, in the end obtains wealth and becomes engaged to Miranda's daughter. João Romão's fortune and his engagement to Miranda's daughter transform Bertoleza into a nuisance which has to be discarded. João Romão contacts her legal owners and they come to take her away. To avoid being taken as a slave again, Bertoleza kills herself.

For this discussion, the moment Bruno dictates to Pombinha—somewhere in the middle of the story—is of fundamental importance, because she is suddenly startled by the man's tears. The narrator informs the reader that "only after the sun blessed her womb, after she felt the first feminine cry from her entrails, had she eyes for these violent and painful miseries to which poets gave the beautiful name of love." It is also at this moment that "[h]er intellectuality, like her body, blossomed unexpectedly, suddenly reaching a lucidity which delighted and surprised her" (100). In this episode in Pombinha's life, several crucial points for the understanding of the novel are mentioned. In his analysis of *O cortiço*, Affonso Romano de Sant'Anna says that the fact that the just-blossomed woman owes her newly acquired poetic sensitivity and intellectual awareness to the powers of the sun aligns the novel's philosophical discourse to one of the foundational characteristics of naturalism: thermodynamics (*Análise estrutural de romances brasileiros* 99-100). The Compact Edition of the *Oxford English Dictionary* defines thermodynamics as "the theory of the relations between heat and the mechanical energy, and of the conversion of either into the other." Here, the thermodynamic medium which awakes Pombinha to the "life of the spirit" is the sun. Even more important—in a novel so conscious of and so insistent on the effects of the environment—it is a *tropical* sun.

For Pombinha, once called the "flower of the *cortiço*" (31) this awakening at the same time both levels and differentiates her from her fellow young women living in the tenement house. It is understood that, because she has had her period, now she is a full grown woman who can therefore lead a full sex life; she is in the same position as women of the tenement house such as Florinda, Rita Baiana, Leocádia and Piedade. She can finally marry Costa, the fiancé who has patiently waited for her to become a woman. On the other hand, becoming a woman thrusts Pombinha into a realm different from the one where her neighbors dwell: she becomes more than a sexual subject—she can think, she can reason, she can write, she can feel what the others cannot: she becomes a rational and literary subject. Here, again, as before with Ana Rosa in *O mulato*, a woman sheds her previous "nature" and enters a new realm of her existence at the moment she is dealing with written matter. The difference in the two novels, besides the obvious one that Ana Rosa does not produce, but consumes written matter—Raimundo's anatomy book—and Pombinha is producing a textual account of another person's desires, is that Ana Rosa is awakened to the life of her *female, procreative*, flesh, whereas Pombinha is awakened to the life of female *sensitivity*. In *O mulato*, the metamorphosis is a passage to nature through culture, and in *O cortiço*, to culture through nature.

Nature and Culture: Where Does One End and the Other Start?

Affonso Romano de Sant'Anna locates the main tension in *O cortiço* within the axis "nature and culture," and divides the action in two units, the São Romão tenement house and Miranda's house. The tenement house "is defined by its elementary composition. Its elements have a primary constitution and are at the level of nature and instinct," whereas the unit 2, Miranda's house, "shows the operation of more well defined cultural rules. Among its elements there is a co-existence based on a malleable regimen of exchanges, which indicates the pre-dominance of interests other than the merely instinctive" (*Análise estrutural* 99-117). Although Romano de Sant'Anna is aware that such a division might be a simplification, he insists on it and leaves aside important narrative undercurrents which point to a more complex structure for the novel. By placing Miranda's two-story house *(sobrado)* on the side of culture and delegating the tenement house to the realm of nature, Sant'Anna is taking for granted a definition of "nature" and "culture" which he does not elaborate. It seems the critic is equating wealth and "aristocracy" to culture; and poverty to instinct and nature. On the contrary, I want to argue that both the tenement house and the two-story house represent culture in two different manifestations.

From the outset, the tenement house is based on the exploitation of an unpaid worker, the negress Bertoleza, who believes that her lover, João Romão, has used her savings to buy her off from her owner. Certain of her freedom,

> Bertoleza representava agora ao lado de João Romão o papel tríplice de caixeiro, de criada de amante... Às quatro da madrugada estava já na faina de todos os dias, aviando o café para os fregueses e depois preparando o almoço para os trabalhadores de uma pedreira que havia para além de um grande capinzal aos fundos da venda. Varria a casa, cozinhava, vendia ao balcão da taverna... à noite passava-se para a porta da venda, e...fritava fígado e frigia sardinhas... E o demônio da mulher ainda encontrava tempo para lavar e consertar, além da sua, a roupa do seu homem. (14)[1]

Whatever João Romão and Bertoleza save goes to the buying of a lot at the back of the tavern, where he later builds three little houses. These houses, made with the material stolen from nearby construction sites, are the beginning of the tenement house. The economic system operating in João Romão and Bertoleza's

---

[1]Now, at João Romão's side, Bertoleza performed the triple role of clerk, maid and lover. . . . At four a.m. she was already going through the daily chores, preparing breakfast for the customers and later preparing lunch for the workers of a stone-pit that existed beyond the bushes at the back of the tavern . . . at night she posted herself in front of the store and . . . fried liver and sardines. . . . And that devil of a woman still found time to mend not only her clothes but her man's as well.

partnership is based on a system in which the relations of employer-employee are regulated by trust and mutual respect. In this case, however, Bertoleza does not have the status of an employee. The fact that she is, first, a slave whose papers have been falsified without her knowledge, and second, a woman without a husband to protect her interests, makes her a choice prey for a man whose only ambition in life is to get rich. She thinks she has bought her freedom from her former owner, but Bertoleza is still a slave, and, as such, subject to the laws which regulate slavery. In fact, a slave could buy his/her liberty and receive a *carta de alforria*—the instrumento of manumission. Stuart B. Schwartz writes that "in this document the slave owner identified him- or herself and then identified the slave being freed." Also part of the instrument was the slave's description: "age, color, place of birth, and, on rare occasions, the slave's occupation. . . . If the master received money or some other form of payment in return for the grant, it, too, would be noted." Schwartz notes also that

> *libertos* (manumitted slaves) would normally keep the original letter in their possession, since the illegal enslavement of people of color was always a danger, but in order to protect themselves and to fully legalize the transition of status, the document was then taken to the nearest notary and transcribed in his register as well. ("The Manumission of Slaves in Colonial Brazil" 605)

In *O cortiço*, because the character Bertoleza cannot read, she does not understand the paper that João Romão shows her as being her *carta de alforria*. She has no reason to mistrust him, since, in order to make the fakery look even more convincing, João Romão even pastes (used) stamps on it (14). Because João Romão is white, Portuguese, and the proprietor of a tavern, he is endowed with a certain social superiority, and any relationship he might have with Bertoleza always implies her exploitation as "beast of burden" (animal de carga). The fundamental irony of the situation lies in the fact that, actually being a slave, Bertoleza works like a slave who believes herself free.

From this starting point, João Romão develops a series of other ways of exploiting both his workers and his tenants. The money from the rent of the first three houses and the profit from the counterfeited goods he sells at the tavern are used to buy more space, more material, and to build more houses which in turn are rented to other people who will be exploited by the inn-keeper. From the capitalization of Bertoleza's work, João Romão begins to generate a machine which has the ability of reproducing itself.

Despite the instability and contradictions in the text's conception of force, it does not take much interpretive pressure to see that the two thermodynamic principles embodied in João Romão and Pombinha represent two different kinds of force: one economical, the other sexual. These two forces are at times collapsed into one another: they represent the two fundamental principles of thermodynamics[2]—the law of conservation and the law of dissipation—which in *O cortiço* are depicted as gendered forces, seen sometimes as atavistic and sometimes as economic forces. But the relations between these two sets of force are not harmonious or even coherent. The novel can be seen as a study of a bipolar situation in which a girl—Pombinha—becomes a woman, and a man—João Romão—becomes a capitalist. Yet, each one of these elements is made up of

---

[2]To speak about thermodynamics is, of course, to speak about force, or, as it came to be known later, energy. First formulated in the 1840's as the Law of Conservation of Force, it provided the theoretical framework for a rush of scientific activity which yielded dramatic results, and one of the most important of them was the correlation of scientific branches which had traditionally been separate. This was an exciting era of scientific discovery, and although the concept of force has had little importance in the twentieth century science, its effects on science, language and culture of the last decades of the nineteenth century are undeniable. One of the most prominent thinkers who helped make the concept known was the English philosopher Herbert Spencer, who conceived a cosmic scheme based on a combination of what he called "the persistence of force" and an equally idiosyncratic concept of evolution (contemporaneous with Darwinism but independent of it). "Force" was the fundamental element of Spencer's universe, and he envisioned force's innate and peculiar pattern of evolution (and devolution) as the pattern of universal process, whether it be in the formation of the solar system, the industrialization of nineteenth-century Europe, or the development of artistic style. Other philosophers and scientists contributed to the study of the concept in mid-nineteenth century. Among them, the most prominent were Sir Charles Lyell, Lamarck, Laplace, Darwin and Comte. Although not considered the most important or even the most famous of these men in other countries, Comte was extremely important in Brazil. His attempts at discovering the laws behind social and intellectual phenomena led him to develop the Law of the Three States, which asserted that the human mind naturally passed through three stages in attempting to develop any branch of knowledge: the Theological, the Metaphysical, and finally the Positivistic. For a more detailed discussion of thermodynamics and its influence on the literature of the nineteenth century, see Martin, *American Literature and the Universe of Force*.

other complex angles which are illuminated both by and through the other characters in their relationships with João Romão and Pombinha.

The outcome of João Romão's actions (and sensitivity to monetary gain) is his introduction into the financiers' world, his title of viscount and his marriage to Zulmira, Miranda's daughter, whereas the result of Pombinha's sensitivity is, on the other hand, profitable prostitution.

It is important to indicate that the significance of such different destinies can be better understood if we consider both characters as tropes for very specific tensions and anxieties of the last decades of the nineteenth century. João Romão, by becoming a capitalist, outgrows the *cortiço* and joins the bourgeoisie; Pombinha, by becoming a prostitute, also outgrows the *cortiço* and becomes a rich woman. These could easily be seen as *gender* distinctions. Nevertheless, I believe that they are also a commentary on the role of the artist as well as a political statement. Pombinha and João Romão are marked by their individuality, which imposes on them a law of truth which each one must recognize in the other and which others must recognize in them. Michel Foucault, in "The Subject and Power," states that "[t]here are two meanings of the word 'subject': subject to someone else by control and dependence; and tied to his own identity by a conscience or self-knowledge. Both meanings suggest a form of power which subjugates and makes subject to" ("The Subject and Power" 781). Both João Romão and Pombinha are subject to the different demands of their individuality—to get rich and to overcome powerlessness, respectively—and both these demands at the same time liberate and tie them to their environment, the tenement house. The question, here, is whether the tenement house is a unitary system.

A Battle of Natures

On a macro level, the universe of the tenement house is opposed not to the two-story house, but to the stone-pit João Romão buys with the profits from his inn and from the rent of the little houses. The tenement house is described as a place where "one felt in that sanguine fermentation, in that healthy hunger of weeds which sink their vigorous feet in the black and nutritious mud of life, the animal pleasure of existing, the exhilarating satisfaction of breathing on earth" (29). At once, the people at the *cortiço* are vegetal and animal, and what unites these two forms of life is their "satisfaction of breathing on earth." Although the persons who inhabit the tenement house existed before in other places, it is here that they come to life as a group. There is a close relationship between who they become and what the tenement house becomes. At this point, the group of little houses acquires the characteristics of the human life that dwells there.

The fact that João Romão initiated the construction of the houses with the money he stole from Bertoleza makes the *cortiço* a "child" which comes from male and female—the tenement is the product of their joint effort—hence the *cortiço*'s animal characteristics. The way the elements within the *cortiço* procreate is characteristic of the way animals reproduce. That accounts for the fact that, up to the end, the tenants continue having children : "The number of children increased at a frightening rate!" (141). Between the time the individuals move to the *cortiço* and their production of new individuals, they go through the rituals of animal reproduction: they are like "eels" (31), have "dogs' teeth" (31), "a monkey's lustful eyes" (32), "cobra" (57) , and "a bull's neck" (35), and they use their animal characteristics to attract each other, so that they can continue with the routine of reproduction, and then, "in that swampy and smoky earth, in that warm and muddy humidity it started to swarm, to grow: a world, a live thing, a generation which seemed to sprout spontaneously, right there, from that mud, (and it began) to multiply like larvae in manure" (21).

An important characteristic of this description of the place where the inhabitants of the *cortiço* procreate is that it is "humid, muddy, smoky." The abundance of water in the place is one of the main points of interest for the families who move in the tenement house. João Romão makes sure the facilities are attractive: "the price of each tub, with water, five hundred 'réis'. . . . The tenants were given privileges and didn't pay anything to wash" (21). Because the tenement house is characterized as a place which has "little houses and tubs for washerwomen" to rent (21), it becomes more than a mere place where people live: it is a work place as well: "and that became a big laundry, excited and noisy, with its stick fences, its vegetables and its three-by-four little gardens which looked like merry spots amidst the blackness of the overflowing tubs and the white cotton tents open over the shiny wash boards" (21).

The nature of the work—washing—determines its predominantly feminine constituency. The only male in the group of washerwomen is Albino, who, unlike his companions who are described as "weeds," is appropriately described as being of the color of "cooked asparagus." It is significant that he is the only member of this group of workers who seems unlikely to be capable of reproduction. Albino, definitely effeminate, has "thin, lifeless brown hair which fell in a single line to his soft and thin neck" (32). He always prefers to live among the washerwomen, with whom he was so familiarized that they treated him as a person of their sex; in his presence they spoke about things which they wouldn't expose in front of other men; they even made him the confidant of their loves and their infidelities (32). The presence of Albino among the washerwomen is more than a mere attempt at portraying an effeminate man: it demonstrates the incongruence of his position as a male working in a female profession, and it exposes the fact of his sterility. Unlike his fellow workers, Albino cannot reproduce himself. The ability to reproduce is tied to the freshness and the rawness which the women display. Being cooked, he is dead; being a man among women, he is a victim of abuses; being unable to relate to women as the other men do, he gets "ants in his bed" (141). In this environment where the reproductive, sexual forces are in full display, Albino functions as a reminder that women and men had better keep within the *boundaries* of their sexual roles.

The other macro-universe, the stone-pit, is placed beyond the "hot and scalding grass" (37) near the tenement house. The stone-pit is fundamentally different from the place where the washerwomen work. The terrain is "made of gravel" (37), where "shoes got dirty with a white dust" (37), and the stone-pit itself "blinded whoever tried to look at it directly" (37). Here the place is not "muddy" nor "swampy" anymore—it is dry, full of gravel, and the sun's rays do not activate the humid exhalations it does at the terrain around the tubs: now the sun is "thirsty" (37) and seems to have drunk the river "in one gulp" (37). Nevertheless, in spite of the dryness, the stone pit embodies the same effervescence seen at the tenement house. The difference is that here, "there was no woman to be seen" (39). The pit:

> dava a idéia de uma atividade feroz, de uma luta de vingança e de ódio. Aqueles homens gotejantes de suor, bêbedos de calor, desvairados de insolação, a quebrarem, a espicaçarem, a torturarem a pedra, pareciam um punhado de demônios revoltados na sua impotência contra o impassível gigante que os contemplava com desprezo, imperturbável a todos os golpes e a todos os tiros que lhe desfechavam no dorso, deixando sem um gemido que lhe abrissem as entranhas de granito. (38)[3]

---

[3][G]ave the idea of a ferocious activity, of a fight of revenge and hatred. Those men, covered with sweat, drunk with the heat, maddened by the sun, breaking, teasing, torturing the stone, looked like a bunch of devils revolted by their impotence against the insensitive giant which contemplated them with scorn, undisturbed by all the blows and by all the shots which they discharged against its back, permitting them to open its granite entrails without uttering any moan.

The text's representation of the stone-pit as a place where the granite entrails of the earth are opened—by men—to bring forth its contents, is a very similar process to midwifery. The difference is that here, the "fecundation process"—the transformation of the stone-pit into a lucrative enterprise—is made by João Romão alone, without Bertoleza's help, and the "entrails" of the giant are extracted without the concourse of women.

In 1852 obstetrician and gynecologist Augustus Kinsley Gardner published *The History of the Art of Midwifery*, in which he argues that,

> [F]rom the foundation of the world man has been born of women; and notwithstanding that his inventive genius has discovered steam, the great Briareus of the nineteenth century, and has harnessed him to his chariot, and sends lightning to do his bidding over the almost boundless extent of the world, yet we cannot hope that any change may be affected in this particular. (1)

Despite man's advances in science, we understand, he is still tied to a secondary role in the procreative process. The solution, therefore, is to either reinforce his role in the process, or play it down by overwhelming the world with much more formidable inventions—such as machines, steam power, and, ultimately, an economic system completely outside the realm of the home. It is not coincidental, therefore, that the images at the stone-pit are fundamentally obstetrical: the earth "delivers" the fruit of its entrails under the direct influence of men who, at this moment, reassert their positions of middlemen who do not need—nor admit—the presence of women. The striking differences between the tenement house and the stone-pit invite some important questions about the gender of force (or the force of gender), about the ultimate force which organizes the universe of *O cortiço*, and, finally, about who or what embodies this force, if it can be embodied.

This novel carries out this discussion through a not very prominent character—Léonie—who lives outside the tenement house but keeps close ties with it. Her house constitutes a space which is not very visible in the story, since it is located "downtown." It might also be little visible because it constitutes an interdicted space. It is a prostitute's house, and only quick glances at it and at the activities performed in this space are permitted in the text. However, I believe the main reason for the interdiction is that it is a "female" space, to which not even the narrator himself has unlimited access. This "femaleness" is due to the fact that it is a woman who *owns* the house, and to keep the house she *exploits* men. Although potentially unsettling, the exploitation of men alone would not make Léonie's house into a completely interdicted space. It is the way Léonie handles her sexuality which baffles the (male) gaze of the narrator.

When Lúcia Miguel Pereira says that "[when it started] to be experimental, and therefore scientific, the novel began to have importance and dignity; it stopped representing a pastime like embroidery" (*Prosa de ficção* 30), she probably is referring more to the kind of depiction of a male gaze existing in *O cortiço* than to an experimental and scientific method. In this novel, on two occasions the narrator uses the plural "nós" (we) in situations when he is clearly referring to a "we" composed only of men. On page 17, when describing the Mirandas' sex life, he says that the husband "discovered [in the wife] the wonderful enchantment which the prostitutes, well trained [*amestradas*] in the science of the venereal pleasure, use to intoxicate *us* (*nos* embebedam)" (emphasis added). On page 61, describing Jerônimo's physical feelings after he has had a strong medicine, the narrator says that this feeling is similar to that "relaxed feeling which precedes sexual satisfaction, when the woman, having had *us* wait for her for some time, finally gets close to *us*, avid for kisses" (emphases added). Besides the fact that these "we's" certainly were not found in the embroidery room, what these passages show is a display of male boasting of superiority: the prostitutes are "well trained" (in Portuguese the verb "amestrar," used here for prostitutes, is the same used for animals: an "animal amestrado"—an animal trained to do tricks at the command of its owner). By whom are they trained? Or, more importantly, *for whom* are they trained? They are trained exclusively to please men. In the passage of page 61, the "we" is so sure of its (his) domination over the woman that he is "relaxed" while he waits for the approach of the woman. She, on the other hand, no matter how long the masculine "we" waits, will surrender in the end, "avid for kisses."

It seems clear that the narrator is trying to inform his presumably male reader that women exist, to a certain extent, to please man, and to complete him. In *The Daughter's Seduction*, Jane Gallop discusses female sexuality and the phallus. At a certain point, she states:

> The phallus is both the (dis)proportion between the sexes, and the (dis)proportion between any sexed being by virtue of being sexed (having parts, being partial) and human totality. So the man is 'castrated' by not being total, just as the woman is 'castrated' by not being a man. Whatever relation of lack man feels, lack of wholeness, lack in/of being, is projected onto woman's lack of phallus, lack of maleness. (22)

In Azevedo's text there is a sharp separation between the "male" reader and the "female" object of this reading. Why is it so important, in a text with so many powerful feminine characters, to state women's dependence on men? I believe that, because the text presents Pombinha, Léonie, Rosa Baiana, and even Leocádia, as strong women, the narrator needs to find some sort of relief for his male readers. As Jane Gallop says, "Woman is . . . the figuration of phallic 'lack'" (22). A solution for the anxiety provoked by the sight of female lack is to transform the female body into a fetish whose parts or whole function in place of the missing phallus. If we apply this explanation to *O cortiço*, it is easy to recognize the narrator's attempts at fetishizing first Léonie—her body, her clothes, her house—and later Pombinha: both women are meant to "complete" man (they are trained, *amestradas* to please man). When they seem to have far too much power, they have their bodies transformed into fetishes. For instance, when Léonie appears at the tenement house, her uniform is a veritable semiotic extravaganza: "Her silk dress of the color of steel, adorned with incarnate bull's blood," her red umbrella seemed "suffocated under a cloud of pink lace," her extravagant hat had an "immense scarlet trim [which had] a whole bird glued to its top"; she wore "capricious jewels, scintillating with fine gems"; her lips were "painted carmine; her eyelids stained violet" (74). The blond prostitute seems at once to embody all the forces which constitute the spaces of the tenement house and of the stone-pit: the color of her silk dress—steel— resembles the material of the pick-axes the stone-pit workers use to "deliver" the stone from the earth; the dress is embellished with a male animal's blood (Jerônimo, the strongest man in the tenement house, is compared to a bull); her umbrella has the spirit of aerial things—clouds; her hat appropriates a whole bird (Rosa Baiana is compared to an *ave de arribação*—birds from the Northeast which fly South every year); her jewels are made of precious stones (stones—of a lesser kind—are the decisive boost for João Romão's fortune); her violet eyelids at the same time suggest Pombinha (the flower of the tenement house) and Rosa Baiana, whose whole body smells of "a sensuous odor of clovers and aromatic plants" (45); and finally, her carmine lips suggest the devouring—or vampiristic—capability of the woman, who can engulf all the others' features in an anthropophagic feast. And all this, the narrator is quick to propose, is done for man's benefit.

Yet, in a novel so obsessed with reproduction, it seems that Léonie is sterile. At least, in spite of her busy sex life, she has no children. The only child she is seen with is her goddaughter Juju, whom she enjoys dressing up more like a doll than like a living human being. A characterization of Léonie as sterile is, however, inappropriate. Like all the others, she procreates, but, unlike them, she processes this procreation in a different way. For example, when she seduces Pombinha (92-5), she awakens the young girl's female body—Pombinha menstruates for the first time after the episode at Léonie's house—and this awakening is responsible for Pombinha's later realization that "she would never give herself to the husband who (wanted to) have a friendly, loyal and dedicated companion"; she knew that she could never consider him "a superior being to whom one gives a whole life; she would never be enthusiastic about him, and therefore would never love him, even though she felt capable of loving somebody—if only there were any men worthy of that" (101). In the afternoon she spends with Léonie, upon seeing photographs of respectable men who let the prostitute dominate and exhaust them completely, Pombinha understands

> sua superioridade sobre esse outro sexo, vaidoso e fanfarrão, que se julgava senhor e que no entanto fora posto no mundo simplesmente para servir o feminino; escravo ridículo que, para gozar um pouco, precisava tirar da sua mesma ilusão a substância do seu gozo; ao passo que a mulher, a senhora, a dona dele, ia...desfrutando o seu império,...prodigalizando martírios que os miseráveis aceitavam contritos, a beijar os pés que os deprimiam e as implacáveis mãos que os estrangulavam. (100-1)[4]

And, although she cannot understand this strange and powerful domination women have over men, Pombinha likes the idea of her own strength, of her own value. She smiles at the thought of exercising this power, and "in her smile there already were fangs" (100). At this point, the first stage of Léonie's self-reproduction is accomplished: Pombinha reaches the knowledge Léonie has known all along. Pombinha is a kind of daughter to whom Léonie has bequeathed her understanding of the world and of men. The second stage is when Pombinha abandons her husband and goes to live with Léonie: "the serpent finally won: Pombinha, hypnotized, walked straight to the serpent's mouth" (154). At this point, Pombinha—"little dove"—becomes a serpent like her creator Léonie: "with only three months of public bed, she had made herself as expert as the other

---

[4]Her superiority over that other vain and braggart sex which judged itself the lord and which had nevertheless been put in the world to serve the feminine; a ridiculous slave who, in order to have some pleasure, needed to take the substance of his pleasure from his own illusions, whereas the woman, his lady, his owner, enjoyed her empire . . . lavishing sufferings that the poor bastards accepted contritely, at the same time kissing the feet which stepped on them and the implacable hands which choked them.

. . . her lips never touched anybody without drawing blood; she knew how to drink, drop by drop, from the mouth of the most avaricious man, all money the victim could have" (155). The metamorphosis is now complete. Pombinha, under the guidance of Léonie—"leonine"—enjoys the power of her newly acquired identity: like João Romão, Pombinha exploits her "clients." The difference is that the adulterated goods João Romão sells to his tenants come from industries, whereas Pombinha employs her own body as a means of extracting money from men. In the end, there is a sense that both the former inn-keeper and the prostitute exploit the same people, because João Romão lends money at high interests to people who frequent the financiers' corner and Pombinha "draws blood" from her clients, rich men who certainly also frequent the financiers' corner.

Pombinha has reached maturity and has equaled herself to João Romão. It is time for a new step. From this point on, like Léonie before her, Pombinha has to start thinking about her self-reproduction. The chosen girl is Senhorinha, who, not coincidentally, also writes letters for the tenement house people and lives with her mother. Senhorinha becomes "her favorite protegé," to whom Pombinha "devoted special attention, similar to the attention she herself once inspired in Léonie. The chain continued and would continue unendingly; the tenement house was preparing a new prostitute in that poor, forsaken girl who was becoming a woman at the side of her drunken mother" (155).

The three modes of reproductive process—the tenement house, the stone-pit and the prostitute's house—manage to highlight the rivalry between the "male" and "female" forces involved in the process. However, although this aspect is relevant to the understanding of the novel, this absolute differentiation of gender powers can function as a way of discussing other issues pertinent to the nineteenth century in general and to Brazil of the nineteenth century in particular. In other words, difference itself may be representative not only of the body as power, but of a strategy of control in a more general economy of body *and* power. In the struggle between these two different—but not necessarily mutually exclusive—fields, the ultimate goal is to command the process of representation. In the case of *O cortiço*, the success in the struggle will be the power to represent the tenement house as an urban living space. In a wider scale, the novel is arguing that the victory in the battle of representation will mean the possibility to determine a specific kind of subject—a Brazilian subject—that will constitute the hegemonic semiotic register for the whole nation.

The representation of the *cortiço* as an urban living space, or as a "city" (opposed to, say, a more rural area) calls to attention the specific characteristics of this space as both a confluence of forces previously scattered in geographically distinct regions, and as an optimal condition for these forces to fight one another over issues of hegemonic representation. Thus, in *O cortiço*, several examples of power keep being presented and studied in order to be dismissed, or to, at least, have their importance relativized in face of other power sources. In the passage where Pombinha realizes that men are mere "bastards" she evidently implies that their control over women as sexual beings can be used by women themselves against male power. The death of the boy Augustinho, Machona's son, in an accident at the stone-pit, is the confirmation of the powerlessness of the male-female power which produced that child. Another source of power in the novel is represented by the old witchlike woman, Paula, called Bruxa,[5] who sets fire to the tenement house in two occasions and ends up dying in one of the fires. In sum, if men's power is nothing, women's power is nothing too, and if the combination of the two is reduced to death by the giant stone-pit, the only thing left, it seems, is the awesome force of nature—the sun and the stone-pit—which revolutionizes human beings' lives and understanding of themselves and which ultimately kills them. Nature is then the colossal mother who has the power of life and death over her children.

However, there is another part of the universe depicted in *O cortiço* which seems to be untouched by these vagaries of mother nature: the financiers' corner at the heart of the big city. The tenement house is the place where nature exacts a payment in the form of a relentless preservation of the species, whereas the financiers' world is governed by different rules. João Romão, initially only interested in his inn and his tenement house, now "started being frequently seen on Direita Street, in the commercial district and in the banks. . . . He started to get involved in large-scale speculation; he accepted stocks from companies with English names and only lent money guaranteed by good mortgages" (104). It would seem that, by accepting stocks and lending money, João Romão is only working on a scale bigger than the tenement house, where he also mortgaged his tenants' salaries and possessions. However, the presence of English companies

---

[5]Paula's characterization as an old "cabocla" who has "teeth cut by blade . . . straight hair, still black in spite of her age" (30) suggests that this woman is either Indian or of Indian origin. The word "cabocla," in Brazilian Portuguese, can mean just a woman from the backlands, but in this case, because Paula still has "black straight hair" in spite of her age, it might signal her Indian origin. It is also significant that she is presented as mysterious and capable of special prayers to cure several diseases. In *O cortiço*, where the main interest falls on the white, black and mulatto characters, this fire setting "cabocla" character might be a reminder of those Indians who have to live repressed in darkness, in solitude, but whose destructive power should not be overlooked.

among his new customers signals an economic scale far beyond the tenement house and the Brazilian financiers' world. Now João Romão is doing big business, he is dealing with a corporate world which is unknown to the other characters. The implication of the brief depiction of this world in the novel is twofold: it is brief because the narrator himself does not know much of it; it has to be depicted because, like Léonie's house, albeit at a much higher level, it constitutes a space of interdiction.

This interdiction, of course, is operative not due to moral reasons; this space is interdicted to those who do not have wealth. Since most of the characters in the story, including the rich neighbor Miranda, do not know the rules for inhabiting that space, the best way to convey its power is to leave it unclear, diffuse. In fact, the financiers' world, blurred to the eyes of common people, represents the ultimate power which commands their lives and all destinies. The way to best represent this unrepresentable entity is through its contraries—the people and the people's lives. In a novel so interested in the subject of force, the financiers' corner in downtown Rio de Janeiro (then the capital of the Brazilian empire) is the very center from which all force emanates, but it is an "absent" center.

"The Most Fateful Force"[6]

In *O cortiço*, the energy for the opposite of the financiers' center—the tenement house—is given by food, and, even more importantly, by the rituals of preparation and sharing of this food. These rituals are divided into three different kinds that represent three different purposes, or three different modes of production and consumption. All of them are embodied by female characters who represent different economic and ritualistic spaces.

In the beginning of the novel, Bertoleza is depicted as "a thirtyish black woman" (13) who makes João Romão's food. She sells porridge in the morning and fried fish at night in order to pay "commission" (13) to her owner, a blind old man who "ate the skin of her body" (13). When she begins her relationship with João Romão, she continues selling the same foods and begins preparing the meals for João Romão's customers, besides preparing João Romão's food. Throughout the novel, Bertoleza will always be associated with the preparation

---

[6]This line is a quotation from Weber's discussion on capitalism and its structures as "the most fateful force in our modern life" (*The Protestant Ethic and the Spirit of Capitalism* 117).

of food: she cleans fish; she fries fish; she cooks porridge; she is always "dirty and full of cinder, always without Sundays or holidays, always around the stove, stirring pans and filling plates" (45). By the end of the story, when João Romão is rich and wants to rid himself of Bertoleza in order to marry Miranda's daughter, the black woman's neck resembles "thick blood sausages" (149). In the last scenes of the novel, Bertoleza kills herself with the same knife with which she has been scaling fish. By cutting her belly open, and falling on the spot she was working, Bertoleza accomplishes her final metamorphosis: her intestines mix with those of the fish she has been cleaning. At this point, she has come full circle and gone another level lower: from the beginning of her life, when her owner "ate her skin" to the time she becomes a "blood sausage," to the final stage when, mixed with fish remnants, she is not even appropriate for consumption anymore. Once she ceases to have any utility for the system which exploits her, she becomes completely "inedible." For the author, Bertoleza's death is the dramatization of the destiny of those who do not recognize the law of truth in themselves. Since she does not have self-consciousness, or, rather, since she is not conscious of her slavery, she is subject not to her own identity, but only to João Romão's designs.

The other place where meals are produced and consumed is Miranda's house, where the meals are prepared by two maids, Isaura and Leonor. Besides Miranda, his wife Estela and the daughter Zulmira, two other people live in the house: Botelho, described as a "parasite," and Henrique, the son of one of Miranda's customers, who is studying in Rio de Janeiro. Miranda despises the wife, whom he knows betrays him, and ignores the daughter, who he thinks is the child of her mother's lover. Estela hates the husband. Botelho, the parasite, listens to both spouses' complaints about one another, and, although diplomatic enough not to tell what the other says, takes advantage of the whole disharmonious situation by flattering each in turn. Even though Botelho is described as a poor devil who, despite everything, is nothing more than a hopeless old man, his characterization reveals a kind of social economy bred both by his financial situation and by his former status of slave trader. He still has "all his teeth, but so spent that they seemed to have been filed down all the way to half their size" (24). The filed teeth connect with other images which define Botelho as a voracious parasite: he has "claws of a bird of prey" (25), he has "round glasses which magnified his pupil and gave to his face the expression of a vulture" (24). The result of all this eating, this devouring, is inescapable: "now old, eaten by disillusion, full of hemorrhoids, [Botelho] sees himself without any resources and [has to] vegetate in Miranda's shade" (25). Like Bertoleza, Botelho has also been "devoured," but, unlike the black woman, the old parasite has also devoured (that explains his filed, worn-out teeth and his hemorrhoids), and now, at least, has the comfort of a haven where he can be a "vegetable."

A special meal is prepared at the two-story house when Miranda receives the title of baron. For this especial occasion, new servants are hired, a great amount of food is bought, marinated and cooked; fireworks are prepared. Still, none of the family members does more than walk among the servants who, later on, "hung a skinned goat by the neck; it had its legs open, sinisterly resembling a child whom somebody had hanged after peeling off its skin" (78).[7] The feast happens, as foreseen, with many people coming to commemorate Miranda's title. It is not a meal, however. People come to dance, to drink, to laugh and, especially, to show off their costumes. There is no description of a set table and of people sharing the food the servants took so long to prepare. Instead, the guests only drink, because the servants still continue "running from the dining room to the cellar and to the kitchen, carrying glasses in silver trays" (84). Although the feast is prepared *by* the poor, it is not prepared *for* them; therefore, it is not theirs. The people for whom the feast is prepared gorge themselves in an orgy of consumption of things they do not produce. It is significant, however, that there is no mentioning of *eating*, only of *drinking* in Miranda's party. It seems that, like Libório, an old Jewish man who lives at the cortiço, they do not have teeth and have to eat their food in liquid form.

The connection between Miranda's guests and Libório can be made through both his avidity for saving money and his incredible appetite: "it caused terror [to see] his implacable, furious and devouring jaw; that enormous, avid and bony

---

[7]This passage seems to be a foreboding of the episode when Marciana tries to grab her daughter's seducer in order to make him marry her. The seducer, a clerk, is forced by João Romão to escape during the night leaving with him all the money he has earned during the time he has worked at the inn. The innkeeper, as soon as the news of the girl's pregnancy is known, promises her mother that either his clerk will marry her daughter or pay her dowry. The day after the discovery of the girl's pregnancy, Marciana goes to the inn in order to see the clerk; João Romão tells her his employee disappeared during the night. Asked about Florinda's dowry, João Romão first protests that the clerk fooled him and ran away during the night, and later threatens to evict Marciana from the tenement house (70-74, 78-79). The almost perfect juxtaposition of the scene of a hanged goat resembling a child whose skin has been peeled off and the cheating of both the clerk and Marciana is a repetition of the same theme and a suggestion that Miranda also cheats people; after all, the expression for both "to skin" and "to cheat" is the same in Portuguese: *arrancar a pele*.

chin without one tooth, which seemed [capable] of swallowing everything starting with his own face. . ." (53). Like Libório, Miranda's guests devour what they have not prepared, and it seems, with more savagery for that same reason.

The third place where meals acquire a ritualistic characteristic is the tenement house itself. The tenants are always buying food at João Romão's store and sharing spices and recipes among themselves. In the novel, the tenants have two ritualistic meals. The first one happens when Rita Baiana returns from her three-month long carnival festivities. Sweet basil leaves and a vanilla stick in her hair, her arrival already presages a commemoration: "She came accompanied by a boy, who brought on his head an enormous basket filled with the things she had bought in the market: a big fish looked through the lettuce leaves with its sad and foggy look, contrasting with the gay colors of the radishes, the carrots and the slices of red pumpkin" (45). She is enthusiastically greeted by all neighbors, who come to hug her and ask about the carnival. After greeting everybody, Rita "told her companions that at night they would have a guitar feast. They could count on that!" All neighbors cheer:

> Esta última notícia causou verdadeiro júbilo no auditório. As patuscadas da Rita Baiana eram sempre as melhores da estalagem. Ninguém como o diabo da mulata para armar uma função que ia pelas tantas da madrugada, sem saber a gente como foi que a noite se passou tão depressa. Além de que "era aquela franqueza! Enquanto houvesse dinheiro ou crédito, ninguém morria com a tripa murcha ou com a goela seca!" (47)[8]

During the dinner, some neighbors gather at Rita's house, others at the Dores's house. There is great noise in the two houses, and, "once in a while, from the window of one of the houses one of the women appeared, calling the neighbor to give her a full plate, thus exchanging between themselves the specialties they prepared" (50).

The analyses between food and group discussed in Susan Kalcic's essay "Ethnic Foodways in America: Symbol and Performance of Identity" is pertinent

---

[8]This last bit of news caused real joy in the audience. Rita Baiana's parties were always the best ones in the tenement house. Nobody was like that devil of a *mulata* to organize a feast that went until late at night; without anyone realizing, the night was gone quickly. Besides, she was "so generous! While there was money or credit, nobody died with an empty stomach or with a dry mouth!"

to the function of food in *O cortiço*. Kalcic writes that "Food has two social functions, namely: to maintain the cohesion of the society and of the group within it; to determine, in part, the relation of the individual to the society and to the smaller group within it" (48). The food Rita Baiana gives her neighbors has the function of maintaining the cohesion of the group, whose members can get together and eat and commemorate. The Miranda household contrasts with the tenement house: although the food is shared, Miranda's family get-together, instead of being reason to commemorate, is just a pretext for heated arguments or for social showing-off. Even though the act of eating is communal, there is no communion of ideas or feelings. Bertoleza, on the other hand, is never seen eating: she prepares and serves, but never eats—she is an outsider to this reunion and cannot share in its benefits of solidarity and friendship.

In the same article, Kalcic also points out that food can be used to express rank or hierarchy within groups: "Eating together or eating similar foods in similar ways are expressions of equality. . . . Reserving certain special foods . . . would clearly indicate a lack of equality" (49). By having the servants prepare, serve, and not share the food, the Mirandas show their separation and their lack of friendship towards them. Bertoleza, in turn, prepares and serves the food, but does not benefit from the amiable society which forms around the tables at the inn. In *Rabelais and His World*, Mikhail Bakhtin states that the banquet and other popular festive forms are linked to abundance and contentment, forces that oppose death. In the act of eating man "tastes the world, introduces it into his body, makes it part of himself" (281). Eating symbolizes joy and triumph because it is an affirmation of man's dominance over death: he devours it, without being devoured himself. In the tenement house, where people are compared to animals and weeds, the fact that these people can feast on *food* shows their inherent superiority over their environment, because they can come together as a group and celebrate even when the only reason for celebration is the mere fact that they are alive and together.

The feast which follows the communal dinner extends and enlarges the meaning of the dinner itself and becomes a mythical celebration of life. The tenants' feast resembles ancient celebrations in honor of Dionysus and Eros, who are characterized by and as the forces of transformation and renewal. Dionysus, a divinity who dies and rises again from the dead, also represents the passage from chaos to cosmos, in an analogy to the decay and rebirth of vegetation.[9] The

---

[9]For an excellent discussion of the meaning of Eros and Dionysus, see Frazer, *The Golden Bough* 38-67.

renewal characteristics of Rita's party also relate it to the Roman Saturnalia. These Roman festivals were "outbursts of the pent-up force of human nature" (Frazer, 58), and celebrated the merry reign of Saturn, a period of abundance, peace, and communal property, and was marked by a mad pursuit of pleasure, together with an inversion of roles and ranks between master and slave (Eliade 68).

Bakhtin, writing about the theme of carnivalization in literature, points out that carnival is the festival of the time that destroys and renews everything (*Problemas da poética de Dostoiéviski* 107). Rita's arrival, the communal dinner, and the party which follows it signal the profound changes the tenement house and the inhabitants are going to experience. This revolution in the dwellers' lives will transform the tenement house from a *locus amoenus* into a place which "hardly seemed what it once was" (140): after Rita's party couples separate, people die, people are killed, and Rita Baiana, at once the spirit and the embodiment of the happiness in the tenement house, moves away with Jerônimo, Piedade's husband. Piedade, until then an example of industriousness and honesty, becomes a drunk who is frequently raped. Her daughter, Senhorinha, has to leave the boarding school and settle in the *cortiço*. After these occurrences, the tenement house begins to resemble a "ferocious machinery in that terrible engine"—*feroz engrenagem naquela máquina terrível*—which "never stopped (and) already started swallowing a new social group which would little by little let itself be completely dragged to its interior" (141).

This last image again reflects the imagery of the communal dinner, at once reinforcing and contraposing itself to it. In the beginning, the people of the tenement house, under the influence of Rita Baiana, feast together to commemorate her arrival and the plain joy of living. In the end, the tenement house, now a machine, swallows new people, whose bodies will be consumed in order to produce more energy for the machine itself. The capitalization of force, throughout the novel, places it as a contrary to female generative powers in favor of, not exactly a "male generative power" per se, but to a generative power which is set in motion exclusively by men: machines, science, and the financiers' world. Thermodynamics, in *O cortiço*, is not represented only by the sun's force, which the narrator says is "the only cause for all that" (127). Rather, it is represented also by the emerging forces of the capitalist machine, which is always hungry, always greedy, always ready to "swallow" a new group of people, and which is capable of operating reproductive consumption; that is, of reproducing itself and its means of reproduction in order to continue consuming people.[10]

Now there are no longer feasts (patuscadas) held outside in the communal yard: in the new *cortiço*, dinners and dances are held inside the houses, and only the people formally invited can participate. The betterment of the tenement house, and the arrival of people from a slightly higher social class looks like progress. It is order and it is progress.

The awareness of force demands that the *concept* of force be bound in order to avoid more proliferation beyond that which already exists inside the tenement house. What ultimately happens is that the boundaries of the tenement house are broken and the incipient seeds of power operating within it spill on to the surrounding spaces: Jerônimo and Rita go to live elsewhere, and Pombinha moves downtown to become a professional prostitute. The forces engendered within the *cortiço* seem to be loose. The traditional ways of containment of these forces—gender, race, and class—are dissolved within the space of the city. The process works itself in the other direction too: now the tenement itself is open to the arrival of a great number of well dressed strangers, bohemians, students, artists and Italians. The São Romão Inn becomes "São Romão Avenue," as a sign of definite adoption of the city and of recognition of the *cortiço* as an undeniable space within the city. It can not be otherwise, because to lag behind in modernization means to revert to the stage where the rival *cortiço* "Cabeça-de-Gato" still remains, completely discredited, raided daily by the police. The ultimate force, the one represented by João Romão and the financiers' corner, is the only one which can see to the containment of the disperse forces within and without the *cortiço*. This containment is operated through the use of human beings them-

---

[10]Ronald E. Martin writes that, in the nineteenth century, it was up to the imaginative writers to explore the significance of the starkly mechanistic views on a human scale. "In addition," he says, "the universe-of-force viewpoint was of a piece with some of the Western world's most pernicious social practices and theories at the turn of the century. Force-thinking generally rationalized racism, class superiority, imperialism, the acquisition of wealth and power, and veneration of the 'fittest.' Explicitly a philosophy of inevitable and benevolent progress, of an evolutionary hierarchy in which some individuals or societies are by nature superior because of their higher organization or greater concentration of power, it is meshed only too neatly with the rampant forms of Social Darwinism and helped to obscure from otherwise responsible men the obligations and even the possibility of social reform" (*American Literature and the Universe of Force* xv).

selves as fuel for the invisible engine which controls the social (and financial) machine.

O cortiço, a novel written only nine years after *O mulato*, displays not only more craftsmanship in its writing, but an acute awareness of both the present situation of the nation and the effects of the emergent capitalistic system whose power is based on the power of machinery, science and stocks. It presents a disenchanted view of the role of the artist in this society where the signifiers of forces are in constant shifting. It is no coincidence that the most literate character, Pombinha, becomes aware of her destiny as a prostitute at the same time she acquires her poetic sensitivity. The ultimate force which dominates all characters is not the tropical sun or the tropical nature; it is not the races or the mixing of them either. What dominates all the levels of significations and all the mechanisms for the formation of subjects is the force which emanates from a system which is far beyond the understanding of all characters except João Romão. It is a force made of stocks, mortgages and foreign titles. The humanity of the tenement house, as the humanity of the nation Azevedo witnessed, is but another source of energy for the maintenance of that machine. The struggle among these elements to represent themselves in this newly created universe, and not the bipolar structure "nature" versus "culture," is the main subject of the novel.

3. *A CARNE*, OR, "DE MÃOS ATADAS"

About thirty pages from the end of *A carne*, the description of the spicy details of the affair between the main characters Lenita and Barbosa is interrupted to give way to the description of an accident in the sugar-cane factory:

> Um crioulinho deixou-se prender nos cilindros do engenho, e teve o braço esmagado. Ao ver a mísera criança segura, atraída pelo revolver lento, implacável, do mecanismo bruto, o pai dela, o negro moedor, tomou uma alavanca de aço que achou à mão, entalou entre os dentes dos rodetes. Ouviu-se um grande estalo metálico, um tinir sonoro de ferros partidos, o engenho parou. (134)[1]

This disaster only merits from the owner of the farm the comment that the little black boy "was [born on] September 28; [he did not mind] his becoming a cripple, it would mean little loss" (134). The accident at this point of the story, when Lenita is already pregnant by Barbosa and the farm is in its most critical moment of production, constitutes the crucial encounter between the private and the public spheres which, I believe, is the most important subject of this much-reviled novel of Brazilian naturalism. This chapter will be a four-step reading of this moment and what it represents. I will concentrate first on the critical reception to the novel both in the nineteenth and twentieth century; next, I will discuss how the matter of language is handled in the novel especially when speech itself is already contaminated by so many other languages and linguistic registers; the following section will be a meditation on the appropriation of the feminine body as a site where history is written; and finally I will discuss matters related to the moment of convergence between public and private history. First, the story: Lenita is the beautiful daughter of a rich widowed man who brings her up sur-

---

[1]A little black boy was caught in the cylinders of the engine and his arm was crushed. When he saw the poor child caught and attracted by the slow, inexorable movement of the brutal mechanism, his father, the negro in charge of the cane crushing, took a steel fulcrum he found nearby [and] stuck it among the teeth of the contraption. A loud metallic groan, the tinkling of broken iron was heard--the machine came to a halt.

rounded by mentors and books. Since childhood, Lenita quickly learns everything, from languages to sciences to sports. After her father's death, the grieving Lenita goes to spend some time at the farm of one of her father's old friends. There she hopes to rest and to evade her many suitors. When the farmer's son—Barbosa—arrives at the farm, he and Lenita discover their common interest in science and in hunting, and they begin spending time together. Although Barbosa is separated from his wife and therefore cannot marry Lenita, she decides to become his lover. Later, when she discovers her pregnancy, she abandons Barbosa, marries one of her former suitors, and leaves for Europe, where she will give birth. Upon receiving a very cold letter from Lenita, Barbosa kills himself with a paralyzing drug.

The Monstrous Childbirth, etc. . . .

A carne, Júlio Ribeiro's second novel, had a unanimous reception among the critics of the time it was published: it was considered obscene, silly, exaggerated, and criticized from all points of view. The object of this criticism ranged from the dedication of the novel to Émile Zola in the Introduction (in French), to the supreme fault of not being "national" or not "national enough."

José Veríssimo, in an essay written in 1889, when comparing *A carne* to Aluísio Azevedo's *O Homem*, says that the latter, "perhaps the only lasting work of Zolean naturalism in Brazil, despite the subject and the principles which inspired it. . ." accepts it as "a respectable book." The same, however, "cannot [be said] about *A carne*. It is the monstrous childbirth of an artistically diseased mind" (*Teoria, crítica e história literária* 188). This criticism, written by one of the most eminent Brazilian critics at the time the novel was published, seems to have dictated the tone for its appreciation from that point on. Even Sílvio Romero, Veríssimo's rival in Brazilian criticism, agrees and joins him in the chorus against the novel. Strangely enough, however, Romero's criticism, as well as much that was subsequently written about the novel, is against one of the characters, Lenita, who, according to him, is "a *precious* and pedantic girl, for whom disoriented readings and studies did not prevent the thrusts of the *flesh* and who eagerly prostituted herself with the first male who came near her and gave her lessons" (*Teoria, crítica e história literária* 114) (italics in the original).

Veríssimo himself also goes on to criticize the character Lenita. For him, she is constructed of the "most corny and vulgar romanticism," and, "far from being a realist or naturalist creation as the Author imagines, Lenita is the least true of all feminine creations of Brazilian novel" (*Teoria, crítica e história literária*

188). To prove his point about Lenita's inadequacy in terms of Brazilian literature, Veríssimo compares her with Alencar's feminine characters, to the latter's advantage, because Alencar's women,

> apesar do exagerado idealismo do grande romancista, são, não há negar, brasileiras por uma porção de circunstâncias que me falta espaço analisar. Têm a simpatia fácil, o amor a um tempo recatado e namorador, a sentimentalidade um pouco piegas mas sincera, o fundo inconsciente de honestidade burguesa da Brasileira. Em Lenita nada disso. (188-89)[2]

In the next paragraph, Veríssimo speaks of Lenita as a "Herbert Spencer in skirts." He soon clarifies that these faults of the novel come from several sources:

> É com uma puerilidade de romancista novo a quem falta absolutamente a intuição artística da arte em que se atreve a ensaiar-se, que o Sr. J. Ribeiro nos apresentou a sua heroína, e o seu prurido de alardear conhecimentos científicos—que é uma nota predominante do livro—não nos poupa sequer a estafadora nomenclatura das diversas prendas que a exornam. E não foram só as ciências que ela... estudou—senão que nenhuma das literaturas mais notáveis lhe é estranha, como não é leiga em nenhum dos exercícios viris... Esta Minerva é também Diana. (188)[3]

Therefore, Lenita is not good because she is not realistic enough and also because she is not like the best romantic heroines created by Alencar. What is it, then, that makes this character so offensive to the critics? Is it the fact that she

---

[2][I]n spite of the exaggerated idealism of the great writer, [they] are, no one can deny, really Brazilian, due to a number of circumstances which I do not have the space to analyze. They have the easy friendliness, the love at once bashful and coquettish, the unconscious background of bourgeois honesty of the Brazilian woman. There is nothing like that in Lenita.

[3]It is with the puerility of a young writer who totally lacks the necessary artistic intuition of the art in which he dares to try his hand that Mr. J. Ribeiro presented us his heroine; and with his craving for boasting scientific knowledge—a predominant note in the book—he doesn't spare us even the tiresome nomenclature of the several talents which embellish her. . . . She studied not only the sciences, but also, none of the most notable literature is strange to her, and she is not ignorant of any of the male exercises. . . . This Minerva is also a Diana.

is not "friendly", not "bashful" not "bourgeois" or not "honest" or all these together? What is it that makes one writer's heroines better than the other's? Veríssimo's answer, in the same essay, is that the author of *A carne* does not try to

> justificar por uma causa aceitável o procedimento de sua heroína... o A. no-la apresenta, com um aparato pedantesco de fisiologia fácil, dominada pela obsessão da carne, comida pelo desejo do homem. Essa fisiologia fácil a que me refiro, apanhada, ao que parece, muito pela rama dos trabalhos *à la portée des gens du monde*, tem levado poetas e romancistas modernos a uma concepção, ao meu juízo, inteiramente falsa, a respeito das fatalidades fisiológicas da carne. (191, italics in the original)[4]

Hence, it seems that Veríssimo's main objection to the novel is centered mainly on the facile, pedantic, and physiological way Júlio Ribeiro developed one character, Lenita. He also cannot understand the presence of certain episodes in the novel: "In his narration there isn't even any unity and the episodes occur without necessity. What is the use, for instance, of the scene of the punishment of the fugitive negro, of the scenes of witchery with the old black Joaquim Cambinda? What kind of connection [do these scenes] have with his novel?" (191).

However, it still seems that the greatest objection Veríssimo has about Lenita is the education Ribeiro accorded the character with. Hers is a "fantastic education (*educação de fantasia*) such as a woman has never been given in Brazil and very few have received outside here" (188). In the last paragraph of his critique, Veríssimo writes that the synthesis of *A carne* is "Jules Verne mixed with Émile Zola—appropriating from him what he has of least estimable—and a copious mixture of Bocage's 7th volume" (192); that is, the novel is science fiction *and* French naturalism *and* comedy.

The only critic of the time the novel was published who was less mordant in his analysis was Araripe Júnior, who says that Ribeiro, in *A carne*, "equipped

---

[4][J]ustify the heroine's actions with an acceptable cause. . . . The author presents her to us with a pedantic apparatus of an easy physiology, dominated by the obsession of the flesh, eaten by the desire for the male. This easy physiology to which I refer—acquired, it seems, from the surface of works *à la portée des gens du monde*—has taken many poets and novelists to a conception, which I believe completely false, about the physiological fatalities of the flesh.

by modern science, conscious of the excellence of Zola's method, tested his muscles and, following the line of his disposition, set himself far beyond the expected." Unfortunately, however, as Araripe says, "in all his audacity and in all paths he went through, (the author) was followed by a lot of things *que hurlent de se trouver ensemble* (*Obra crítica*, italics in the original)." Unlike Veríssimo and Romero, Araripe Júnior admits that the science that Ribeiro professes in his novel is "modern," and that the method used comes from excellent origins—Zola himself. But, these things which *hurlent de se trouver ensemble*—which do not match—what are they? Araripe mentions that "Zola's disciple rises at each step to crush the author of *Padre Belchior de Pontes*—traces of the former romantic are still so accentuated"(123). Hence, here again, what the critic presents as Ribeiro's main shortcoming is his attempt to eliminate the romantic residues from his first novel, *Padre Belchior de Pontes*. As for the novel's main character, Araripe Júnior writes that "Lenita has a vigorous, sensuous, meditative temperament." "She renounces [something] when she wants to, but she never annuls herself; [she] faints for a moment under the influence of an occasional illness, but she thinks, analyzes the phases of her eroticism and finally gives in [: she is] the complete negation of hysteria" (123). Romantic, not romantic enough, realist, not realist enough, or a mixture of all these characteristics: which is Ribeiro's main problem in this novel, after all? Lúcia Miguel Pereira states that the problem with *A carne* is that because of her "excessively" demanding body, Lenita "is as nonexistent as the bodiless romantic heroines." Lenita, "[l]ike the majority of characters of our naturalism . . . was a romantic inside out; that is, she was created not according to observation, but according to preestablished formulas which prescribed the substitution of feelings by instincts" (*Prosa de ficção* 131).

It seems that the fifty years after Veríssimo and Romero's time were not enough to call the critics' attention to the fact that *A carne* is not reducible to the character Lenita. In the middle of the twentieth century, an important critic *still* insists on the romanticism of the character, *still* centers her critique on only one character, without taking the time to analyze the reasons and the implications for what Nelson Werneck Sodré calls the novel's "hybridism."[5] Up to our own time,

---

[5]It is Sodré who also compiles the several critiques written about the novel, and affirms that Araripe Júnior "had just discussed the clinical case [the novel discusses] and not the literary problem; as a clinical case, the novel failed. It is possible that such had really happened . . . —but the fact is that *A carne* would have a long life, in spite of all its deficiencies" (*O naturalismo no Brasil* 185).

it seems that Veríssimo's and Romero's first words about the novel still echo in most critics' ears when they analyze *A carne*. Sodré all but totally dismisses the novel as "an example of falsity in literature." For him, in *A carne* Ribeiro "took intentionality in art to disproportionate levels. The book, marginal as literature, does not resist the slightest analysis, be it of form or of content" (*História da literatura brasileira* 394-95). Even its hybridism is yet understood in terms of binary oppositions centered basically on the concepts of naturalism/romanticism—the way Lenita conducts her sex life versus the way the romantic heroines conduct theirs. One other critic, Massaud Moisés, concedes that *A carne* is neither "the monstrous childbirth of an artistically diseased mind" as José Veríssimo says, nor "out of literature" as Álvaro Lins wants ("Dois naturalistas" 165). For Massaud Moisés, in spite of its shortcomings, the novel needs to be placed among other defective romantic and naturalist novels, because to ignore its existence would be to "contribute to the impoverishment of our literary spoils (*espólios*) and to collaborate on a deficient vision of our naturalism" (*Realismo* 137).

How Many Languages Can There Be in a Novel?

In "The Order of Discourse," Foucault remarks that in appearance speech may well be of little account; however,

> the prohibitions that surround it very soon reveal its links with desire and with power. There is nothing surprising about that, since, as psychoanalysis has shown, discourse is not simply that which manifests (or hides) desire—it is also the object of desire; and since, as history constantly teaches us, discourse is not merely that which translates struggles

---

It is interesting to note that Sodré, although seemingly agreeing with Araripe Júnior, still considers that Lenita, as well as Magdá, the leading female character of Aluísio Azevedo's *O homem*, can "serve as a model for the particularization of this common type in naturalism, the hysterics" (185). Neither Sodré nor Araripe, nor any of the other critics for that matter, venture to comment on the novel's popularity for such a long time. The insistence that the character is a hysteric points to a very obvious point in the novel, and, in itself, the presence of hysteric women does not explain the appeal works such as *A carne*, and *O homem* have for the Brazilian audience.

> or systems of domination, but is the thing for which and by which there is struggle, discourse is the power which is to be seized. (110)

In *A carne* there is a close relationship between language and the material and social conditions displayed in the novel. About *A carne* there has been a discursive battle carried on by critics and self-appointed language specialists who have contended that the language of the novel is inadequate.[6] Although there is the lure of taking the language of the novel on its face value, as if the language "means what it says," there is also the possibility of taking language as a far more radically vexed device—a powerful force which actually defines or even creates social, political and gender constituencies.

There is a moment in Bakhtin's discussion of discourse in the novel, where he states that:

---

[6]The controversy about the language is by no means limited to *A carne*. One interesting case is the one presented by José Veríssimo. In "Questões da língua portuguesa," he starts by protesting that the subject, the Portuguese language in Brazil, exceeds his limited (*escassa*) competence. But, since Veríssimo doubts the existence of competent philologists in Brazil (33), he decides to tackle the discussion himself. Further ahead, he concedes that a language is made by the people and not by grammarians and literati. However, he insists that if anybody besides the people can have a role in the formation and institution of a language, it is the poets, "especially those who, by the nature of their aesthetic and sentimental functions are closer to the people" (44), and who are the "true representative of (the people's) emotion and feeling" (44). When he writes this passage, however, he seems to have forgotten what he has written some pages before: "some of our most important writers, such as *José de Alencar* yesterday, and *Joaquim Nabuco* today, *gravely sin against the correct usage* (of the Portuguese language) either on purpose or because of carelessness, or (because) they have a wrong conception of linguistic evolution" (34) (my emphasis). What Veríssimo himself does—criticize writers for their "poor" Portuguese—he doesn't want others to do: he takes issue both with Portuguese writer Cândido de Azevedo, because he dared to write a series of articles in the *Jornal do Comércio*, "teaching us what we should not say" (35), and with Brazilian jurist and scholar Rui Barbosa, because he criticized the writing of the Civil Code of Law (35-36). Previously, José de Alencar also showed his concerns with the situation of the Portuguese language in "A língua portuguesa no Brasil," *Obra completa*. For another example of the continuous discussions on the situation of the language, see also Antonio Houaiss's "Política lingüístico-cultural," *Estudos vários sobre palavras, livros, autores* 9-22.

> any concrete discourse (utterance) finds the object at which it was directed already as it were overlain with qualifications, open to dispute, charged with value, already enveloped in an obscuring mist—or, on the contrary, by the "light" of alien words that have already been spoken about it. (*The Dialogic Imagination* 276)

What I want to do here is to open up the dispute, and to show that alien words have already been spoken when the text is written, and that the display of several languages and sub-languages in *A carne* constitute a medly of competing strategies for the discussion of the arguments which embody the polissemic instance of the reality/realities which the novel tries to represent.

In the beginning of the book, there is/are one/two dedications to Zola, in French, followed by a Latin citation. I pass over the question of the fact that the text, as printed, is full of mistakes. The dedication/s read/s:

> Quoi qui'il en soit, voici mon oeuvre. Agréerez-vous la dédicace que je vous en fais? Pourquoi pas? Les rois, quoique gorgés de richesses, ne dédaignent pas toujous les chéfits cadeaux des pauvres paysans. Permettez que je vous fasse mon hommage complet, lige, de serviteur féal en empruntant les paroles du poéte florentin:
>
> Tu duca, tu signore, tu maestro.
>
> St. Paul, le 25 janvier 1888 [sic].
>
> Jules Ribeiro

On the next page, facing the above quoted text, there is still what seems to be another dedication, followed by a Latin quotation given as number one:

> A. M. ÉMILE ZOLA
>
> Je ne suis téméraire, je n'ai pa [sic] la prévéntion de suivre vos traces; ce n'est pas prétendre suivre vos traces que d'écrire une pauvre étude tant soit peu naturaliste. On ne vous imite pas, on vous admire. "Nous nous échauffons, dit Ovide, quand le dieu que vit en nous s'agitei": eh bien! le tout petit dieu que vit en mois s'est agité, et j'ai écrit La Chair. Ce n'est pas l'Assomoir, ce n'est pas la Curée, ce n'est pas la Terre;

mais, diantre! une chandelle n'est pas le soleil et pourtant une chandelle éclaire.

(1) Est Deus in nobis, agitante celescimus illo [sic].

One can immediately ask what these two pages in French, before a work obviously written in Portuguese by a Brazilian, are doing in the beginning of a novel. Several possibilities can be suggested, and among the most obvious is the fact that Júlio Ribeiro wants to pay homage to his master, as he himself says in the dedication. But why can't he write this homage in Portuguese? Or, if Ribeiro ever sent the novel to Zola, is the homage an end in itself, destined only to flatter the French writer who might not be able to read the contents of the novel? But then, if Zola could not read the novel, why does Ribeiro indulge in his subservient affirmation that he does not imitate him, only admires him as the candle the sun? Obviously, it is also possible that, by initially framing his novel with three foreign languages—French, Italian and Latin—Ribeiro is at once establishing the polysemic character of the work while disclosing more linguistic barriers. Although it is commonly understood that the Brazilian elite of the time—1888—had at least rudimentary knowledge of French, it is a little unlikely that *all* prospective readers could understand French, Italian and the Latin quotation at the bottom of the page. The fact is that, up to the time of the 1975 edition of the novel the typist and the proof-reader do not know the language well enough to catch some obvious mistakes—even the page-setting of the dedication is placed in wrong order, with the end of the letter being printed *before* the beginning. (For that matter, they do not even know Portuguese well enough, as the many misspellings in the book show.)

How could Ribeiro expect to be understood by his audience at the end of 1888? The answer is: he cannot, and therefore he does not. The novel constitutes a series of linguistic and cultural codes which are not easily accessible. On the other hand, in a time of much needed consensus and centralization about what Brazil meant, Lenita constitutes a focal point because the material which underlines the novel is much too powerful and potentially disruptive to be allowed to come to the surface. We need to remember that the novel was not written at a time when the linguistic vernacular had some kind of autonomy. It was decades later before it attained it. According to Neil Larsen, as late as 1930 the Brazilian "[l]anguage would appear to be, formally speaking, a model practice of consumptive production by virtue of its capacity to 'produce' the world by engulfing it whole" (*Modernism and Hegemony* 83). At the time *A carne* was published, the

Portuguese language, as it was practiced in Brazil, could not be a model practice of any kind of consumption, or not even of consumption, much less production.[7] By writing his flattering—some might even say subservient—dedication to Zola in French, Ribeiro marks the extremely important role languages play in his novel, and discloses the necessity of the incorporation of these other languages as a function of the Portuguese language itself, while at the same time he stresses that these languages were not available to be consumed. Paradoxically, it seems that the ability to speak French, or any other European language, constitutes the hegemonic mark of those who can speak proper Portuguese.

In point of fact fact, nobody understands these levels of the novel, and the critics attack Ribeiro for the dedication[8] and for the presence of foreign languages.[9] Veríssimo is adamant: "in descriptions, speaking about a plant, [he]

---

[7]It is interesting to observe how the same preoccupation with linguistic purity was very much on the mind of other Latin Americans. Andrés Bello, in the "Prólogo" to his "Gramática Castellana," adverts that "the worst evil, the one which, if not checked, will deprive us of the great advantages of a common language, is the avenue of neologisms of construction which inundates and obscures much of what is written in America" ("El castellano en América" vii). Commenting on this aspect of Bello's concern for a pure language, Julio Ramos writes that in Bello the national language "regulated by the letters—more than a supplementary instrument for the passive transmission of the contents of the law, designs the map where the limits and the hierarchies of the territorial State are written" ("Saber decir: lengua y política," *Desencuentros de la modernidad en América Latina* 49).

[8]See, for instance, José Veríssimo's outrage at Júlio Ribeiro's calling Zola "duca, signore e maestro": the critic's anger is not caused by the presence of a foreign language, but by the terms of the homage Ribeiro pays to the French writer ("O romance naturalista no Brasil" 182).

[9]Among those who do not understand is twentieth-century critic Giogio Marotti, who seems to be deeply irritated by what he calls "a continuous flowering of foreign terms and scientific citations" (41). At one point in his discussion of *A carne*, Marotti wonders whether the use of foreign terminology is Ribeiro's way of "trying to confirm his Nordic origins (he was the son of a North American)," or his way of showing off his culture ("Sex under the Sun of the Tropics: *A carne*" 41). Not coincidentally, although foreign terms such as "*ètageres, netskés, vide-poches, huit-ressorts, pur-sang, kirchwasser, black town, bric-à-brac, choke-rifled, struggle for life*" (41) provoke the critic's wrath, he says

puts in parentheses . . . the scientific name, [and that] is original in a work of art" (*Teoria, crítica e história literária* 191).[10] Veríssimo, in fact, is so interested in what he calls Ribeiro's "fixed idea" of showing off his scientific knowledge, that he misreads an important distinction in the novel: "Barbosa apart from Lenita, when he had just made her his lover—and what a lover!—writes her, instead of a letter . . . a long report about the geology of the coast region of the province, with a technical description of the railroad from São Paulo to Santos" (*Teoria, crítica e história literária* 191). The letter Veríssimo mentions is actually a long report Barbosa sends from Santos. It does constitute a "study" of geology and of railroad technicalities one would rarely write to a lover, but, in fact, at this point, Lenita and Barbosa *are not* lovers. This distinction, as I shall demonstrate later, is very crucial for the understanding of the text's imbrication of several languages.

These languages appear in the text not always as linguistic acts to which the status of a language is given. Some of them appear as registers of certain ways of speaking and as written codes. In a sense, however, all of them contribute for the extreme destabilization of the linguistic matter in the novel.

About the language, Veríssimo says that "it is in fact pure and good, as suits a grammarian, but [it does not have] distinctiveness, and there is an abundance of false expressions such as 'sensuous lightning'" (191). Veríssimo also ridicules Ribeiro because of certain idiosyncratic orthographic uses:

> [O]utra puerilidade, em que aparece o gramático, é a ortografia especial das palavras em que entra o grupo *ch*, todas escritas com *kh*, assim melankholia, kharacter, etc. Kilômetro é khiliometro, e à capital da

---

nothing of Ribeiro's rendition of the slave Joaquim Cambinda's language in *A carne*.

[10]Veríssimo's concern with the proper usage of the Portuguese language was by no means restricted to *A carne*. Machado de Assis himself doesn't escape criticism, even when Veríssimo means to be favorable to his friend: "To be perfect (Machado's) language only needs sparkle (*brilho*), eloquence, color, and not just the ostentation that pleases so much our poorly refined taste." However, he later concedes that Machado's language "is . . . the best, the healthiest, the most numerous, the most expressive and the most beautiful ever written here. Since (his language) is one of the most vernacular, it is so without the indiscreet sacrifice of correction (*casticismo*)" ("Das condições da produção literária no Brasil" 109).

> Baviera, que foi sempre traduzida em português por Munich, conserva o Sr. Ribeiro a sua forma alemã München. (191, italics in the original)[11]

Such antics do not appear in the 1975 version of the novel, but it is possible to imagine the critics' surprise at their occurrence in a time the Portuguese language was going through accommodationswhich deemedsuch orthographic mannerisms at least obsolete. However, their presence in their original edition serves to show one more degree of linguistic destabilization. Since the main linguistic code, Portuguese, was not stable enough to decide for one unified orthography, the text becomesa linguistic extravaganzaat once showing its porosity and its inadequacy to convey precise meaning. The fact that both Lenita and Barbosa have long "scientific" conversations about the nature and origin of trees, and proceed to give their Latin names, is but one register of this unsteady characteristic. In *A carne* language has no center, and the addition of scientific language only heightens its de-centered existence in another language. In a sense, the Portuguese language, *although* it is the main language in the novel, becomes a "supplement" to the other languages displayed in the text. Or, on the other hand, *because* the main language is Portuguese, the others are the necessary supplement.

There are other registers which signal even more instability. When the old black witch-doctor Joaquim Cambinda gathers some slaves in his shack and starts to perform his ceremony, he is greeted as "mganga." The editor explains in a footnote that "'mganga' is an "African word" (63) which means "'lord of the time, distributor of rain' and, by extension, "theologian, priest, teacher" (63). The black "teacher", however, speaks an impossible Portuguese:

> —Zelómo, disse Joaquim Cambinda, ussê pensô bê nu quê vai fazê, lapássi?
> —Pensô, *mganga.*
> —Intossi, ussê qué mêmo si rissá ni rimanári ri San Migué rizáma?
> —Qué, *mganga.* (63, italics in the original)

[11]Another puerility in which the grammarian appears is the special orthography of words in which the group *ch* appears, [he writes] with *kh.* Thus melankholia, kharacter, etc. Kilômetro is khiliometro[;] and the [name of the] capital of Baviera, which has always been translated in Portuguese as Munich, [in] Mr. Ribeiro it is written in the German form München.

A footnote immediately follows, giving a Portuguese version of the dialogue:

> —Jerônimo, você pensou bem no que você vai fazer, rapaz?
> —Pensei, mestre.
> —Então você quer mesmo alistar-se na irmandade de São Miguel das Almas?
> —Quero, mestre. (63)[12]

Joaquim Cambinda's language is a departure from the accepted Portuguese norm, and, because of the person who speaks it, it constitutes a language with its own authority within his group, since it is backed by power: the witch-doctor knows his environment, controls it through this knowledge and uses it to dominate and impose rules on his fellow black people. When a slave woman dies in the farm, Barbosa recognizes in the symptoms a type of poison which he has studied in France. Joaquim Cambinda is the main suspect of the killing, because he has been seen gathering seeds and leaves of local plants which, concocted, become that powerful poison. The suspicion is confirmed, to the amazement of both blacks and whites. Cambinda confesses the killing of that slave and at least five others. His speech, a departure from the Portuguese norm, is of a piece with his handling with natural products of his environment: he derives his power from both. However, since he is a slave and not a white man, he can be accorded neither scientific honors for his knowledge in herbal chemistry nor recognition for his language formation. His death comes as a punishment both for his actual crimes and for his handling of a scientific knowledge which "belonged" to the whites. His speech, therefore, is the first sign of his danger and, in fact, constitutes the symbol of the potential disruptiveness of such knowledge acquired through the collection and adaptation of things existing in the Brazilian environment. Both his language and his scientific knowledge are "brasileirismos," a form of degeneration which cannot be permitted to flourish, since it represents danger. On the one hand, we have languages—Portuguese, Latin, Italian, and especially French—which are all high status, and on the other hand, we have a language which has none: in *A carne* language proliferates, as if to make up for the absent

---

[12]—Jerônimo, have you thought carefully about what you are going to do, my boy?
—Yes I did, master.
—Then you really want to join the brotherhood of Saint Michael of Souls?
—Yes I do, master.

center, because no one single language can encompass all the others. As Bakhtin remarks,

> [E]very concrete utterance of a speaking subject serves as a point where centrifugal as well as centripetal forces are brought to bear. The process of centralization and decentralization, of unification and disunification, intersect in the utterance; the utterance not only answers the requirements of its own language as an individualized embodiment of a speech act, but it answers the requirements of heteroglossia as well; it is in fact an active participant in such speech diversity. (*The Dialogic Imagination* 272)

The text's own departure from the norm, that is, its choice of a different orthography, is a rupture or a "break with" the accepted orthographic norm; the penchant for giving the Latin names of plants is a rupture with the accepted norm for the novel in the Brazilian literature of the end of the nineteenth century. In sum, these deviations were just as unacceptable for a "work of art" as Joaquim Cambinda's private branch of knowledge was unacceptable for the scientific community. What seems clear is that in the structural abstraction of language from concrete experience, a certain kind of concession of concrete experience to linguistic form is made, but not the concession that that form, itself, has the status of a language.

Other languages appear in the text. Starting with the dedication in French, Latin and Italian, the text continues its journey through more French, English and Latin. Barbosa writes to Lenita that he is looking forward to giving her a "a strong, energetic *hands-shake* (sic), in the English fashion (83, italics in the original); later, Lenita is reminded of Rabelais when she realizes she is pregnant: "*Les bêtes sur leurs ventrées n'endurant jamais le mâle masculant*" (141, italics in the original), and finally, she chooses a Latin expression to explain to Barbosa why she is marrying another man: "*pater est is quem iustae nuptiae demonstrant*" (154, italics in the original). These languages, English, French and Latin, however, constitute a common heritage which can be shared by all educated people. Lenita chooses to use French and Latin to give respectability to her plight. When she wants to get down to their relationship, she uses a secret code in her letter to Barbosa: "[the words] were followed by some cryptographic lines drawn in some code which Barbosa and Lenita had agreed upon since the first time of their acquaintance" (154). Both are initiates in this secret code. Similarly, Joaquim Cambinda's followers are initiates in his secret linguistic and ritual code. Joaquim Cambinda is punished with death; Barbosa is punished with death too.

The ideology which informs these languages seems not to represent any immediate empirical consistency. However, there is a sense in which the death of Barbosa and Joaquim Cambinda are played in contrast to Lenita's survival and departure from the country as soon as she finds out about her pregnancy.[13] Why is it that, although a partner in all deviances—linguistic, sexual, social, intellectual—she is not punished? There is a sense in which the author preserves her from the common death given to the two men in order to transform her into a trope for other instances of both novelistic and social dangers.

The Body of a Woman as the Body of History

Few novels in the whole of Brazilian literature constitute such a powerful exploration of the question of pregnancy and consequently of the feminine body as a site of conflict for the continuation of society; pregnancy represents at once the making of new beings, the perpetuation of society as both a physical and a social entity. In these circumstances, what does it mean for a woman to get pregnant in Brazilian literature at the end of the last century? What it means can be stated very clearly: a woman is immediately subject to two simultaneous discursive roles—that of an object and that of an agent-subject.

A pregnant woman is immediately comprehended as a consummately immanent being: pregnancy comes to dominate both the way she sees herself and the way she is seen. She is, exactly, a Pregnant Woman, a woman "in the flesh," whose very body discloses both its difference from other, "normal" bodies as well as its own differences from itself. When she becomes pregnant, Lenita, whose educational privileges heretofore rival those of a man, is suddenly and irrevocably a woman: one who gives birth.

More important, now pregnant, she is subject to the imperatives of conventional social rules. Just as her maternity must eventually be converted into motherhood, her pregnancy, out of wedlock, must be converted into marriage. Lenita, in this sense, joins the gallery of "fallen women" notable in so many other Bra-

---

[13]Here, again, it is convenient to compare the destiny of this baby to that of Iracema's child, Moacir. Unlike José de Alencar's character, Lenita's child has both father and mother from the same white race. However, they have two things in common: both are generated outside the law—in Moacir's case, the law of racial purity, and in the case of Lenita's child, the law of marriage—and both will somehow become viable through the agency of an outside, Europe.

zilian texts whose unconventional behavior finally assumes the character of a punishment, like ostracism or/and death (Luís Felipe Ribeiro).

Lenita's pregnancy can be understood as a provocation for the domestic economy in which it must sustain itself; the energies that the very fact of her pregnancy releases, or perhaps confirm, must be contained. Just so, the very fact of her identity as a woman must now, and definitely, be subjected to the paternal power of a man; an unmarried pregnant woman must have a husband, as a condition of society itself having, once again, each time, a discursive order into which the crucial expectation of a new member can be processed, as well as the woman out of whom the child must pass.

Although it registers everywhere on the body of its heroine the necessities of social discipline and paternalistic power, *A carne* could not help being considered a scandal in its own time. The fact that critics reacted against it so quickly and so vehemently seems to indicate that the novel was read as being *for* the things that, if it does not outright condemn, at least does not totally condone. That is, the text of pregnancy—as I have been considering it—is misconceived: its origin is wholly corrupt, its emergence into the world has resulted in the birth of a monster.

What is compelling about Veríssimo's outcry—"monstrous childbirth"—is that it expresses two things that the novel enacts: the effacement of the motherhood of the woman and the dramatization of the moment that this out-of-wedlock motherhood comes to represent in society. It is as if Veríssimo has discerned pregnancy in *A carne* not merely as an object upon which a whole social formation must proceed to act. More crucially, Lenita's pregnancy embodies quite literally an agency that at least incipiently challenges the very basis upon which this society is formed. Even in Veríssimo's words, something of this challenge can be seen: does a man produce a child? What role does a man have in producing a child? Does he represent "mind" to the woman's body or "flesh"? But what if the child thus engendered is a monster?

Or, and I believe this is one of the crucial points of the novel, could there be something monstrous about such a woman as Lenita, who enjoys the education normally accorded to men and who subsequently starts treating men as her inferiors? It first happens when her father, stunned with her brilliance, lets her make decisions on her own, and later to Barbosa, the lover, who accords her not only intellectual freedom but also the freedom to chase him sexually. It is significant that Barbosa is the one who continues her education after Lenita's father dies, and that he himself dies when she is about to start another phase of her life and learn other things. In other words, Lenita's flesh, from one perspective the very material that activates the various mechanisms for social control is, from another perspective, the material which engenders new possibilities that challenge this control. Lenita is an object in terms of which differences recreate themselves: she is finally a woman who is not a man—female flesh which takes control of her destiny and heads for unknown territories. Yet Lenita is also an agent who suggests new configurations of these same differences—and hence, I want to maintain, critic José Veríssimo is scandalized. In terming the text a "monstrous childbirth" he discloses its register of monstrosity (which always arises when two things normally kept apart are combined into one thing) and, moreover, the complicity between monstrosity and childbirth.

What I want to do in the remainder of this discussion is, first, to set out the basic differences that the figure of monstrosity locates in *A carne*. There are three differences: those between men and women, between gender and race, and between nature and history. Secondly, I want to consider the last of these as the source of the text's peculiar provocation when it was published.

A carne was published one year before the proclamation of the Republic; the moment of its publication was then almost simultaneous with the birth of a set of new free Brazilian citizens, finally separated from a political model and a ruling royal family originated in Portugal. This "birth" was, to a large extent, operated by a woman, Princess Isabel who, with the signing of the Lei Aurea (Golden Law), at the same time determined the beginning of a free life for those previously kept as slaves, and also the beginning (or, should we say, the confirmation) of her ruling powers.[14] Princess Isabel's first really important act was the signing of a literal text which had the consequence of definitely inscribing her in Brazilian history, and of determining, at the same time, her involvement with the Monarchy, and the Monarchy's role in bringing about the Republic. As a document of its time, it may be, indeed, that it is history itself which is born in *A carne*, although what the text emphasizes is how history is incarnated, and how a body has to be incorporated into social institutions so that what issues from it can proceed with due health and right reason.

---

[14]The matter of Princess Isabel's signing of the "Lei Aurea" can be seen as an aftershock of the "religious question", occurred at the end of D. Pedro II's government. The strengthening of the emperor's powers, with the diminishing of the Church's, ended up being politically damaging for the monarchy. Arthur Cezar Ferreira Reis argues that "the emperor was not just a symbol of the regime. He governed and administered. The daughter, D. Isabel, when she occupied her father's place during his absences, was even more 'executive' than him; [she] imposed her will, and thus demonstrated what the Second Empire could become" (*Aspectos da formação brasileira* 217).

A final point. Must there be a break between the natural and the historical? That is, is there a moment, before one becomes the other, when what there is simply exists, or has happened, or becomes manifested? Or is it that there is a moment when there is such instability that what exists is neither natural nor historical? If so, how is this break, or rupture, traversed? Who or what force precipitates the fact? Let me begin my consideration of differences in the text by locating its most significant and formal difference: the shift in point of view from Lenita to her lover once Lenita becomes pregnant.

Prior to Lenita's pregnancy, *A carne* expresses an extreme absorption with female sexuality. In the very beginning of the novel, for instance, Lenita's father tries to convince her that "a man is made for a woman, and a woman for a man. Marriage is, not so much a social, but *mainly* a physiological necessity" (9, italics in the original). Later, after her father's death, Lenita retires to an old friend's farm and there, after a nervous breakdown, she realizes that "in spite of her powerful intelligence and all her science, she was, in the species, nothing more than a mere female, and that what she felt was the desire, the organic need for a male" (16). Since there is no male available at the moment, Lenita starts having fantasies and dreams about a statue of a male body she has in her bedroom. When Barbosa finally comes to the farm, he is overwhelmed by her beauty, her intelligence, her ability with guns. He provides her with the best places for hunting; he assists her in her pursuit of wounded animals—he finally takes up her education from where her father left it. The difference is that now, where there was theory, there is practice; where there were lectures on chemistry, there is a chemistry laboratory. Their friendship becomes more intense because, besides being an intelligent woman, Lenita can also ride horses and hunt like a man. Her ecstasy upon seeing the bloody bodies of the animals she hunts can only be compared to his ecstasy in collecting their bodies for her. However, one day Lenita does not show up to talk to him. Barbosa concludes: "menstruation—that was the reason: menstruation: *tota mulier in utero*, Van Helmont has said" (53, italics in the original). Thus, in spite of all her intelligence, the truth of Lenita is embodied in the last frontier which demarcates her as a female: her womb.

As the transition between the previous theoretical lessons Lenita had with her father to a more practical kind of teaching she is having with Barbosa, there is a point when sex, and not conversations about sex, is due. After Barbosa cures Lenita from a snake bite, she goes after him in his bedroom. He cannot resist her: "a horde of disordered ideas agitated him; [they] confounded themselves in his excited brain; his thoughts exited; desire won; the suggestion of the FLESH was victorious" (121, capital letters in the original).

As the story continues, the narrative does not shy away from describing the most private moments Lenita shares with Barbosa. Sometimes it seems that the narrator himself is either overwhelmed by what he is describing, or that he is afraid to put in words the full expression of Lenita's sexuality. Such is the case of a scene in the woods, when Barbosa, inspired by the memory of Michelangelo's *Aurora*, undresses Lenita, lays her down on a stone, adjusts her limbs to imitate the picture's pose and, "slid a little bit, laid on his stomach and, crawling like a serpent. . ." (131). The description of the scene is then engulfed by twelve lines of suspended periods interrupted only by the candid affirmation that "Lenita fainted in a spasm of pleasure" (131). In a novel where languages abound, it is interesting to notice that the narrator momentarily appears lacking: he cannot find the words to describe the scene. Or is it that the mere suggestion is more powerful than real words would be? Or is this another example of editing by the typists or publishers? What is possible to know is that the mere suggestion of such scene was transgression enough for the literature of the time, especially because it is a woman's pleasure which is being described.

However, the narrator's proximity to Lenita ends at the moment she discovers her pregnancy. "What was she going to do?" (142), the narrator says she asks herself. Next, the narrator himself says that Lenita answers to her own question "without hesitation" (142): "take the pregnancy to a good term, give birth, raise, educate the son, see herself in him, be a mother" (142). There are two important points in this assertion of Lenita's: first, the determination of the child's gender, and second, the choice of the verb "parir" for "to give birth." In Portuguese the word "filho," when used in the singular, means "son"; when used in the plural, it can mean children—daughters and sons—or only sons. The narrator could have chosen the word "criança" instead of "filho"—this word would mean "child" without implication of gender. The choice of "filho" points clearly to the fact that Lenita thinks she engendered a male child. The verb "parir" is used when animals give birth; when one is talking about humans, a more elaborate form—"dar à luz" (give to the light)—is used. By choosing these two words—"filho" and "parir"—the narrator might be either equating the birth of males to the lower level of animals, or suggesting that, when she gives birth, Lenita will be just an animal.

However, the time when Lenita discovers her pregnancy and makes plans for the birth of the son is the last time she appears "live." Flora Süssekind remarks that this moment signals Lenita's appropriation of the power of diagnosing. In her analysis of other naturalist novels, Süssekind stresses the fact that it is either the doctor or the narrator who names the disease and prescribes the treatment: "[the] disease functions as a stage for the doctor to shine. . . . The more pathologic the cases described and the language in the novels, the greater the desire to reaffirm the power of those who speak a medical, therapeutic language" (*Tal Brasil, qual romance?* 128-29). By investing herself with the power this scientific language entails, Lenita is appropriating another male prerogative, because she not only "diagnoses" her pregnancy, but also "prescribes" the treatment, that is, she decides that she has to leave the farm and get married so that the child can be born within an acceptable family. In this family, however, the child will be a reflection not of the father but of Lenita, who will see *herself* in him. From this moment on, Lenita will only appear through her letter describing the city of São Paulo or through Barbosa's eyes. Süssekind affirms that the insistent presence of doctors in the naturalist novel does not mean that

> os "autores" falem por meio dos "médicos" de seus romances. Falam nos textos é de sua própria busca de um poder maior dentro da sociedade brasileira. Se, nos seus romances, dão voz àqueles que detêm um discurso científico, parecem sugerir que se faça o mesmo no país, que detenham poder aqueles que têm saber... O médico dos romances naturalistas possui traços que o aproximam dos intelectuais brasileiros da virada de século. Enquanto um possui poder de intervenção no espaço familiar, a ponto de ordenar internações e casamentos, o outro desejaria estar investido de idêntica possibilidade de transformar a vida nacional. (129-30)[15]

Since Lenita appropriates this scientific language and uses it for her own personal diagnosis, there is a sense, therefore, that, like the Brazilian intellectual of the time, she also would like to be capable of influencing public life, or, at

[15]The "authors" speak through the "doctors" in their novels. What [the authors] speak about is their own search for greater power within Brazilian society. If, in their novels, the writers give voice to those who command the scientific discourse, they seem to suggest that the same be done in the country—that power be accorded to those who have knowledge. . . . The doctor in the naturalist novels has many characteristics which equate him to the Brazilian intellectuals at the end of the century. If one has the power of intervention in the familial space—he can prescribe hospitalizations and marriages, the other would like to be invested with identical possibility to transform the national life.

least, that part of public life, the medical arts, which is overwhelmingly male.[16] In part, the narrator's interest in Lenita's development prior to the moment of her self-diagnosis has served to mark sexual difference. Lenita acts, the narrator reflects. Lenita is a woman, the narrator is a man. Lenita indulges herself, the narrator lets her indulge herself while enjoying the titillating details of everything. Lenita does as she does, the narrator provides a framework for whatever she does. This framework, however, is only explicitly foregrounded after Lenita's pregnancy—as if her pregnancy requires it. It is not so important to note that the unavoidability of the social consequences of Lenita's pregnancy is suggested by the abrupt switch in point of view. Far more crucial is the fact of the switch itself, momentarily disruptive on the formal level, yet decisive and lasting on the ideological level: in *A carne* it is fundamental that being pregnant be something that takes place as an event in male, not female subjectivity.

Indeed, it is crucial that Barbosa proceeds to undergo a process of self-pity so exacerbated that it can only be compared to an overwrought woman's: "(nature) had given him—handcuffed—to the caprices of a hysterical woman who offered herself to him, who gave herself to him, as she would have offeparared herself, as she would have given herself to anyone, to a negro, to a slave of the fields, not for psychic love, but just to satisfy her hungry flesh. . . ." And, what seems to hurt Barbosa the most, "[o]nce replenished, satisfied, this woman abandoned him" (159). Barbosa's curses of Lenita can easily be taken as displacements of her own reviling of herself. It is not lost to the reader the fact that here, unlike in the episode of Joaquim Cambinda's transgressions, the narrator is presenting "negro" as a sign of lack: this time of capacity for "psychic love." Alternately, these same curses can be understood as how Lenita, pregnant, gives birth to the subjectivity of the narrator. Since she leaves the farm and is not available for the narrator's study, her pregnancy is something whose consequences cannot be foreseen. The existence of this pregnancy and her absence unsettle the very differences which it appears to confirm. The lover then languishes in a "feminized" position until he kills himself with a paralyzing poison. With her "hungry flesh," Lenita unsettles the text of the social grammar. Just so, with this novel former grammarian Júlio Ribeiro can be understood to have upset the rules

[16]According to Roderick J. Barman, "the first Brazilian woman to practice medicine obtained her degree from the New York Medical College in 1881. In Brazil itself, a female physician graduated from the Bahia Medical School in 1887 and another from the Rio School in the following year" ("Politics on the Stage: The Late Brazilian Empire as Dramatized by França Júnior" 255).

of the Brazilian novel, which generally contended, up to that point, that the subject of the novelistic sentence was male, and the object female, and that the subject should always come before the object for the sentence to be readable.

Where the Public Meets the Private

It is significant that the accident at the sugar-cane factory mentioned on the first page of this discussion—the breaking of the cylinders by a black man whose son's arm was caught in the machine—happens at the time when Lenita is already pregnant. As I pointed out earlier, this is the moment in the novel when the private sphere of the narrative meets the public sphere. It is not the only moment, but it is the single most important instance in the mapping of the ideology which informs the text in its implication with the Real as a historical configuration of the moment the narrative is placed.

Again it is convenient to stress that the year the novel was published, 1888, marks the date slaves were officially freed with the signature of the Golden Law by Princess Isabel. From that moment on, the labor market was flooded by a whole contingent of human beings who had known only the life of servitude. Arthur Cezar Ferreira Reis writes that the signature of the Golden Law was a "a romantic solution." "To the eyes of the world," he continues, "a moving step had been taken, [and the world was] startled [with the fact that] the measure [was] voted without any legislative difficulties. . . . The antecedents of the measure did not foretell the solution which was adopted so quickly" (*Aspectos da formação brasileira* 218). It must be stressed, however, that most of these newly freed persons not only did not know how to read and write, but also did not even have any professional training besides that necessary for their work in the farms and in the houses. The arrival of European workers, considered more fit for the handling of the new kinds of agricultural techniques and machinery that were being introduced,[17] reduced even more the prospects of work for the freed

---

[17]The importation of European immigrants was defended by many as the solution to the problem of population control and racial improvement. In *The Control of the Tropics* (1898), Benjamin Kidd wrote that "in dealing with the *natural* (indigenous) inhabitants of the tropics we are dealing with peoples who represent the same stage in the history of the development of the race that the child does in the history of the development of the individual. The tropics will not, therefore, be developed by the natives themselves" (qtd. in Curtin 36-37). In Brazil, the same principles determined that Chinese workers, although believed

slaves. If the freeing of the slaves was, on the one hand, an act destined to win for the monarchy the support of liberals and positivists, on the other hand it estranged those men who composed the rural patriarchy which was one of the main supporters of D. Pedro II. Since the signature of the Law was not backed by any other act which would provide the former slaves with some sort of social security or compensation, the liberals themselves were taken aback at the sight of the proliferation of homeless, jobless people in the cities. Arthur Cezar Ferreira Reis remarks that

> [a] classe de homens libertos...à qual não se concedera qualquer possibilidade para uma realização moral e material dignificadora, passaria a compor os quadros de uma nova classe: a dos marginais, peso morto na vida do país, incapaz que era de criar-se uma condição ou uma posição levando-a a incorporar-se à dinâmica nacional. (*Aspectos da formação brasileira* 219)[18]

Writing on the same subject, Lúcio Kowarick remarks that in 1888, "with the collapse of slavery, there were all kinds of workers available to the farmers willing to pay them, although in São Paulo, at least, Brazilian workers continued being the least desirable class of workers" (*Trabalho e vadiagem* 63).[19] In a

---

to be more docile than the Europeans, should not be imported. For more information on the reasons why Chinese workers were not imported, see Greenfield; Dean; and Conrad, "The Planter Class and the Debate over Chinese Immigration in Brazil."

[18]The class of freed men, to which no possibility for a moral and material dignifying realization was offered, became a new social class: that of the marginals—a dead weight in the country's life, since the country was incapable of creating conditions and positions which would facilitate this class's incorporation into the national dynamics.

[19]Kowarick continues that, "marginalized since colonial times, the free or freed man usually does not pass through the 'work school,' and is frequently transformed in an itinerant who wanders through the countryside and the cities. They are seen by the farm-owners as the incarnation of a worthless mob that prefers idleness, vagrancy, vice and even crime to the discipline of the work at the farms" (65). The European immigrants, on the other hand, were treated with respect and were given official incentives in the form of loans from the federal government. In *Triste fim de Policarpo Quaresma*, a novel first published in

sense, white society could feel good about the humanitarian act the Golden Law represented; however, there was no way of denying the existence of these new citizens and their basic needs for housing, food, and work. History, described by Althusser as a "process without a subject or *telos*" (*Lenin & Philosophy* 145), cannot recuperate the depths of these problems in order to show the poignancy of the private tragedies the liberation of the slaves represented. The place for the recuperation of such situations is ideology, which, according to Fredric Jameson,

> must always be necessarily narrative in its structure, inasmuch as it not only involves a mapping of the real, but also the essentially narrative or fantasy attempt of the subject to invent a place for himself/herself in a collective and historical process which excludes him or her and which is basically nonrepresentable and non-narrative. (*Fables of Aggression* 12)

The need for the narration of ideology is, still according to Jameson, closely connected to the subject's anxiety "at the moment of truth— moments of personal crisis and of the agonizing political polarization of revolutionary situations; and from such an approach to the Real the subject then tends to retreat again, at best in possession of abstract or purely intellectual schemata when not of personally charged narrative representations" (13). The crucial "moment of truth" in *A carne* is represented in the alignment of the existence of two different sets of young Brazilians: one, the black son of a black slave—"28 of September", born after the Law of the Free Womb—and the other, the child conceived by Lenita and Barbosa. This white child, whose natural father kills himself when he knows about its existence (154), will be born in Europe, where the fact of its conception outside the marriage structure can be camouflaged. Which of these two children—the "28 of September" crippled black boy and the bastard white

---

1919, Lima Barreto dramatizes the different treatment given to Brazilians and foreigners. One of Quaresma's workers says: "The land is not ours. . . . We don't have tools . . . this is good for Italians or Germans, [to whom] the government gives everything. . . . The government doesn't like us. . ." (120). Later on, Quaresma himself, who in the beginning of the story is an idealist who believes that in the Brazilian land, "if one plants, everything blooms," remarks: "the [governmental policy of] *self-help* was valid only for the nationals; for the others [the government provided] all sorts of help and facilities" (120). For an illuminating discussion about this novel and the role of Lima Barreto—a mulatto—in Brazilian letters, see Wasserman, "Lima Barreto; The Text and the Margin."

child—represents Brazil better? Ultimately, the Brazil which would be represented would be what Jameson calls "a fantasy." Nevertheless, there is a sense in which, having approached Brazil as the Real, it is as if the narrative does not know how to put distance between itself and this Real without representing it in a dual form: the white and the black child. However, the matter of representation of Brazil is re-problematized once again in both Barbosa's and Lenita's letter-accounts from their trips.

When Barbosa writes the long letter to Lenita, relating his trip to Santos, he gives a detailed description of the situation of both the city and the technological advancements of the region. After referring to Brazil's independence from Portugal as "the functional disarrangement which led Mr. D. Pedro de Bragança to dismount [by the Tietê river], at four o'clock p.m. on September 7, 1822 " (76), Barbosa describes the English railroad which unites Santos to Jundiaí. This description does not spare praises for the English genius which cut the mountain and placed powerful machines on its slopes: "in the Santos mountain, man's work is harmonious with the land where it is placed; the careful power of art is worthy of the threatening magnitude of nature" (81). Here, *man* is equated to *English*, since the railroad system is a product not of the Brazilian, but of the English genius. The mighty work of engineering, whose financial funds came from several sources—"the federal government guaranteed five per cent of the capital used in the construction, and the provincial [government guaranteed] two per cent" (82)—cannot help but give wonderful profits:

> Ganham, ganham muito dinheiro, ganham riquezas de Creso os ingleses, e merecem-nas. O progresso assombroso de São Paulo, a iniciativa industrial do paulista moderno; a rede de vias férreas que leva a vida, o comércio, a civilização à Botucatu, à S. Manuel, ao Jaú, ao Jaguera, tudo se devė à *Saint Paul Rail Road*, à Estrada de Ferro de Santos a Jundiaí. *Rule, Britannia! Hurab for the English!* já que o nosso governo não presta para nada [*sic*]. (82, italics in the original)[20]

[20]They make a lot of money; they make Creso's fortunes, these Englishmen, and they deserve [fortunes]. [Behold] the awesome progress of São Paulo, the industrial initiative of the modern *Paulista*; the railroad takes life, commerce, civilization to Botucatu, to S. Manuel, to Jaú, to Jaguera—all thanks to *Saint Paul Rail Road*, The Estrada de Ferro Santos to Jundiaí. *Rule, Britannia! Hurrah for the English!* since our government is worthless.

From the point where Brazil's independence from Portugal is considered a "functional disarrangement" to the dismissal of Brazilian government as "worthless," Barbosa states his clear preference for things British, that is, European. The fact that the "English" make lots of money from the exploitation of Brazil's underdeveloped railroad system seems not only right but praiseworthy, and whatever civilization São Paulo can boast is owed to the English and to their modernizing machines. But if this "civilization" is a counterpart to some previous state existing before the arrival of the English, can this previous state be said to represent an untouched, "natural" Brazil? There is a strong sense in which this representation of the railroad—after all made by Barbosa—constitutes another moment when the private meets the public, disclosed as being inseparable from the public.

The description of the mountains around Santos resembles, to a certain extent, the description of the stone-pit in Azevedo's *O cortiço*. Here, too, the mountain provokes "the delirium of the heights" (79)—*o delírio das alturas*—and, when Barbosa starts going down the mountain,

> a paisagem abre-se, rasga-se de vez. Por entre os contra-fortes, por entre as alturas da serrania, que se erguem de um e de outro lado, como bastidores titânicos, alonga-se a perder de vista uma planície extensa, chata, lisa, nivelada, pardacenta. De dois outeiros à direita que, simétricos, redondos, suaves, emparelhados, lembram os seios de uma virgem, parte uma linha horizontal, muito escura, muito tersa; é o mar, é o oceano, cuja vista dá o nome à serra—*Paranapiacaba*. (79, italics in the original)[21]

The anthropomorphization of the mountain and, especially, the feminization of the landscape, is of a piece with the overwhelmingly male characteristic of the railroad which "like a furrow stretches itself along the plain, cutting here and there mirrored surfaces of calm water; on this furrow an enormous, stooped down thing, with a disproportionate glyptodont which comes and goes." The train

---

[21]The landscape opens itself, tears itself open at once. From among the columns, from among the heights of the mountain which stands in both sides like titanic theatre wings, there is an ample, flat, smooth, leveled, grayish plain. From two hills on the right which, symmetric, rounded, soft, one on the side of the other, resemble a virgin's breasts, a horizontal, dark and tense line departs; it is the sea, the ocean, whose sight gives name to the mountain—*Paranapiacaba*.

is "a flat thing which slides quickly, vomiting smoke: the furrow is the railroad; the glyptodont [is] the engine" (79).

The phallic engine, sliding back and forth in the furrow, is a clear representation of a sexual act, and the smoke it vomits is the sperm which fecundates the previously virgin Brazilian landscape.[22] Since the Brazilian government ("governo"—a masculine word in Portuguese) is worthless, impotent, it is necessary that foreign devices be brought in order to fecundate the incipient nation. That explains why the text is so adamant in stressing that it is the railroad which brings "life, commerce, civilization" to São Paulo and surrounding areas (82). The important detail, however, is that the images of this fecundation are closer to those of rape than to lovemaking, and they echo the same brutality displayed by Barbosa in his first intercourse with Lenita: he "quickly sat at the side of the bed [and] without letting the girl free, pulled her to him, close to his breast, held her head with his left hand and, nervous, brutal, glued his mouth on hers, pressing his harsh mustache against her soft lips; [he] drank her breath" (121).

The economy of fecundation displayed in *A carne* exists, therefore, both on a sexual and on a political level, as the result of the brutal male taking possession of a virginal space which needs and expects this brutality in order to surren-

---

[22]In *The Octopus*, a novel published in 1900, North American writer Frank Norris presents the locomotive through the character Presley. For him, the engine has nothing of the fecundating characteristics Júlio Ribeiro portrays in *A carne*; rather, it has an "enormous eye, cyclopean, red" and it advances "throwing a glare far in advance; shooting by in a sudden crash of confused thunder, filling the night with the terrific clamor of its iron hoofs" (41). Unlike Júlio Ribeiro, Norris does not present the engine as a symbol of life; rather, "it is now the symbol of a vast power, huge, terrible . . . the echo of its thunder reaches the valley, leaving blood and destruction in its path; the leviathan with tentacles of steel clutching into the soil, the souless force, the ironhearted power, the monster, the colossus, the octopus" (42). For Latin American writers, machines, factories, and technology went from a first moment of wonderment with Martí: "So many inventions (in the printing business)! Such wealth of machines, these iron workers!" (*Obras completas* 12:419-20), to estrangement and a sense that machines fundamentally disturbed literature with Gutiérrez Nájera: "The asthmatic cough of the locomotive, the sharp shriek of the rails, the whistle of the factories [prevent us] from speaking about the gardens of Academus, about the fiestas of Aspasia, about the tree of Pireo in the calm and gentle language of the poets" (*Obras. Crítica literaria*, 1:192). For more detailed discussions on the reception of growing technology among novelists throughout the Americas, see Julio Ramos; Leo Marx; and Barbara Novak.

der its own procreative forces. Both São Paulo's mountains and Lenita's body can only become fecund if brutalized and torn open. It seems that Barbosa's letter welcomes foreign imperialistic forces just the text welcomes the outside in the form of foreign languages. It must not be forgotten, however, that on the textual level, this opening up for foreign—"acceptable," "civilized"—languages, also leaves room for the inclusion of the foreign within, that is, Cambinda's language.

In contrast to this description of the awesome forces represented by the British influence in Santos' mountains, Lenita's letter, although coming from the same state of São Paulo, dramatizes the more enclosed space of the city itself, which is having its old shacks demolished to make space for "hygienic, comfortable, modern houses" (150). Lenita does not agree with all the new constructions, especially with the "small palaces of the transitional period, [built in] the farmers' fashion," the cosmopolitan fashion, and which "constitute a grave fault which will not disappear anymore" (150). There are, however, "constructions . . . made in these past five years by the architect Ramos de Azevedo, by the *Italian* Pucci and by *other foreigners*, which are real works of art" (150, my italics).

Yet, the crucial point for Lenita is that the destruction of old historical buildings not always give way to real works of art. Commenting on the new "Palácio do Governo" (Palace of the Government), she says: "to put down the old, solid, historical, legendary construction of the Jesuits to stretch on its place that dreadful building!" (150). The fact that she defends the Jesuits' constructions against the new, awful styles decreed by Brazilian government signals to a kind of nostalgia for a time when the Portuguese ruled the country and determined its destiny. The only other acceptable architectural styles have necessarily to be of a foreign origin: if it is not Portuguese, it has at least to be European.

These architectural considerations are, I believe, another foregrounding of the political turmoil the country was going through in 1888. Lenita might, like Barbosa and like part of the Brazilian elite of the time, believe that the independence was a mere "functional disarrangement." She abhors the Brazilians and their dubious taste; even more important, she dislikes the small palaces built on the farmers' fashion. Theirs is the influence which, although solidly built, "constitute[s] a grave fault which will not disappear anymore" (150)—their houses and their architectonic preferences stand as a metonymy for their influence on the whole nation. It is important to keep in mind that the "coffee aristocrats"—certainly the farmers who built the little palaces Lenita refers to—were responsible for the settling of the state of São Paulo and its transformation into the new economic and political force at the end of the nineteenth century. Hence, Lenita's dismissal of their houses as in bad taste implies both that she herself is against the idea of the free Brazilian state these farmers represent, and that, since the Portuguese were not a world power anymore, other European powers such as England were welcome to "fecundate" Brazil. This is another instance, on the architectural level, of Bakhtin's point about "alien words": which "style" is more adequate to Brazil, when Brazilian buildings themselves have always already been "overlain with qualifications, open to dispute, charged with value, already enveloped in an obscuring mist"? It also resembles the question about the "style" in which the book should be written, about which should constitute the master language ordering the narrative. The point is, I believe, that the Portuguese language, itself a late offshoot from Latin, has become inseparable from the other languages which had infiltrated it at the time. The Brazilian Portuguese, a still later offshoot of the "original" Portuguese, cannot but dwell in these oscillations resulting from its settling in America in the sixteenth century and its inevitable "contamination" by sounds and vocabulary of the Indian and African languages.

Amid all this struggle there are two children. One of them, conceived out of wedlock, will be born in Europe; the other belongs in a family whose status of servitude does not prevent the father from breaking an expensive machine in order to protect him from being crushed to death. Who is the real Brazilian? Who will speak the language of Brazil? This is why, once again, we see that *A carne*, like *O mulato* and *O cortiço*, proposes a central question, but has no center in which to literally write the question, much less the answer. Is there in this text an idea of totality? Or is the book even more radical because it does not exactly aspire to the idea of totality? Because the text clearly does not have any center, Lenita has been traditionally seen as this center, since she constitutes the vortex of all these contradictions, tensions and pulsions. The obviousness of Lenita's privileged positioning in the novel has caused the critics to see her, not as a refraction where all the forces converge, but as the only point about the novel, and finally as the novel itself. Because she is the site of this convergence, Lenita is spared from the death given to Joaquim Cambinda and Barbosa. Because she is a vortex, critics have traditionally applied to her what Jameson, in *The Political Unconscious*, calls "strategies of containment" (52-3), which "can be unmasked only by confrontation with the ideal of totality which they at once imply and repress" (53). As a representation for these forces circling around an empty center, Lenita's potential disruptiveness has to be contained, and this containment can only happen within ideology. This is what has happened both to the novel and to the character, as we have seen, through the agency of critics such as Giorgio Marotti, who says that the author confronted the presence of slavery "as a slave master" (45), or as Veríssimo, who dismisses the novel for its "obscenity" or for its being "a monstrous childbirth of an artistically diseased mind."

4. *BOM-CRIOULO*, OR, "CONTRA SI PRÓPRIO"

Adolfo Caminha's *Bom-Crioulo* is the first Brazilian naturalist novel to be totally conceived and written after the inauguration of the Republic, but the text looks back in history. When the story of Amaro, the Bom-Crioulo, starts, the text says that "the victory of the movement for the freedom of the slaves was still very, very far away" (17). This technique of providing a historical background in which Amaro's story is embedded, besides situating him as a runaway slave, serves the purpose of providing the story with a perspective which functions in the text as both background and foreground for the development of the plot, and which operates on several levels within the narrative.

In 1895, when the novel was first published, the Brazilian Republic was in its sixth year; the phase of self-congratulation for the freedom of the slaves and the euphoria for the beginning of the new political regime had given way to very practical matters. Important economic and social changes were in force, and what seemed at first a very easy transformation from a monarchical to a republican society threatened to become a nightmare with the Encilhamento,[1] the spots of

[1]In "Brazil's Bourgeois Revolution?," Steven C. Topik writes that the Encilhamento "began under the Empire as a response to the abolition of slavery and booming international capital markets" (269). The Encilhamento "was not simply the artifice of policy makers bend on self-aggrandizement. Rather, it was built on the foundation of an economy that was rapidly developing in the 1880s" (248). The rising of prices for coffee and rubber made these agricultural products extremely important for exportation. Favorable market conditions, and the freeing of capital provoked by demise of slavery encouraged planters to diversify their investments. This situation led to more industrial and urban investments, and to railroad building in the 1880s, and also to the development of a financier class which dealt with the monies necessary for these enterprises (248). Although the Empire's last ministry had political motives for the implementation of the Encilhamento (to placate ex-slave owners who were not compensated after the Lei Áurea, and to strengthen the newly emerging financier class), there were also real developmentalist objectives involved in the process. With the beginning of the Republic, especially during the government of Marechal Deodoro da Fonseca, the imperial policies were maintained, with the continued favoring of centralizing banking enterprises. These enterprises at the same time strengthened Rio de Janeiro's financial stronghold over the whole country and propitiated several

resistance to the new regime, and the urgent need for housing and for jobs created by masses of newly-freed slaves immigrating to the cities. *Bom-Crioulo* pointedly ignores these monumental problems and concentrates on a small slice of Brazilian society.

What I want to propose is that *Bom-Crioulo*, once the first layer of the narrative is transposed, opens itself as a meditation on Brazil as the site where the text was produced *as* the effect of an intricate process of projection, compensation, repression and displacement. I believe that this omission of the external reality, is, in itself, an attempt to render this reality not as a common-sense external reality, nor even as the most conventional historical narratives encountered in History manuals; rather—as Jameson remarks when referring to the relationships between the Real and the literary or aesthetic act—*Bom-Crioulo* is the rendering of this historical Real as "the rewriting of restructuration of a prior historical or ideological *subtext*" which must itself "always be (re)constructed after the fact" (*The Political Unconscious* 81). I will try to uncover the rifts and discontinuities which constitute the text as a heterogeneous and multifaceted artifact and which, ultimately, represents the Real as an "absent cause." In other words, it does not matter that the text chooses to ignore the historical circumstances in which it was produced; what does matter, however, is the fact that they are ignored, because this omission itself points at these rifts and discontinuities I want to discuss in the present chapter.

Bom-Crioulo has traditionally been seen as a love story. Lúcia Miguel Pereira writes that "in this novel of passion and death . . . there is hardly a breath of lyricism, rarely does the poetic resonance elevate the crawling creatures which move in it" (*Prosa de ficção* 171), and the way the theme of the novel—"sexual inversion among sailors"—"is treated in a way which makes it extremely shocking, with the same crudeness with which Júlio Ribeiro registered the details of normal sexuality, with the same paradoxical repugnance for reality which one notices in Aluísio Azevedo" (171).

For Pereira, therefore, no matter how repugnant the creatures in it, or how shocking and crude the treatment of the theme, this is a love story. Nevertheless,

---

shady negotiations. Paulista concerns with centralization, European suspicions of corruption, and Marechal Floriano's hostility to the imperial plutocracy still in command (270), brought about the collapse of the Encilhamento, and the consequent discrediting of the model of organized capitalism. For more details on the Encilhamento, see also Nelson Werneck Sodré, *História militar do Brasil*; Hélio Silva, *O poder civil*.

to see *Bom-Crioulo* only as a story about homosexual love is to give the novel the character of a unitary, totalized universe, which impoverishes the work and denies its extremely comprehensive discussion about the ideological constructs underlying the Brazilian life of the time. The plot of the novel is seemingly very simple: a black sailor, Bom-Crioulo, falls in love with a white cabin boy, Aleixo, and starts living this love in the ship where they work, and in a rented room at the house of a Portuguese woman, Carolina. This love is eventually transformed into crime when the black sailor, coming back from a hospital, finds out that the cabin boy is having an affair with Carolina. Bom-Crioulo then kills the cabin boy. In the last scenes of the novel, the black man is taken away by the police while the crowd looks at Aleixo's bloody corpse. On this level, it seems that the story does not present any novelty—there are countless stories of mad loves and passionate crimes. However, some more complex factors woven into the text transform this novel—only 80 pages long in the original version—into a very special case in Brazilian literature.

Although it might seem surprising that as early as 1895 a Brazilian novel deals with a love triangle involving homosexual love, in itself, the treatment of a homosexual love is not a new subject in the literature of the Portuguese language, since this was the theme of Abel Botelho's *O Barão de Lavos*, published in Portugal in 1891.[2] However, *Bom-Crioulo* is the story of a homosexual love between a black and a white man; more novel still, the black man is a former slave, and perhaps most novel of all, the third party in the triangle, Carolina, is Portuguese. In the working out of this love story, several gender alignments and re-alignments are in operation, and they represent other levels of displacement which include class and race relations which, in their turn, point at even more complex matters of ideological alignments.

In general, critics of the end of the nineteenth century ignored the publication of *Bom-Crioulo*. According to Lúcia Miguel Pereira, even the always alert critic José Veríssimo never mentioned its existence, and Romero only mentioned it briefly. Pereira elaborates on this indifference to Caminha's work:

> o feitio agressivo e a amargura de homem que se conhecia superior ao seu destino lhe valessem antipatias que explicariam o silêncio em torno dele. É porém mais provável que, surgindo quando já começava a murchar a voga do naturalismo, os seus livros tivessem sido acolhidos com

---

[2]For more details on this novel, see Jacinto do Prado Coelho, *Dicionário de literatura portuguesa, brasileira e galega* 116-17.

> o enfado que não poderia deixar de causar a monotonia de processos literários que se vinham repetindo desde a estréia de Aluísio de Azevedo. (*Prosa de ficção* 167)[3]

Nelson Werneck Sodré agrees with Pereira: "when compared to Aluísio Azevedo, Adolfo Caminha is not at any disadvantage. . . . *Bom-Crioulo* is, really, one of the great books of naturalism" (*O naturalismo no Brasil* 192-93). Dorothy Scott Loos compares *Bom-Crioulo* with other naturalist novels and with Caminha's *A normalista* and concludes that "at times *Bom-Crioulo* takes on epic aspects, with the protagonist a symbol of man, the admixture of good and evil, wanting to do good, but impelled to evil by forces beyond his control" (*The Naturalist Novel in Brazil* 88). David Brookshaw, on the other hand, reads *Bom-Crioulo* as a racist novel: "The message . . . is basically that the company of blacks is not salubrious as they have no control over their animal instincts, and having therefore no morality of their own, they can create havoc with the lives of those who have" (*Race and Color in Brazilian Literature* 39). Among the critics of the time the novel was published, Araripe Júnior seems to have been the only one to greet it with some enthusiasm: "The new writer, as anyone can see, chose the naturalist brush. From his palette come loud colors, which many times resemble an obscene realism, and the language of some of his characters exceeds the limits of what usually is permitted in books" (*Obra crítica* 325).

Because Araripe Júnior's is one of the first examples of *Bom-Crioulo*'s initial reception, it invites some further analysis. First, Araripe Júnior assumes that everyone knows what "naturalism" is and that the author is in complete control of whatever naturalism prescribes. If the author has the naturalist palette at his command, that implies that all colors are at his disposition. It is the combination, at once unusual and scandalous, of these colors, which cuts through the accepted mode of even naturalist novels. Araripe also says that Caminha's language "exceeds the limits of what is usually is permitted (*se permite*) in books." The use of "se permite," a Portuguese construction which denotes an indefinite subject, immediately diffuses and equivocates the matter of who does the permitting in

[3]The aggressive manner and the bitterness of this man who knew himself to be superior to his destiny resulted in antipathies which explain the silence around him. However, it is more probable that, since his books appeared when the naturalist fashion was withering, they were received with the boredom caused by the monotony of a literary process which had been constantly repeated since the appearance of Aluísio Azevedo's first works.

terms of which language is adequate in novels. Are the critics like Araripe Júnior the ones who decree what is permitted and what is not? Of course it is convenient for the critic not to elaborate on this subject.

A recent critic, Francisco Caetano Lopes Jr., argues that "[*Bom-Crioulo*] progressively deconstructs all possible stereotypes found in the Brazilian society, transforming its narrative fabric into an arena where the strongest contradictions fight among themselves and the black element is shown as fundamental" (233). Flora Süssekind also says that the master trope for the novel is "negro." She stresses that Bom-Crioulo's description calls attention to his exceptional physical force; this technique, according to Süssekind, "reinforces a racist theory [because] it does not let the Negro speak and [instead] lets theories of racial inferiority speak for him" (*Tal Brasil, qual romance?* 139).

It is interesting that Pereira refers to the artistry of the text as "invisible threads," Lopes refers to "fabric," while Araripe Júnior chooses "color." For both Araripe and Miguel Pereira, the text is very much the product of one author; for Lopes, a critic influenced by the post-structuralist critique of the subject, the idea of an individual author is beside the point: there is no author anymore, just an ideological war in the text; a fabric is, after all, a complex encounter of several threads, which can come in several colors. There is a sense, however, in which the three readings can converge in showing the same totality operating within the fictional universe of *Bom-Crioulo*. In other words, the "threads" which pull the characters might be exactly the same which compose the "narrative fabric." The understanding of the threads which compose this narrative fabric can be made only by first locating the one master thread, or, shall we say, organizing pattern, which determines the distribution of all the others—threads and colors—for the disposition of the very intricate pattern represented on one level by the novel, and on another by the editorial apparatus of the 1983 edition of *Bom-Crioulo* which guides the reader to pre-established conclusions about the novel.

Here I Am Emperor! [4]

---

[4]The name for this subtitle is a reference to one of Machado de Assis's characters, Rubião. At the end of *Philosopher or Dog?* (*Quincas Borba*), we see the character Rubião back in his native Barbacena after his escape from a sanatorium in Rio de Janeiro. Rubião begins hallucinating again, and starts repeating "To the victor, the potatoes," which had been taught to him by his deceased friend and "philosopher" Quincas Borba. Only now, at this phase of his hallucination, Rubião adds "Here I am Emperor!" ("*Aqui estou Imperador!*") The text then continues: "This obscure, incomplete phrase was repeated out in the street; and it was

Halfway through the novel, Bom-Crioulo goes back to his room in Carolina's house. The room, furnished by him and Aleixo, the cabin-boy, has a number of odd objects collected around the city. Bom-Crioulo lies down on the bed and starts inspecting the walls. On one of them, there is a "picture (which) showed the Emperor smiling tenderly, with his beard of an indulgent patriarch. He was his man. People, these so-called 'republicans,' spoke evil of him, because the old man had feelings and liked the people. . ." (49). The fact that the sailor has the Emperor's picture in his room is in itself no great surprise: both Amaro and Aleixo, being lower class, collect pictures from magazines and plaster them on the walls of their little abode. However, the choice of a picture depicting the Emperor smiling indulgently as an old patriarch points at other levels of significance. It is not clear, at this point of the development of the story, if the Emperor is still in power. The text has stated that Amaro escapes the farm where he is kept as a slave when he is eighteen—when "the victory of abolitionism was still far, very far" (17)—and he meets Aleixo when he is thirty. In the twelve years of Amaro's life in the navy, the freedom of the slaves and the beginning of the republic might have taken place, but the text makes no reference to such public affairs. The tone of the story—published in 1895—leaves this matter in suspense, as if the external political life, or any social life outside Amaro and Aleixo's relationship does not have to be explicitated. Since this is, after all, the story of a Negro man, why does the text choose to fall silent about these important details of Brazilian social life while clearly mentioning the highest figure—the Emperor—which commands (or commanded) this life?

The text, by consciously avoiding such references, calls attention to the novel's special grammar; in other words, the text proposes to re-create the outside world in a more intense and minute way, and the saturation of the sailors' lives with historical references would interfere with the intensity of the issues the text wants to discuss. Another reason is, I believe, due to the fact that the Emperor, with the beard of an indulgent patriarch, functions in the place of an

---

examined; but its meaning could not be apprehended" (270). The pun of Assis's text, namely, the use of verb *estar* in a situation where *ser* would be expected, is meant to call the reader's attention to the extreme instability of one's being Emperor. However, neither the "crazy" Rubião can explain the meaning of his words nor the others can understand it. I believe that, in the case of Bom-Crioulo, his relationship with his lover Aleixo is the more poignant because the more fragile. But Bom-Crioulo does not know this. What he knows is that, at a certain moment of his life, he *is Emperor* in the fullest sense of the Portuguese verb *estar*.

organizing principle under which Bom-Crioulo and his story can take place. However, Bom-Crioulo goes beyond this point, when he says that the Emperor is "his man." Why does Bom-Crioulo choose to identify with a man who, obviously, was responsible for the continuation of the state of slavery into which many like him were born? And why stress the Emperor's "benign" patriarchal mien?

In *The History of Sexuality*, Michel Foucault writes that

> [T]he power over sex is exercised in the same way at all levels. From top to bottom, in its over-all decisions and its capillary interventions alike, whatever the devices or institutions on which it relies, it acts in a uniform and comprehensive manner; it operates according to the simple and endlessly reproduced mechanisms of law, taboo, and censorship: from state to family, from prince to father, from the tribunal to the small change of everyday punishments, from the agencies of social domination to the structures that consitute the subject himself, one finds a general form of power, varying in scale alone. (84-85)

What Foucault talks about in *History of Sexuality* is a dispersion to the point where the mechanisms of power are everywhere at the same time. *Bom-Crioulo*, on the other hand, locates these mechanisms in only one figure—the Emperor—which becomes the site of power—the ultimate signifier of power.

In the novel, however, the mechanisms of law, taboo and censorship mentioned by Foucault work themselves out in various ways. For Amaro, the Bom-Crioulo, his homosexuality is beyond interdiction: it is a *fait accompli*. He has completely assumed his sexual orientation and even conquered a partner, Aleixo. His life, whose beginnings are dimmed in his memory and in the text itself—"Amaro came, nobody knows from where" (17)—has always been organized around the fact that he was, nonetheless, born a slave, and even the ritual of his examination for admission in the navy is just a replay of the examination slave buyers gave to the prospective merchandise: "they ordered him to take off his clothes . . . they examined his back, his chest, his thighs, and gave him a sailor's blue shirt" (17). The fact of Bom-Crioulo's inescapable powerlessness extends itself even to the very property of his body. As a slave, he does not have right to possess anything—he is, instead, a thing possessed; as a sailor, although he has a small salary, he is the property of the navy. The only realm in which he has freedom is in the choice of his sexual orientation.

It is, however, not a freedom which was given to him as his birthright. In the beginning of his life in the navy, he *did not know*: "He didn't recall having ever loved or having ever risked one of these adventures so common in youth, in which easy women are involved." Rather, "he had always been indifferent to certain things, preferring his parties on board, with the boys, far away from the intrigues and falseness of women." But, until he was twenty, unaware of his immanent homosexuality, once "he was forced to sleep with a girl in Angra dos Reis," where he "ended up being a most pitiful copy of a man; and, later, completely drunk, he went to the house of a Frenchwoman at the Rocio. He left the house ashamed, and swore to never again being led to care about these things" (24).

Bom-Crioulo's hesitant attempts at trying to know what he wants, and even his frustrated attempts to have intercourse with women, may be a trope through which the text orients itself politically, thus going beyond issues of sexuality itself, as well as it may be the reason for Bom-Crioulo's identification with the Emperor. At least, in the representation of D. Pedro II he can see something stable. Nevertheless, it is odd, to say the least, to have a text in which the old imperial regime is figured in the form of a black homosexual revering the king.

In his study about authority, Richard Sennett points out that the need for authority is basic, and that "assurance, superior judgment, the ability to impose discipline, the capacity to inspire 'fear'" (18) are the qualities of an authority. Sennett continues:

> In society as in private life, we want a sense of stability and order, and these benefits a regime possessed of authority is supposed to bring. This desire appears in the monuments of authority in public life: massive churches, shrines, government buildings, all symbols that the ruling order will last beyond the generation which now rules and the generation which now obeys. Indeed, one meaning of one Latin word for authority, *auctor*, is that the authority can give guarantees to others about the lasting value of what he does. It is solid. But the social bond is no more timeless than the personal. It is historical, it cannot help but change. The strength those monuments of authority symbolize is a defiance of history, a defiance of time. (*Authority* 18-19)

By having a picture of the Emperor in his most private living space, Bom-Crioulo is certainly evoking the stability and order the Emperor represents. Here we have a classic example of what Max Weber calls "traditional authority." In fact, since Bom-Crioulo never can reasonably expect to meet the Emperor in person, it suffices to him to bask under the glow of the Emperor's authority personified in that picture. Because this authority based on heredity even has a name, a face,

Bom-Crioulo can relate to him on the level of his charisma. This explains why Bom-Crioulo says that "the old man had feelings and liked the people." At this moment, more than ever, Bom-Crioulo *belongs*: he is no longer a former slave, no longer a poor sailor; he is one with the people, and, as such, the Emperor likes him too. Moreover, this tiny "monument" to the Emperor may also represent Bom-Crioulo's awareness of the political instability of his time, as well as his "horror" to those—the Republicans—who agentiate the instability.[5] Accordingly, Amaro does not want to be involved in feminine "intrigues" and "falsities," preferring, instead, the company of his own colleagues in the navy. Besides expressing his preference for bonding with males, Amaro is expressing the need to be closer to the center from where power emanates. Being powerless, he wants to at least associate himself with the most powerful; better still, he wants to be close to a powerful being who can be "benign" to him: "he desired to embark in a certain ship, whose commander, an aristocrat, was said to be friends with all robust sailors; [he was] an excellent educator of youth, a perfect gentleman in his pleasant and severe dealings [with people]" (20). Besides all these advantages, "Commander Albuquerque rewarded his people's work, and never failed to promote his favorites" (20). And Bom-Crioulo, just as he does with the Emperor, definitely defends his commander-to-be: "What people said about him, that he preferred one sex to the other in his love relations could be a calumny like many others invented [by people]" (20).

Women, with their "intrigues" and "falsities," do not represent any source of power in a social environment where the main figure has a "benign patriarchal smile" as his principal asset. What I want to investigate now is what sense this patriarchal system represents Amaro's choice of sexual orientation and of a partner in Aleixo. More importantly, how are his choices reflected in the representation of a Brazilian society which has just emancipated itself from an imperial to a republican state?

Before he meets Aleixo, Bom-Crioulo is "a sweet and tolerant character" (22); after the cabin boy becomes his lover, "nobody saw in him certain scruples

---

[5]Obviously, this is a complicated issue, which exposes Bom-Crioulo's ambivalence, or ignorance, in political subjects. As history books tell us, the republicans were the ones who pushed more for abolition. The Emperor, although "benign," was the one who kept postponing the complete freedom of the slaves. But to Bom-Crioulo, born to slavery and raised who knows how, a smiling, kind face sufficed to make him side with the Emperor against those republicans who had no face, at least not for him.

of obedience and seriousness; he had lost that air, that posture of respect which won him the esteem of the officials in Villegaignon and which distinguished him from the other restless and shameless sailors" (22). His love for the cabin-boy gives Bom-Crioulo the first free impulses in his life. However, these *free* impulses, which lead him to free choices, work in the contrary direction of his liberty. This structure can start with a comparison between his time at the farm and at the navy, before the appearance of Aleixo:

Farm	**Navy**
slavery (17)	freedom (18)
cotton clothes (17)	sailor's shirt (17)
work from dawn until dusk (18)	good bed, good food (18)
the trunk and the whip (18)	no punishment in a year (18)
a negro who flees is hunted down as an animal (17)	"nobody cared about a sailor's colour" (18)

After twelve years in the navy, after having "travel[led] all the world, risk[ed] his life fifty times, sacrifice[d] himself uselessly" (20), Bom-Crioulo wants to stay on land. However, it is not the trips, nor the dangers, nor the sacrifices which tie him to land: it is the need to be closer to Aleixo. At this point, the dismantling of the dichotomy farm/slavery-navy/freedom comes as the onset of Amaro's consciousness that, what he believed to be freedom—the navy—now is only a yoke on his neck, an obstacle to the full expression of his affection for the cabin-boy. This love represents, at the same time, his first free action, and the beginning of his real slavery. Now, he is whipped (15-6) and continually punished on the ship; now he bullies his colleagues, criticizes the officials and challenges their orders (22). It is necessary for Amaro to be free in order to be born as a homosexual, which, itself, becomes another form of subjection. The moment he enters the "free world" *is not*, therefore, the moment he discovers his subjectivity; rather, the moment he discovers his subjectivity is the moment he discovers his sexual orientation (only to have it simultaneously transformed into the denial of this subjectivity).

However, Bom-Crioulo's admission to the navy is as involuntary as his birth to slavery. Upon his escape from the farm, he manages to avoid the slave-hunters and,

> depois de curtir uma noite, a mais escura de sua vida, numa espécie de jaula com grades de ferro, Amaro, que só temia regressar à "fazenda", voltar ao seio da escravidão, estremeceu diante de um rio muito largo e muito calmo, onde havia barcos vogando em todos os sentidos, à vela, outros deitando fumaça, e lá em cima, beirando a água, um morro muito alto, em ponta, varando as nuvens, como ele nunca tinha visto... (17)[6]

The pain of Amaro's physical constraint inside that cage with iron bars is only made on the one hand more constraining because of the proximity of boats sailing free, and on the other hand more bearable because now he *knows*; he *has seen*; therefore he can desire. His first glimpse at a free life is so exhilarating, "that he even wanted to cry, but to cry frankly, openly, in front of other people, as if he had gone crazy. . ." (17). It is significant that, when Amaro escapes the farm, he has to spend a whole night in the cage before he is accepted into the navy. It is as if, to become a free citizen, he has to be born again. The cage is a womb from which he sees the wonders which await for him outside: a free country where boats sail free, crisscrossing the river in all directions. And Amaro is born as everyone is born: naked. His crossing of the boundary between his previous slave-life and the new free life gives him two things: his body, and a new identity, a new name. Now he is not only *Amaro*—"bitter" in Latin—he is *Bom-Crioulo*—Good Black Man. There is a sense in which the only thing a "crioulo" can be in this society is "bom"—good. There is another sense in which the only body this "bom-crioulo" can have is a sexless body, or a body which is not aware of itself as a sexual body—a body which is one with the ship, a body which *works*.

Yet, the bodies of the men who work in the ships do have a sexual dimension, in spite of all interdictions. In the complete absence of women, this sexual

---

[6]After spending one night, the darkest one of his life, in a kind of cage with iron bars, Amaro, who only feared going back to the "farm," going back to slavery, trembled in front of a wide and calm river, where there were boats crossing in all directions; [some were] sail boats, others vomited smoke, and there yonder, close to the water, [there was] a very high sharp mountain [which] crossed the clouds. He had never seen such a sight. . . .

dimension is lived in un-reproductive ways. The day Bom-Crioulo is whipped, two other sailors are whipped as well. The narrator is as explicit as he can be about the reason for the punishment:

> Ora, aconteceu que, na véspera desse dia, Herculano foi surpreedido, por outro marinheiro, a praticar uma ação feia e deprimente do caráter humano. Tinham-no encontrado sozinho, junto à amurada, em pé, a mexer com o braço numa posição torpe, cometendo, contra si próprio, o mais vergonhoso dos atentados... No convés brilhava a nódoa de um escarro ainda fresco. (13-14)[7]

The sailor's masturbation is motive for much commentary, and a fight starts between sailors Herculano and Santana. Although the two of them are punished because of their fight, the ultimate reason is Herculano's masturbation. Herculano's crime, the text tells the reader, "was not in the judicial codes; it was a crime against nature; [since] he *unnecessarily* spilled, on a dry and sterile deck, *the man's generative sap* (*a seiva geradora do homem*)" (14, my emphasis). What is a crime against nature? More precisely, what is crime? If there is a *crime* against *nature*, it is implied that nature has been de-codified and that it constitutes a set of fixed laws against which crimes can be committed. The fact is that "generative sap" has been wasted. This, and not the fight between the two sailors, is the act that deserves punishment.

Bom-Crioulo also receives a severe beating on the same day Herculano is whipped. The apparent reason for Bom-Crioulo's punishment is also a fight: he has beat a colleague because he dared to "mistreat the cabin-boy Aleixo, a beautiful blue-eyed little sailor, [who] was very esteemed by everybody and about whom 'things' were said" (16). Here, again, the superficial reason covers a more serious reason, namely, Bom-Crioulo's love for another man.[8] The structure of

---

[7]On the eve of that day, Herculano was caught, by another sailor, practicing an ugly and depressing act of the human character. He had been found, close to the bulwark, standing, alone, moving his arm in a vile position; he was committing against himself the most shameful offense. . . . On the deck a fresh stain of spittle still shone.

[8]In fact, as David William Foster points out, "if Bom-Crioulo is postulated as a naturally decent man despite his white masters, his masculine sexuality is counterbalanced by the white adolescent whom he pursues. Aleixo is the character in the novel who reveals the stereotypic androgynous or effeminate features

sexual interdiction operating in the novel is dependent on the fact that the sailors, living as men among men only, are destitute of other possibilities to express their sexuality. Not even the officers are free from such predicament, since one of the most important commanders is also said to favor the beautiful sailors and have homosexual relations with them (20, 54-55). All of them, sailors and officers alike, are evading a procreative sexuality and practicing "fruitless" pleasures. The level of interdiction operates even in Bom-Crioulo and Aleixo's room, where the sight of the proof of their lovemaking—the stains on the bed—has to be hidden under "a thick red blanket" (38). One question begs to be asked here: what use can sex be put to when it is still in hiding? One of the uses can be the enforcement of a notion of political conservativism which goes back to the moment when Bom-Crioulo looks at the Emperor's picture on the wall. By the same logic, something keeps sex in hiding, and something (else) determines that it be driven out of hiding.

Writing about the production of a multiplicity of discourses on sex in the eighteenth century, Foucault states that

> from the singular imperialism that compels everyone to transform their sexuality into a perpetual discourse, to the manifold mechanisms which, in the areas of economy, pedagogy, medicine, and justice, incite, extract, distribute, and institutionalizes the sexual discourse, an immense verbosity is what our civilization has required and organized. (*The History of Sexuality* 33)

For Foucault, the attention given to such "perversions" is motivated by one basic concern: "to ensure population, to reproduce labor capacity, to perpetuate the form of social relations: in short, to constitute a sexuality that is economically useful and politically conservative" (36-37). It might seem that the sailors' "perversion" is due in part to the absence of women who could center their sexuality in a possibly more "reproductive" pattern; Aleixo, at least, is so young that he seems not to have ever entered into contact with any woman, and cannot therefore make a free choice. Later in the story, he is given the chance to choose, when he is confronted with Carolina.

---

routinely associated with the images of Greek boy-love" ("Adolfo Caminha's *Bom-Crioulo*" 17).

Here I Am Empress

Carolina, the woman who rents rooms at the Rua da Misericórdia, is an old friend of Bom-Crioulo's. Once he saved her from the attack of two burglars, and since then she has felt indebted to him. A former prostitute, Carolina knows that "the Negro was not a man for women. . ." (36), and treats him with the intimacy of somebody who knows the other's sexual preferences and does not fear them.

When they go together to Carolina's house for the first time, Bom-Crioulo remembers the night he saved her life. On that occasion, she "came from the performance of *Drama on the High Seas*, which was presented at the *Phoenix*" (36). The attack by two burglars, narrated immediately after the name of the play she has just seen, and the mentioning of the mythological bird phoenix which, according to the legend, resurrects from its own ashes, provokes a curious interplay with the situation Carolina and Bom-Crioulo live in the episode with the burglars. For one thing, the drama she lives happens not *at sea*, but very much on land. Since the name of the theatre house is mentioned in the text, it leads to the question of who the phoenix might be, Carolina or Bom-Crioulo. Because she is the one who can almost count herself as dead when the sailor saves her, Carolina might be the representation of the legendary bird. On the other hand, since Bom-Crioulo almost dies too, he might be the bird. However, precisely because the first reference, "drama at sea" marks a contradiction, there is a sense in which "phoenix" might be taken as an ironic device used to call attention to its contrary: whoever might represent the phoenix will not be resurrected from ashes; rather, he or she will go to ashes. It is important to remember that, in the episode the phoenix is mentioned, there is a woman defending herself against the attack of two burglars—referred to as "dois indivíduos" (two individuals), an indefinite plural masculine; Carolina is, then, first seen as a female fighting against two males. Therefore, besides opening up the question about the identity of the phoenix, the episode underlines the possibility that the gender category is also undergoing a bloody struggle for control.

This matter is left unclear for a while, and the very idea of the phoenix will be made more complex throughout the story, because, just as what happened to the mythical bird, metamorphoses begin to occur with the characters. Aleixo is the first one to be metamorphosed: his descriptions, up to that point, stress his feminine qualities: he is "pretty" (*bonitinho*); he is "very light, with rounded forms. . . . Bom-Crioulo had never seen masculine forms so well built, never such arms, such firm and fleshy hips like those. . . . Breasts would make Aleixo a real woman" (38-39).[9] It is interesting to observe that Bom-Crioulo's seduction of the cabin-boy also starts with a trick aimed at calling his attention to his physical body. Boasting to know "the world," Bom-Crioulo first strokes Aleixo's vanity, giving him a cheap little mirror he bought in Rio de Janeiro—"so that he could see how beautiful he was." The little cabin-boy "looked at himself and . . . smiled, lowering his eyes" (23-24). The calling of Aleixo's attention to his own beauty aims at transforming him into a "vain girl," thus softening him to Bom-Crioulo's sexual approach. However, when he becomes aware of the power of his appearance, Aleixo starts taking advantage of it and accepting money from other sailors. Bom-Crioulo, by trying to conquer the boy, unleashes his sense of worth and uncovers the reason of his power: his ambiguous sexuality.[10] The playing out of this ambiguity happens when Carolina, momentarily free from Bom-Crioulo's presence and influence (he has been sent to a hospital after the flogging at the ship), seduces Aleixo. But her seduction of the cabin boy sets in motion a second metamorphosis, a second rebirth. She "closed the door and began undressing quickly in front of Aleixo, while he stood there, motionless, startled in front of this man-woman who wanted to deflower him there, vilely, like an animal" (46). At this moment, Carolina is not only the old prostitute knowledgeable in the arts of sex; she is a man who rapes a young innocent woman. After their first sexual encounter, Carolina herself is transformed: "Aleixo rejuvenated her like a strange elixir, miraculously aphrodisiacal." Following the encounter, "her nerves were firm; her appetite was back; the extraordinary

---

[9]Aleixo is depicted here as a monster; that is, he combines characteristics of the two genders. This inherent monstrosity might be what first baffles and finally attracts Bom-Crioulo to the cabin-boy. Being in the position of a monster himself, the sailor cannot help being attracted by Aleixo, who displays the same characteristics.

[10]Foster comments about Bom-Crioulo's changes and states that, when Bom-Crioulo becomes a demanding master, he is "both echoing contemporary narratives concerning master-slave relationships and inverting radically the pattern of white master and black slave. Caminha is unflinching in narrating the details of sexual enslavement of Aleixo by the older man, and one cannot help but wonder if his portrayal held a doubly morbid fascination for readers who might have been contemplating for the first time both the possibilities of homoerotic passion and a scandalous inversion of the roles of slavery" ("Adolfo Caminha's *Bom-Crioulo*" 17-18).

joy of a bride during the honeymoon entered her soul; all her being vibrated in a strange exuberance of life, in a torrential explosion of happiness" (58).

The metamorphoses in operation are, therefore, of a very complex nature: from woman, Carolina becomes a man in order to seduce Aleixo,[11] only to later be transformed into a woman again by the same seduction. Furthermore, from a friend, as she was seen at first, she is briefly considered a mother to Aleixo, then, she is a man seducing a young girl, and finally, after she seduces Aleixo, she is a bride, a woman in full bloom.

However, the text still vexes the matters further, by metamorphosing Aleixo a second time. From a beautiful boy he becomes a beautiful woman; as a beautiful woman he is seduced both by Bom-Crioulo and Carolina. The process does not stop here, because as soon as he is seduced by the woman, Aleixo starts acting as a "man." He replays with Carolina the same scenes of jealousy Bom-Crioulo plays with him. First, he demands that Carolina stop seeing the Portuguese butcher who pays her rent and sends her meat, and later, upon finding the front door to her house closed, Aleixo "ran his gaze over the furniture, the bed, the bedroom and the living room, as somebody who tries to find vestiges of infidelity" (68).

In addition, the relationship of the three characters throughout the story suffers a series of changes. When Bom-Crioulo saves Carolina's life, he gives her life, thus, in a sense, fathering her. When he brings the young cabin-boy to the house, the three of them become a family: "they were like a small family, they didn't keep secrets from one another; they esteemed each other" (40). However, Carolina's lust for Aleixo breaks this familial harmony, and Bom-Crioulo is considered the extraneous element, the one which has to be discarded.[12]

---

[11]Massaud Moisés also comments about this aspect of the novel. Carolina is the "tertius" of the triangle, but she acts "as a man, because she conquers Aleixo instead of being conquered" by him (*Realismo* 67).

[12]Of course, the concept of "family" has never been completely stabilized. Ever since Plato suggested the abolishing of the family in *The Republic*, discussion about what can be considered "natural" about the concept, and examinations about the role of the family in the private and public life have been an important part of social, political and psychological studies throughout the ages. For a very lucid presentation of the history of the concept of family, see Jean Elshtain, *The Family in Political Thought*. For a study of the influences of capitalism on the family, see Eli Zaretsky, *Capitalism, the Family, & Personal Life*.

The characteristic of this "small family" is, of course, a parody of a bourgeois family both in its constitution and its functions. Here, the roles of father and mother, although played by a man and a woman respectively, do not have the function of what Foucault calls the "deployment of alliance" which is primarily the function of the family: "a system of marriage, of fixation and development of kinship ties, of transmission of names and possessions" (*The History of Sexuality* 106). Instead, the problematized nature of the characters' sexuality, their complex origin, and the very absence of "real" family ties make Bom-Crioulo, Carolina and Aleixo free to try different arrangements of the sexual and familial model.

This fluidity permits the sexual model to constitute a series of pulsions between the bourgeois model and a different, "deviant" model in which it is conceivable to have Bom-Crioulo "fathering" Aleixo in the world of the navy only to transform him into his lover; Carolina posing as the mother just to be able to get closer to the boy and seduce him as if she were the man and he a young inexperienced woman; and finally, Aleixo accepting both Bom-Crioulo's and Carolina's seeming parental care in order to be seduced only to, later, start mimicking Bom-Crioulo's "husbandly" jealousy. This re-arrangement of family relations, far from being merely accounted for by instincts and some other determinism, demonstrates a deeper level of combinatory systems, very much based on the characters' knowledge of previously learned social roles. The kinship ties the three characters develop, no matter how caricatured, are variations of the traditional family; they do exist and resemble to a certain extent the bourgeois family. Even what Foucault summarizes as "the transmission of names and properties" exists in this family: Bom-Crioulo uses his salary to buy Aleixo his first possession, the mirror, and later he uses his money to furnish their room, understood as a joint property. The cabin-boy also "inherits" Carolina's house, her bedroom, and even the meat the Portuguese butcher sends her.

The difference between the property these "parents" transmit to their "child" and the property the bourgeoisie transmits to their offspring is of kind, not of nature. It is also significant that, for Bom-Crioulo, what signals Aleixo's sexual betrayal is the latter's destruction of their little room—their joint property—that subsequently prompts him to kill the cabin-boy. This equation of course extends itself to the fact that Bom-Crioulo also considers himself the "owner" of Aleixo, especially in the scene when he says that he is "as good as the Emperor" (71).

The relations of ownership—of goods, of bodies, of sexual orientation—are established against the framework of a tragedy—*Othello* (71), himself a black man. By making Bom-Crioulo a *black* man, the text focuses on his color as the point of departure for all the other questionings. If his blackness is a central point, against whose "whiteness" can it be played, Carolina's or Aleixo's?

Carolina is a multi-signifier: she is a woman, a Portuguese woman, a white Portuguese woman. Her positioning within the narrative functions as a source of tensions and combinations both among these categories and within themselves: she is a woman who sometimes acts like a man; she is a Portuguese who chose to live in Brazil; she is a white who befriends a black former slave. Aleixo, although a white man, is employed on the same ship Bom-Crioulo works, and shares with all the other sailors, white and black, the same disciplinary rigors so close to slavery. Moreover, in this economy of metamorphosis, he is one of the principal assets, because he triggers Bom-Crioulo's and Carolina's metamorphoses.

Süssekind writes that what Adolfo Caminha does in *Bom-Crioulo* constitutes a contradiction to naturalism because the author "chooses a protagonist [who is] negro, poor and homosexual at the same time [the author] privileges the work relations and the perverted passions instead of family ties" (*Tal Brasil, qual romance?* 139). However, there *is* a family in *Bom-Crioulo*, only it is not based on the model of the bourgeois family, and therefore it does not, it cannot, operate under the same principles. Süssekind continues her commentary of *Bom-Crioulo* by saying that "naturalism recomposes itself, however, when in [the novel's] text racist theories reinforce a racist science when the negro is not permitted to speak and when, instead, theories of racial inferiority are permitted to speak for him" (139). I believe that the fact that the text portrays a strong black homosexual does not necessarily mean that the text is enabling racist theories to speak for him. Rather, I believe that the operative category here is the semantic oscillation that such a combination implies in face of the volatile political situation of the time the novel was written. Values such as family, sexual orientation, place of origin, race, are all being put under discussion and scrutiny in the extensive and intensive attempt of the Republic to represent (and dominate) Brazilians.

Who Rules, After All?

Bom-Crioulo has been hailed as a celebration of homosexual love. However, I believe that there are other considerations pertinent to the matter of the underlying ideologies operating in the novel and to its intricate network of signification. Of course, the story depicts the homosexual love between two sailors, but the text poses other issues besides the complexities of this love. Certain questions related both to the literature of the end of the nineteenth century, and to the social situation of the time are pertinent: why would such a story appear at the end of the nineteenth century? What social conditions propitiated its appearance at the time? What kind of argument does the text want to discuss?

Foucault, in *History of Sexuality*, again is helpful. He writes:

> [T]here is no question that the appearance in nineteenth-century psychiatry, jurisprudence, and literature of a whole series of discourses on the species and subspecies of homosexuality, inversion, pederasty, and "psychic hermaphrodism" made possible a strong advance of social controls into this area of "perversity"; but it also made possible the formation of a "reverse" discourse: homosexuality began to speak in its own behalf, to demand that its legitimacy or "naturality" be acknowledged, often in the same vocabulary, using the same categories by which it was medically disqualified. (101)

Naturally, Foucault is taking as the point of departure for his analysis countries where the matter of a stable nationality was not in question during the formation of these discursive practices about homosexuality. When we deal with a country like Brazil, which in the end of the nineteenth century was struggling to forge a political identity, Foucault's affirmation has to pass through more filters so that the occurrence of a novel like *Bom-Crioulo* can be properly understood. The struggle between various signifiers to become the master signifier of the nation in process of being stabilized develops in several levels.

Again, the matter of slavery, which at the time of the publication of *Bom-Crioulo* had just been officially written out of Brazilian history with the Golden Law, comes back at full force, like the return of the repressed. It is significant that, in this novel, the main character is not a mulatto, that is, in his veins there is no trace of white blood: Bom-Crioulo is a full-blooded Negro. Moreover, unlike Azevedo's Raimundo of *O mulato*, Bom-Crioulo, besides being a Negro, has an indefinite origin: he comes "nobody knows from where" (17). The indefiniteness of his origin points out to a diffuse teluric characteristic: if nobody knows where he is from, he can be from anywhere, from everywhere. Bom-Crioulo comes from the whole of Brazil, and his beginnings are lost even to his own memory. There is a sense in which Amaro, the "Good Black Man," is this unknown Brazil which lurks behind every Brazilian's Brazil—ever more interesting because mysterious, uncomprehended, uncategorizable within the bourgeois system. The depiction of Bom-Crioulo as a homosexual can be understood on two levels: first, he is a homosexual because he is black; his blackness, understood in this context, would therefore place him close to a more animalistic, unsocialized nature; and second, since his origin is undifferentiated, he is a combination of all Brazilians who, through the figure Bom-Crioulo represents, can be convertable to the signifieds attached to homosexuality: the ignorance of its beginnings and the uncertainty about its practical political and social purposes.

The tensions wrought by such alignments can stand out in an optimal scale within a predominantly male institutional system, the navy. The navy, which receives the former slave among its troops, points to the fluidity, instability of the new world Bom-Crioulo gets on. Everything in this new world is volatile: "The lieutenant continued pacing around the deck, as if everything were wonderfully well in that *little floating world* of which he was, now, a kind of *provisional king*" (11, my emphasis). The relationships between the world of the ship and that of the land, sporadic but inescapable, make the little floating world's reality at once contradict and adopt the laws of the stable world in land. Thus, like the highest authority on land, here the lieutenant is a king. His kingship, however, although derived from the model established in land, is, unlike that one, just a provisional one. Nevertheless, in spite of the temporary quality of the lieutenant's "reign," he still reproduces the laws established by the inland king—he is the father who punishes the three sailors who are involved in sexually related acts. The "system of alliance" of which Foucault speaks is legitimated both by the authority conceded to the main official on board and by the more comprehensive authority of his being the Law and the Father.

Unlike the officials' authority, Carolina's is an amicable and forgiving authority, a "feminine" kind of authority. On land, since there are no powerful navy officials to determine the system of rewards and punishment, and the depiction of the Law is diffuse among the police members and the other members of the army, Bom-Crioulo takes refuge under the shelter of the feminine authority represented by the woman. When he saves her life after she has just seen *Drama on the High Seas* at the Phoenix, Bom-Crioulo's relation with Carolina is both that of her father-savior and her son, since she looks after him in a motherly fashion, and later accepts his bringing Aleixo to her house as if the young cabin-boy were Bom-Crioulo's girl-friend.

That authority is dispersed between a "male" and a "female" kind is in itself nothing new in literature. What matters is the peculiar kinds of tensions and mediations homosexuality has to go through in each one of these "male" and "female" modes of authority. In other words, why is it that on the ship sailors are whipped when caught performing a sexual act, whereas in Carolina's house such acts are known and accepted? After all, Bom-Crioulo's love affair with Aleixo, which lasts one year, is carried on mainly in Carolina's house, with her absolute knowledge of it. Carolina's way of treating homosexual love seems to be in sharp contrast with the way the Navy treats it. In reality, what the text portrays is two different kinds of authority, whose common ultimate goal is to discipline homosexuals. In the ship, Bom-Crioulo and the other sailors are physically punished immediately. On land, his punishment takes many different tones, and he himself ends up destroying the reason for his punishment—the cabin-boy. What this represents in the deployment of force in the novel can be understood in two ways: first, the punishment given by men is more immediate, and aimed at a more public system of humiliation (the whippings are done in front of all the other sailors), whereas the punishment inflicted by the woman is more private; second, precisely because more immediate and more physical, the punishment administered by men is more superficial, less lasting: Bom-Crioulo has been whipped several times and still continues doing the things that bring about his public punishment. The kind of punishment given by Carolina not only is more private, more lasting, but it is also more decisive: it is because of her transforming Aleixo into a heterosexual that Amaro kills the cabin boy and is definitively arrested.[13] It is no coincidence, therefore, that the play Carolina sees before the last appearance of Bom-Crioulo is *The Fall of the Bastille*: Bom-Crioulo's fortress is destroyed at last. Carolina, or the power system she comes to represent, finally distributes justice by having Bom-Crioulo kill Aleixo and propitiating the black man's imprisonment for good.

At one point in *Discipline and Punish*, Foucault is discussing the disappearance of public executions and the substitution of this form of punishment for other more reticent punitive practices which aim at "reach[ing] something other than the body itself": "The body now serves as an instrument or intermediary: if one intervenes upon it to imprison it, or to make it work, it is in order to deprive the individual of a liberty that is regarded both as a right and as a property" (*Discipline and Punish* 11). In these terms, the mode of punishment that the navy employs—the public flogging of its sailors, belongs to the category of spectacle and aims primarily at disciplining through physical suffering. This suffering is,

[13]Foster says that "although she explicitly turns against Bom-Crioulo as a black man, and, in her words, a pederast, D. Carolina is not really conscious of having undertaken a form of social revindication against Bom-Crioulo.". As Foster correctly points out, however, "what in effect does take place is a form of rehumiliation of the black man, such that in the course of the second half of the novel he is reduced once again to his status as a slave without dignity, respect, or rights" (18). The special kind of punishment Carolina inflicts on Bom-Crioulo is, therefore, more effective because on the surface it seems to be devoid of political intentions.

of course, at least superficially shared by the other sailors who have to watch it and fear the same treatment for themselves. The punishment Carolina mediates—Bom-Crioulo's imprisonment—belongs to the economy of suspended rights: now Bom-Crioulo loses the liberty to come and go which he acquired when he left the farm; he is definitively separated from the object of his love, and, more important, because he is separated from Aleixo, he is severed from his own subjectivity which was born as a result of his love for the cabin-boy. In sum, without liberty, without Aleixo, and without his subjectivity, Bom-Crioulo reverts to a purely animal level.

Therefore, in this novel which does not portray a conventional family structure, nor a stable social structure which might perpetuate the "system of alliance," the lawlessness is merely apparent. The structures of control are very much in power and exert their force in the several ways discussed above. Still, an important question remains: what specific social conditions made possible the emergence of *Bom-Crioulo* in the *Brazil* of the end of the nineteenth century?

Bom-Crioulo, as previously seen, admires the Emperor, calls him "his man" and abhors "the republicans" who criticize him. Later, Bom-Crioulo equates himself with the Emperor, by saying that he is "as good as the Emperor." From the point of view of the social and political formation which the Emperor represents—aristocratic, patriarchal—it would seem that the former slave has nothing to do with the structure of domination represented by him. Yet, once he conquers Aleixo, Bom-Crioulo becomes a replica of the Emperor: he rules over his charge, Aleixo, both as father and king, and as a lover. The structure of domination reproduces itself endlessly, like in the phenomenon of the facing mirrors: even the seemingly least powerful person—Aleixo—provides a replica of the patriarchal system embodied in the Emperor when he starts trying to dominate Carolina. It is as if, once fallen, the Emperor rules more pervasively by having the power system he embodies reflect itself more decisively on several levels of society. Because Bom-Crioulo, after all a black homosexual, is shown as the Emperor's loyal admirer, it seems that homosexuality, at this point, is the figuration that the text proposes for the structure of power. Precisely because the word "homosexual" does not appear in the text, because the perpetration of this homosexual love is hidden under blankets or behind locked doors (38), it is more "installed," more "real," and can represent that which is not named in the text: the Republic itself, already set in motion at the time the novel is published for the first time.

It's Not Over Until It's Over

In the Preface to *The Political Unconscious*, Jameson remarks on the impossibility of confronting a text in all its freshness as a thing in itself: "texts come before us as the always-already-read; we apprehend them through sedimented layers of previous interpretations, or—if the text is brand-new—through the sedimented reading habits and categories developed by those inherited interpretive traditions (9)." The 1983 edition of *Bom-Crioulo* is exemplary for the uncovering of these layers of interpretive tradition,[14] as well as for the analysis of the systems of domination previously discussed. The system of "policing" the text, already present in Caminha's effort to avoid the word "homosexual," comes back at full force in the twentieth century. It is important to notice that the book I am using for this study is from the "Série Bom Livro" of the Atica publishing house. It is meant to be an "affordable" edition for students of high schools: every copy

[14]One example of another Latin American writer is helpful when we speak about the fortunes and misfortunes behind the layers of interpretive tradition. In an essay about Sarmiento's *Facundo o civilizacióny barbarie*, Diana S. Goodrich writes that "as *Facundo* was translated into French and English, it was exposed . . . to telling forms of productive misreadings" ("From Barbarism to Civilization: Travels of a Latin American Text" 446). These misreadings, according to Goodrich, range from the excision of significant chapters to the addition of "presentational devices such as prefaces, footnotes, glossaries, and appendixes" (446). About the English translation, made by Mary Mann and published in 1868, Goodrich stresses the telling nature of the translation of the title itself which reads *Life in the Argentine Republic in the Days of Tyrants; or Civilization and Barbarism* (450). But *Facundo*'s adventures in the fairy land of productive misreadings doesn't stop there. In his review of the novel in the *Revue des Deux Mondes* (1846), Charles de Mazade self-servingly (for the purposes of French colonizing enterprises) reads the book as "an undeniable evidence of the need to conquer these barbarous republics." In a final twist, Mazade's review was read in Latin America (obviously stripped of its political agenda) as a gesture of approval for Sarmiento's book ("From Barbarism to Civilization" 460-61). In the case of this specific edition of *Bom-Crioulo*, what we have is an editor who intends to "translate" the novel for twentieth century readers, especially the young readers who presumably will use this edition as required course reading. This text, as well as any other text, can be subject to telling forms of "productive misreadings," or, to put it other words, the text can travel not only in space and in different languages, but also in time and within one same language.

comes with a "work sheet."[15] The book is published in cheap paperback, but there are no typos or other errors. It is a careful edition meant for adolescents; however, because there are no other editions of this novel available for sale in Brazil at present, it is *the* edition of *Bom-Crioulo* most people have access to.

Since this novel has many nautical terms, there is the need for some sort of "editor" who explains the peculiarities of the terminology. But what happens is that the editor enlarges his role and becomes the book's second conscience, a sort of alter-ego of the narrator. The editor's text, marked as usual by different typeface placed at the bottom of the page, soon surpasses its functions and starts *reading* the novel for the reader. Some of the editor's comments are comic, as when, on page 15, Bom-Crioulo appears for the first time, and the editor uses the occasion to place a note which reads: "here we have the introduction in the narrative plan of the central character of the novel, the one who gives name to the book" (15). If anybody has had the ability to read up to this point of the novel, this person can be said to be capable of knowing, first, that in a novel called *Bom-Crioulo*, the character called "Bom-Crioulo" is the main character and that his name is the same as the novel's; and second, that the first time this character appears in the novel constitutes its "introduction in the narrative plan," all without any need for the editor to tell this person the obvious. But the "editor" continues his/her "editorial" practices up to the moment when, some five pages later, he/she enters in direct conversation with the reader, as if looking for an alliance against Caminha, the author. The editor writes: "observe that the narrator sees the fact [the commander's homosexuality] as natural. The preference for the same sex does not shock him nor constitute an aberration" (20). The editor is clearly shocked by the narrator's acceptance of homosexuality among the sailors. It seems that, for a book in an edition for high-school children, "perversions" as the one the novel describes cannot appear without protest. The editor's voice continues appearing throughout the novel, always providing a sure reading of the matters discussed by the novel. There are "(N.E.)"s—"notes of the editor"— on almost every page. The two most important of these intrusions are

[15]These "work sheets", adequately called "suplementos de trabalho" (work supplements) in Portuguese, usually consist of loose pages which come with the book. A work sheet usually displays ten questions which help high school students find out things such as "plot," "main characters," and "type" of the novel just read. As a supplement, this work sheet unfailingly directs the readers' attention to the points it considers more important. The parts considered "obscene" or unfit for adolescent consumption are simply not mentioned at all.

on pages 24 and 60, and both reveal important things not only about the editor but about the system of domination, or "the system of alliances" behind the editor.

After he is punished for the first time, Bom-Crioulo starts thinking that, maybe, it was not such a good idea to seduce the cabin-boy, after all. He struggles against both his desire for Aleixo and his scruples: "Hadn't he lived so well without that? Then, hell! It was not worth it to sacrifice the cabin-boy, a child. . . . When he felt the 'need,' there were women from all nations, French, English, Spanish . . . he could choose anyone!" (24). The accompanying footnote says: "Bom-Crioulo's interior conflict is notable: [it is] his struggle against the latent homosexual instinct" (24). Again, the editor's interference serves only to second what the text very clearly states. These cumulative assertions must have a cumulative effect in the reader, who has to forcibly become aware that his/her reading is not a "solitary" reading, the same way that, in the novel, the sailors' masturbation is never completely private. Another of the editor's important interventions appears at the end of the novel, when Bom-Crioulo is having an attack of jealousy. The text of the novel reads:

> The Negro was filled with hatred at the same time he felt more desire to possess the boy eternally. He desired him, yes, he did. But he desired him virgin of any other contact besides his own; he wanted him as before, he wanted him exclusively to live at his side, to obey his caprices, so that they could have a regime of a common existence filled with serenity and mutual dedication. (60)

The editor's comment to this passage reads: "Notice how Bom-Crioulo conceives of his liaison with the cabin-boy *the same way a man conceives marriage to a woman*" (60, my emphasis).

In this comment, there are at least two very revealing things. The first one is the obvious attempt at "heterosexualizing" a clearly homosexual relationship. The second one reveals something about the editor's own beliefs about a heterosexual relationship; better yet, it reveals that what is at stake is what the editor thinks about marriage itself. By saying that the way Bom-Crioulo conceives his liaison with Aleixo is *the same way* a man conceives a marriage to a woman, the editor is taking for granted that *a man*, *any man*, therefore *all men* believe marriage to a woman entails exactly what Bom-Crioulo believes his relationship with Aleixo grants him: total fidelity, obedience, and a common existence filled with mutual dedication. Installed as a technical editorial device which provides necessary vocabulary explanation in a book ostensibly for adolescents, the disciplinary ideology, as much political as educational, personifies itself as an "editor" who becomes first the alter ego to the narrator, then the voice of the Law which condemns homosexuality, and finally, the authority who tells the young readers what a heterosexual marriage consists of. In a moment I want to clarify how this "editorial" voice is implicated in the novel's fabric itself.

In his chapter on T.W. Adorno in *Marxism and Form*, Fredric Jameson remarks that "the novel is always an attempt to reconcile the consciousness of writer and reader with the objective world at large; so it is that the judgments we make on the great novelists fall not on them, but on the moment of history which they reflect and on which their structures pass sentence" (42). In the case of our discussion of the role of the "editor" in this edition of *Bom-Crioulo*, what we have is clearly a second degree of the writerly instance: the understanding of the novel is manipulated, directed, foreclosed by the editor's intromissions in the text. The causes for this intervention reflect an already existing judgment on the novel and on its subject matter, and, mainly, although this is not the case with all editorial voices in all novels, in *Bom-Crioulo* the narrative provides the space for this intervention.

The reader's understanding of the novel will, therefore, be the result of a double filter which will open up a series of problematized instances of responses, acceptances and, possibly, rejections of the subjects discussed in the novel. Following this track, one can say that the text, no matter how revolutionary its politics, depends not so much on the writer's beliefs as on the possibilities for its development already present in the organizational principle available to the novelistic instance itself. In this case, both for the author of the novel, Adolfo Caminha, and for the "editor," the organizational principle available is the Brazilian society—of the end of the nineteenth century for Caminha and of the end of the twentieth century for the "editor." It is from this society which both the novel and the editor's comments come. Since, as the editor's notes demonstrate, the feeling about homosexuality is still nugatory, the question about the reason for the existence of this novel which talks openly about homosexuality *in the end of the nineteenth century* still holds. How can we explain this novel?

We are told that Adolfo Caminha was a "revoltado," and a Republican, and that during his short life he met hardships and scandals.[16] His first novel, *A*

[16]His romance with the wife of a colleague, followed by their decision to live together and face the prejudices of the Fortaleza society led Caminha to resign from his position in the Navy and to move to Rio de Janeiro, where he obtained a humble clerk position. He died of tuberculosis before he was 30 years old.

normalista (1893), is usually considered what Massaud Moisés calls "an X-ray of the Cearense society" (*Realismo* 61-65). Two years after the publication of *A normalista*, work which saw him through a catharsis of his "wrath against the Cearense society" (*Realismo* 65), Caminha was ready to tackle more difficult issues. There was a new and more complex reality to discuss. *Bom-Crioulo* is this discussion. In his study of "the naturalist episode," Nelson Werneck Sodré correctly points out that "reality . . . has never been in that which constitutes the surface of the external world, or in that which is immediately perceived by observation, or in what is momentaneous, isolated, circumstancial. . . . The servile copy of the visible and perceptible signs of social life does not translate the consciousness of reality" (*História da literatura brasileira* 382). In the case of *Bom-Crioulo*, written after the fall of the Empire and during the effervescent first years of the Republic, with all its pulsions of conflicting categories, the novel becomes an attempt to recreate homosexuality as a figure for a number of things which give the novel its "terrible greatness" (*terrível grandeza*) (*Prosa de ficção* 173). Bom-Crioulo's homosexuality functions as a space for the discussion about the passage of the old imperial regime to the new republican regime, about the difficult matter of slavery, and about the oscillation of gender. But finally, I believe, homosexuality is a figure for History itself, precisely because homosexuality cannot be mentioned as such. The fact that *Bom-Crioulo* cannot be explained is the most interesting thing about it. The very fact that the twentieth century "editor" has to supply history—now ours, not Caminha's—by rewriting the novel through his/her interventions, is an indication that there is a space in the novel for this re-writing, both the editor's, and finally, my own. History, then, *causes* everything to happen, but this causality cannot be represented in itself; it must always be posited as a kind of horizon. In the case of *Bom-Crioulo*, especially with the reading the editor gives to the novel, this horizon is enacted not only as something society can look back upon in order to learn about its past, but, precisely, as something from the past which can enable practices of the present which, on their own turn, will be legitimated—or not—in the foreseeable future.

5. *DONA GUIDINHA DO POÇO*, OR, "A LETRA DA LEI ESTAVA MORTA"

Manoel de Oliveira Paiva's *Dona Guidinha do Poço*, a novel with a singular history in Brazilian letters, constitutes an example of what Flora Süssekind, in a poetic use of a Brazilian expression, calls "uma literatura só lâmina" (*Tal Brasil, qual romance?* 198). Although written in 1897, *Dona Guidinha do Poço* was put in book form only in the twentieth century. Lúcia Miguel Pereira, responsible for the "finding" of the manuscript and subsequent publication of the novel, says that Paiva "died without having published the book; only later fragments of it appeared in the *Revista Brasileira*" (*Prosa de ficção* 195). Before the publication of the novel, Manoel de Oliveira Paiva's work was known through comments made by Antônio Sales, Araripe Júnior and Tristão de Ataíde. Despite the many years it took the novel to become available to the public, this text has kept its importance, because it not only discusses extremely important issues pertinent to the historical moment in which it was produced, but, especially because of the novel's own unusual history, it constitutes a crucial example of the same issues the text dramatizes. The "sharp blade" used by Paiva cuts through several layers of the history of the formation of Brazil as a country, through the many implications of the history in relation to the distribution of power within the polity, and finally, through the extremely complex matter of charisma in society, especially when this charisma is embodied in a woman.

The plot, in simplified form, consists of the following: Guida, the rich heiress of land and other valuable property, marries an older man, Quinquim. She is generous with the drought victims, the *retirantes*, but keeps everybody, even her husband, under the power of her authority. The people of Cajazeiras, a village close to her main farm, Poço da Moita, respect her and do not challenge her decisions, even when they concern her protection of criminals. One such criminal is Quinquim's nephew Secundino, who finds shelter at the farm and obtains financial help to start a business at Cajazeiras. A love affair between Guida and Secundino develops; the husband leaves the farm and tries to obtain some legal counseling about a divorce; Guida hires a hit-man to kill Quinquim. When the hit-man is arrested, it is discovered that he has in his possession a prayer (*fecha-corpo*) written by Guida. She is arrested for ordering the murder of her husband.

Although this is certainly a work of fiction, Paiva found elements for the novel in legal documents. Rolando Morel Pinto writes that the material for *Dona*

Guidinha do Poço was collected from the archives of the county of Quixeramobim, where Manoel de Oliveira Paiva spent some time "in search of a better climate for his health." During this period, Paiva not only read the archives, but also contributed chronicles to the newspaper *O Libertador*, in favor of the republic and of the freedom of the slaves. Morel Pinto remarks that, later, Paiva might have even met personally the woman whose history composes the saga of Guidinha do Poço, and who, at the time, "roamed the streets of Fortaleza as a tramp" (Apresentação, *Dona Guidinha do Poço* 5, 10).

Who Is Who

The text of *Dona Guidinha do Poço* is covered with both references to and literal transcription of written documents. In the first pages of the novel, there is the transcription of the inventory of what Guidinha inherits from her father. The transcription, divided in six parts—gold, silver, copper, iron, "*bens móveis*" (goods which can be transported), and "*bens imóveis*" (real estate, "non-moveable" goods)—immediately inscribes Guidinha's existence as textualized subject: that is, she is already enmeshed in the description of her property. In other words, she *is* her properties, and the best proof of this is that, once she is arrested for her husband's murder, her properties are destroyed too. On the formal level, Guida can be seen as a completely textualized entity; this textualization starts with the very first paragraph of the novel, when the narrator, after having referred to the Poço da Moita farm, says that, "if it were not for the unfortunate event which serves as the principal subject of this narrative, [the farm] would still stand with its iron and its symbol" (11). However, the "unfortunate event" itself is not the destruction of the farm, but another occurrence, which, as in a chain-reaction, dooms both the farm and what it means.

By starting the narrative of a story from its end, the text accomplishes two things: first, it prepares the reader for its foreclosure; that is, no matter what the reader reads in the development of the story, he/she already knows what the ultimate result will be, namely, the destruction of the farm; second, the narrative reminds the reader that this is a narrative, a story, and does not have referential sanction in reality; that is, the narrative emphasizes its *fictional* character.

By recurring to the technique of eliminating any claims to its being a historical—as opposed to fictional—narrative, and subsequently loading the fictional text with names and dates related to the history of Brazil, the text immediately posits the matter of the validity of any written texts as historical documents; in other words, since both historical and fictional documents are *written*, and the only way to have access to them is through texts, both exist on the same level either of historicity or fictionality. The narrativity imbricated in historical and fictional texts belongs to the same category; that is, both are stories *told by somebody after the fact.*[1]

This explanation is very crucial to *Dona Guidinha do Poço,* where questions of the genealogy of the Poço da Moita farm, as well as of the village of Cajazeiras, are explained in terms of written documents and dates related to the history of Brazil itself. The fictional space, defined as fictional since the beginning of the novel, nonetheless entertains close ties with a historical, "Real" space which, at the same time, delimits and explains it.

The first instance of this historicization of the fictional space occurs when Guida, Quinquim, and Dona Anginha, are informing Quinquim's nephew Secundino, a newcomer to the region, about the life of the inhabitants of Cajazeiras village. They start discussing the exact date of the creation of the village. They do not agree on the date, because "one [insisted] that the village was created at D. José's time; the other, that [it was created] at D. Maria I's time" (40). In order to clarify this point, a "folder with a poorly glued leather cover, tied with a little ribbon" (40) is brought to the room. The folder contains the papers of Dona Anginha's late brother, the priest Costinha, who, she says "wrote everything in those papers" (40).

At this point, however, Dona Anginha wants to know if her brother's papers refer to another historical event, the "Constantina," which "is from [the episode of] the republicans of 1824" (40). A dutiful (and well-read) editor offers an extremely clarifying footnote: "In January of 1824, in the city of Quixeramobim, in protest against D. Pedro I's dismissal of the constitution, the people of Ceará refused to recognize the imperial political authority and tried to organize a republican government." But this revolt was frustrated, because, "in December of the same year, defeated by the imperial forces, they were forced to pledge allegiance to the constitution granted by D. Pedro I" (40).

It is important to notice both the intention of the revolt mentioned by the editor—to organize a republican government—and the cause of the revolt itself:

---

[1]This assumption leads to Jameson's reformulation of Spinoza's idea of the Real as the "absent cause," and of Althusser's antiteleological formula for history: "history is *not* a text, master or otherwise, but . . . as an absent cause, it is inaccessible to us except in textual form, and . . . our approach to it and to the Real itself necessarily passes through its prior textualization, its narrativization in the political unconscious" (*The Political Unconscious* 35).

the dismissal of a text, the first constitution written after Brazil's independence from Portugal. For the purposes of clarifying some aspects of *Dona Guidinha do Poço*, it is useful now to look at the events related to the momentous occasion of the writing of Brazil's first constitution after independence.

Although the occasion for the writing of this constitution was the birth of a free political entity, a new country, the textualization of this beginning came already enmeshed in other, older texts. Historian Arthur Cezar Ferreira Reis writes that Antônio Carlos Andrada, part of a commission in charge of the first draft of this first document, in 1840 referred to the 1823 constitution as something that "was completely worthless" because, Andrada says, among the men in charge of drafting the constitution,

> um copiou a Constituição Portugueza, outros pedaços da Constituição Hespanhola; à vista destes trabalhos, a nobre comissão teve a bondade de incumbir-me da redacção da nova Constituição: e que fiz eu? Depois de estabelecer as bases fundamentaes, fui reunir o que havia de melhor em todas as outras constituições, aproveitando e coordenando o que havia de mais aplicavel ao nosso Estado; mas no curto prazo de 15 dias para um trabalho tão insano só pude fazer uma obra imperfeita. (*Aspectos da formação brasileira* 145)[2]

It is not clear whether it was the first draft's "worthlessness" or its characteristic as a patchwork of other constitutions which caused, first, the commission to dismiss it and, later, the emperor himself to dismiss the second draft and then grant *his* constitution. The revolt in Quixeramobim might have been based on the emperor's attempts at becoming a totalitarian ruler and/or on the desire of the people of Quixeramobim to install a separatist republican regime. Once the revolt was crushed, its leaders had to "pledge allegiance to the constitution" granted by Pedro I. The issue, therefore, revolved around a document, around its capability to represent the country generally and the distant state of Ceará specifically. It

---

[2]One copied the Portuguese Constitution; others [copied] parts of the Spanish Constitution; at the sight of these works, the noble commission was kind enough to put me in charge of the writing of the new Constitution. And what did I do? After establishing the fundamental bases, I gathered the best of the other constitutions, [while] taking advantage and coordinating whatever was more applicable to our State. However, in the short period of 15 days to perform such an insane task, I could only come up with an imperfect work.

is significant that the first draft rejected by Pedro I was a document based on a view of Brazil both as a country in itself and as a country modelled on Portugal and other countries; this, even more than their lack of talent or time explains why the legislators copied prior constitutions. Was it because Brazil could not generate its own laws? Or was it because the legislators, out of touch with the "real" Brazil, could only understand it in terms of European states?[3] These questions reveal the depth and complexity of the issues which faced the Brazilian State at its foundational moment, in 1822, when it finally broke loose from the mother country Portugal. A country could not be understood without a constitution—the letter of the law which determined the country's political and national characteristics.[4] However, how Brazilian could this constitution be when all the distant states were represented by men who, in some cases, had never even been to those states, and in others had left their provinces in early youth to study in Portugal? Yet, especially in face of the separatist movements in Spanish America, it was necessary to keep Brazil together, and the constitution was the best way to accomplish this unity in law form.

Another important point about the "Constantina" is that, no matter how important for the people of Ceará, it had little or no resonance in the country at large. For *Dona Guidinha do Poço*, however, the revolt becomes a seminal episode: the fact constitutes the foundational moment of the consciousness of the state of Ceará in an independent country.

It is relevant that the novel, written in 1892, is located in relation to the proclamation of the republic (1889) analogously to the moment the "Constantina" was located in relation to the independence (1882). Like similar measures taken

---

[3]It is of course significant that most Brazilian magistrates were trained in law in Coimbra, and that, in most cases, their knowledge of an entity called Brazil composed of different regions happened through their contact with Brazilian fellow students in Coimbra. It seems "natural," then, that their very knowledge of Brazil, because agentiated through the occasion facilitated by a foreign (European) educational institution, would come "filtered" by this circumstance. It comes as no surprise that, when the time came for them to draft a constitution, the only idea that occurred to them was to copy European constitutions.

[4]Actually, Pedro I summoned a "Constituinte" on July 3, 1822, even before the Independence on September 7, 1822. This summoning was the result of a widespread revolt against the Portuguese constitution, which "insisted on ignoring the Brazilian reality and started taking decisions that made the situation even more tense" (Reis, *Aspectos da formação brasileira* 142).

by Pedro I after the proclamation of independence, the republican regime quickly deposed the governors of the provinces, dismissed the senate, and took the first steps to legitimize the new government: the drafting of a new constitution. *Dona Guidinha do Poço* represents, or is temporally situated, at the same time of the "Constantina"; that is, it constitutes one more attempt to show that the people of Ceará were not happy with the new (republican) constitution. Paiva expressed his concerns about the upcoming new regime in August 1889, three months before the proclamation of the Republic: "It is convenient to remember that whatever the regime may be, especially the republican . . . the law has to be executed by men; and who are they? Almost always the people adapt the law to their habits, their instinct, their temper. When the law does not accommodate itself to the people, they reject it and force it out. How will our people, the backwoodsmen, interpret the future regime? Will they understand the thing in itself?" (Apresentação, *Dona Guidinha do Poço* 7-8).

There are at least two very important considerations about Paiva's worries about the new regime: its adaptability to the people's temperament and its execution, "by men." Obviously, Paiva is not aware of the implication of his choice of a predominantly masculine subject for his republic. His was a pre-politically correct time, after all. However, as *Dona Guidinha do Poço* makes clear, the law is applied by *men* and by the standards set by *men* throughout history.

How can this lack of confidence about the way the new regime handles its power be represented in a fictional level? For Paiva, the solution is, quite simply, to reduce the stakes to a minute, local level. The village of Cajazeiras becomes a "sharp" picture of Brazil; only here, certain figures of the historical theatre have been transvestited: the main head of the state is not embodied in the generals who proclaimed the republic, but in a woman who, like the generals, has her own captains, her lieutenants, her private soldiers, and, most importantly, her "iron and her symbol" (11). Guida's masculine traits, as well as her power over her charges, is undeniable. She is described as capable of "swimming . . . like men [swim], and not like women" (15), her intervention on all matters is considered "golden" (79)—*áurea*. When she comes to the village, Guida is always received by a committee composed of the most important people in the village, because "it was habitual for that generous, respected, festive and influential lady to free criminals, order marriages, and to always be honored by long retinues to her arrival and her departure from the village. . ." (105). As an embodiment of this power, Guida has her supporters and her detractors, whom she manipulates at will in order to obtain what she desires. She sometimes provokes fights between the village judge and her nephew Secundino, sometimes forces reconciliations between them. As a result, during the period of elections, the Poço da

Moita farm becomes "an army's barracks" (81), much to the despair of the other ladies, for whom "the word *elections* . . . had lost its original meaning; it was as if it meant: *noise, confusion, disorder*" (81, emphasis in the original). Although Guida's faction does not win the elections, she still retains the power conceded to her both by her placement as a rich, influential woman, and by her charismatic nature. Max Weber's definition of charisma is, of course, fundamental for our understanding of Guida. As Weber writes,

> the term "charisma" will be applied to a certain quality of an individual personality by virtue of which he is considered extraordinary and treated as endowed with supernatural, superhuman, or at least specifically exceptional powers or qualities. These are such as are not accessible to the ordinary person, but are regarded as of divine origin or as exemplary, and on the basis of them, the individual concerned is treated as a "leader." (*Economy and Society* 241)

Guida's charisma emanates not only from her privileged social and economical position. Her superhuman qualities, namely, her man's strength (15-16), added to her almost supernatural ability to recognize plants and to her capacity for distribution of food and justice, reinforce her qualities of leader in her home and in the political life of Cajazeiras. As the priest says in the novel's final page, Guida is (used to be, before her fall) for the people of Cajazeiras, "more than D. Pedro II's wife" (139); that is, in this minute version of Brazil, Guida is more than a queen.

As a woman who is more than a queen, she exists in a level beyond localized political struggles. That is why, even though her candidate is not elected, she continues being accompanied by a committee of important citizens every time she goes to the village, continues being greeted as "Illustrious Mrs. Dona Margarida, who embodies in herself all the highest virtues of a worthy wife and exemplary mother." She is, in sum, the town's "most prominent citizen" (105). Guida, then, transcends an essentialism which would characterize her as a woman only, and becomes a *citizen*; better still, she is an *exemplary* citizen, in other words, she has a sexed female body that enjoys an empowered voice. But it must not be forgotten that this empowerment is only possible when she conforms to the recipe: *dona*, "wife," "mother."

The person who addresses Guida with such flattering terms is the judge of Cajazeiras, whom she transformed into an ally, later into an enemy, and presently into an ally again. In fact, she is, finally, above politics, precisely because, above her political dimension, Margarida is "mother" and "wife." Indeed, even though

Guida is an incontested political leader, she bases her leadership on minute interventions on the personal level too. This is clear on the way the poor people express their feelings towards her: they call her "Guida" or "Dona Guida," ask her for tobacco (48), thank her for promoting a "rodeo"—*vaquejada*—(86), and are deeply moved by her efforts to comfort the family of a young cowboy killed in an accident (98). From the position of an "other"—because she is a woman—she can be said to have ascended to the position of centrality. The important point here is to inquire what this ascension means in terms of the organizational structure of Cazajeiras.

When Guida is acknowledged as being the "center," this process of discovery and self discovery brings to light what has previously been hidden from her and, even, from her fellow citizens of Cajazeiras: the political workings which make her an "eternal other." The very forces which converge upon her end up transforming her into a specific institutional figure that clashes with the predominantly male power relations. These relations are, in turn, engendered and maintained by an ideological formation which, although seeming to derive from her, constitutes an ensemble of patriarchal symbolic values which are, themselves, above and beyond politics, precisely because they represent the forces which enable politics itself.

Guida's Well

Guidinha's farm, "Poço da Moita"—the very site from where she commands men and politics—requires an explanation of Brazilian slang for sexual terms. The word "moita"—literally "bushes" in English—is commonly used in colloquial Brazilian Portuguese to mean "to suspect" and "to ambush," as in the expression "estar na moita"— to be "in the bushes." "Moita" also means hair, as in "uma moita de cabelo." By analogy, "moita" came to signify "pubic hair." The word "poço"—in English "well"—can mean a "well" both in the sense that it is manmade and that it is a natural formation, like the cavity formed by erosion caused by a spring. I believe that the analogy with female genitalia, in this context, does not need to be emphasized. Poço da Moita, however, is not the only farm owned by Guidinha; the inventory of her inheritance lists also the farms called Amparo, Bom-Sucesso, Mazagão, Mulungu e Imboatá. The names of Guida's other farms suggest a network of signification. Although these properties stand in the background of the story, they can be understood to be part of the economic rural enterprise that Poço da Moita represents. The translation of the names, and some attempt to understand about their usage is helpful: Amparo—support; Bom-Sucesso—good success; Mazagão ("meu zangão"?)—untranslatable, perhaps a phonetic combination of "my" and "drone"—drones do not work in the bee community; they are used for sexual purposes and, once the queen bee is fecundated, they are killed; Mulungu—African sounding name; Imboatá—Indian sounding name. Although I cannot recover the exact meaning of "Mulungu" and "Imboatá," it suffices that their existence, together with the Portuguese names "Amparo" and "Bom Sucesso," suggests that the mixture of the three racial elements stands as supportive semiotic pillar to the main farm, "Poço da Moita."

The fact that Guida chooses to reside in Poço da Moita, and that she becomes known as "Guidinha do Poço" implies that her relation to the meaning of the farm name is more than circumstancial. The other farms might constitute the basis of her fortune (and of her process of signification), but it is "Poço da Moita" which better represents her. We must now ask what else, besides being a representation of Guida herself, the name of the farm means in the extremely charged political context of *Dona Guidinha do Poço.*

Writing in *Gender Trouble* about "Subjects of Sex/Gender/Desire," Judith Butler remarks that

> *politics* and *representation* are controversial terms. On the one hand, *representation* serves as the operative term within a political process that seeks to extend visibility and legitimacy to women as political subjects; on the other hand, representation is the normative function of a language which is said either to reveal or to distort what is assumed to be true about the category of women. (1)

In the case of the Poço da Moita farm, due to its obvious relationship with the main character, there is a kind of metonymic exchange: not only is the farm part of Guida and can be seen as representative of Guida, but she also stands as a part for the whole which the farm constitutes. In this sense, the representation implied in the process does serve as a means of extending visibility to Guida within the political body of Cajazeiras. However, as Butler warns us, representation is the "normative function of language" too. This regulatory characteristic, therefore already conserving in a general sense, becomes highly pre-determined when the object of such representation is a woman. In terms of this novel, Guidinha did not choose either her own name or the name of the farm; this choice is made for her, and, from this starting point, she is recognized *as* the farm.

In "Ideology and Ideological State Apparatuses," Louis Althusser discusses the practice of ideological recognition—how people are interpellated—and he concludes that "the existence of ideology and the hailing or interpellation of individuals as subjects are one and the same thing" (175). By the same logic, the person who is interpellated is a person whose name was given to him/her. Althusser again: "every individual is called his name, in the passive sense, it is never he who provides his own name" (177). This name, given to the individual in accordance to the parents' taste, and to the family lineage, installs the individual in an ideological order from which he/she never escapes. That explains Althusser's last proposition: "*individuals are always-already subjects*" (176). Indeed, in *Dona Guidinha do Poço*, although the protagonist is a woman who can command power enough to transform enemies into friends and friends into enemies, protect criminals and change verdicts, she is always subject to an ideological apparatus which ultimately determines her destruction. The nature of this operation, its rules and specific workings within the polity of Cajazeiras, constitute the main problem the novel articulates.

To review the plot of the novel: Guidinha, a powerful middle-aged woman, falls in love with a younger man, Secundino.[5] In order to be able to keep her lover, she orders the murder of her husband and she is eventually arrested. As a consequence, her properties, as the narrator tells us in the first paragraph of the novel, are destroyed. However, there is a sense in which it is not the husband's murder itself the cause for Guidinha's arrest: it is the *way* the husband is murdered. And this *way*, *her* way, inscribed in the novel in several instances under different tropes, is what makes Guida dangerous.

Poço da Moita is primarily a cattle ranch. As such, it has families of cowboys who tend the cattle. Poço da Moita is also an estate located at the side of the road through which the *retirantes* pass on their way to the coast. The nature of the farm and its geographical location make it an almost inevitable stopping off place for the *retirantes*, who obtain food and water from Guidinha. She feeds them and asks them to leave. She treats them more kindly than most other farm-

---

[5]It is significant that on the very first day Secundino arrives at the farm, he goes to the well that gives name to the farm. The site constitutes a *locus amoenus*: "the atmosphere was soothingly fresh. He sat under the caressing shade of the trees. Soon he started slowly undressing. As in a painting, in the great silence of nature the chirping of the birds, the sounds of wind and water, pictured themselves in harmonious conspiracy. . . . In a gentle current [the water] entered the well and, continued ahead, murmuring. . ." (31). After experiencing the enchantment of the well, it is not surprising that he does not resist Guida, begins having an affair with her, and later helps her plot the murder of his uncle, Guida's husband.

ers, but she demands respect for her property. In the case her property is violated, the punishment is certain: "one day she ordered the cutting of the balls of a guy from Lavras de Mangabeira . . . who one day meddled with a favorite little slave" (31). The castration of the cowboy, however, is not an isolated episode; it is very much part of the routine of the farm, since bulls are also castrated, it seems, with some frequency. The matter, here, is that Guida seems to be disturbingly inward about these practices. On one occasion, when Guida is talking with her husband, "Seu Antônio interrupted the scene, asking whether the *boss* (*amo*) agreed on the *improving* (*beneficiar*) of Muniz. —'Go, Seu Antônio!'—determined Guida with some boredom. . ." (33, emphases added). The euphemistic verb used for castration is "beneficiar"—to benefit, to improve; although Seu Antônio asks the "amo"—masculine boss—for the permission to castrate the bull, it is Guida who gives the permission, "with some boredom." This boredom arises from the fact that presumably so many castrations are performed in the farm. After Quinquim discovers Guida's betrayal, he becomes weak: he becomes afraid of ghosts (99), goes to ask for advice from the local priest, and finally goes to the capital to speak to priest Brasil in order to obtain instructions of how to deal with Guida. His murder is only the last step in her process of unmanning her husband.

The murder is attempted twice. The first time, Guida hires Lulu, a man who, not coincidentally, has just killed his own wife because she betrayed him (113-14). But Lulu cannot kill Quinquim because, although he "had hit and been hit many times; had knifed, beat, and slapped [people]," he "had never attacked anybody in cold-blood" (129). For Lulu, the previous killing of his wife does not belong in the category of murder: "Lately he had sent the wife to the other world, but how? What kind of (macho) man wouldn't do the same? Ah, he was not an assassin; his nature didn't agree with that kind of thing!" (130). Lulu then decides to turn himself in to the police because "everybody said he would be acquitted by the jury, because his crime was dictated by his honor. No jury had ever condemned the defendant in these cases" (130).

We need to keep in mind the contrast of how the actual killing of Quinquim is finally committed, and how it is portrayed by the text. When the murder itself occurs, it is described by a woman from the village: "it was Naiú who killed him! . . . It was that renegade, the Major's godson; [and] the Major had freed him at baptism!" (133). In this description of the murder, the most important point is that the murderer *was freed* by the Major during the ceremony of baptism, and is therefore, his spiritual son (and presumably also his former slave, since the Major freed him). The text chooses not to disclose whether Naiú, as Lulu before him, has had pangs of remorse before killing his benefactor. Instead, the fact is presented as already finished, and the proof of Guida's involvement with the crime is disclosed not only because Naiú has confessed, but especially because Naiú has in him a *fecha-corpo*—prayer to "close the body"—written on Guida's handwriting. At the sight of the written prayer, the judge and the sheriff comment: "Poor one! She had been gotten. The prosecutors of Cajazeiras were going to reach a great success in that crime" (138).

Guida's action immediately becomes not a private matter to be judged by the common justice, but a political act: "the newspapers and the opposition deputies, they could continue saying that the county was left to the flies, that crime was on the rise, that the authorities had no prestige, that *the letter of the law was dead*. . . . They were going to prove the contrary" (138, my emphasis). What determines Guida's imprisonment is not, therefore, only the murder of her husband. It is, rather, the text which the murderer Naiú has in his possession at the time of his arrest: more than a form prayer, this is a prayer written *by Guida*, and it bears her symbol, her handwriting. The prayer reads:

> Senhor da minha vida, Pai do divino cordeiro, dai-me a vossa claridade, para seguir os vossos passos: as portas e as escadas do céu abertas, para ver o anjo da Trindade, o cálice d'água benta, e a hóstia consagrada. Quem esta oração trouxer no pescoço e rezar todas as sextas-feiras não sofrerá privações algumas; estará livre de todas as pestes, fome, guerra; bala não matará, faca não furará, também nunca será preso, estará sempre livre da tentação do demônio... (137)[6]

Guida's is a criminal letter played against the regulatory letter of the law. By directly addressing the ultimate father—God—she is bypassing several layers of religious male authority and incorporating in herself the power this authority represents. Naiú, the murderer, has on him a letter which, because of Guida's signal—her handwriting—implicates her both in the murder and in the ultimate transgression, the contempt for other authorities in charge of "speaking" to God.

---

[6]Lord of my life, Father of the divine lamb, give me your light so that I can follow your path: the doors and the stairs to heaven are open for me to see the angel of Trinity, the chalice of blessed water, the consecrated host. The person who brings this prayer on his neck and who prays every Friday will not suffer any hardships, will be free from plagues, hunger, war; bullets won't kill him; knives won't cut him; neither will he ever be imprisoned; he will always be free from the devil's temptations. . . .

Thus, her act, initiated as the kind of private business not uncommon in Cajazeiras—one spouse getting rid of the other—becomes a major political issue. The narrative, aware of the disparity, comments on this aspect through a character, Seu Domingos: "[h]e bet that if she had ordered Quinquim killed from behind a tree, at the roadside, or around the woods, by surprise, as it was usual among the bandits (cangaceiros), people wouldn't be so upset" (136). For Seu Domingos, "what they were doing [to Guida] was cowardice! Everybody wanted to condemn the woman to be hanged! And what about This Man, and Another, and The Other One, who ordered these and those murders, and didn't get even the penance of saying an 'Our Lady,' and continued strolling freely on the streets?" (136).

In sum, for the townspeople speaking through Seu Domingos, Quinquim's murder, in itself, does not constitute a crime; rather, it is the style of the murder, the way it is perpetrated, which determines the criminality of the act. By choosing to not ambush the husband as is usual in the Cajazeira's community, Guida crossed an important boundary which is *understood*, if not *written*. Guida does not remain as the instance of a "poço" which constitutes her into "the highest virtues of a worthy wife and exemplary mother," nor does she take in consideration the idea of "amoitar"—to ambush. By breaking both sets of expectations, even the symbols of her power—her whip, her clothing, her figure, her horse—which before Quinquim's murder were accepted and loved by the people of Cajazeiras, now serve as an offense to them: "Guida looked at the crowd with admiration, and that, to the people, seemed to be arrogance; and because she whipped her horse, the people said she waved the whip at them" (138). Her charisma, acceptable only insofar as she continues as an embodiment of those traits which constitute a woman, a wife, and mother, has a reverse result once she breaks with the organizing discourse ruling the distribution of power. And *her letter*, a proof of her contempt for the *letter of the law*, is the most important detail in her list of crimes, which now are seen for what they are and not as signs of her generosity, or her inclination to protect those persecuted by the police. At this point, the people of Cajazeiras have to "exorcise" Guida from themselves. After all, she has been their mistress for so long, the legitimacy of her power over them has to somehow be eradicated. To accomplish such feat against a woman who has been their protector and their ally, the people of Cajazeiras subject Guida to a process of de-legitimization: they begin equating her with the lowly hit-man who shot her husband. The people gathered to see her being taken to prison yell at her: "Look at the Naiú! Look at the Naiú! There goes the Naiú! Another one repeats: Look at the Naiú! and still another one [repeats], and the name of the crass assassin fell like rain in the ears of the illustrious heiress of the Reginaldos" (138).

In "The Fear of Authority," Richard Sennett explains that "freedom comes from pushing out the 'master within,' whatever his claims. By disbelieving in his legitimacy, you drive him out; at least your mind is free" (*Authority* 42). What the people of Cajazeiras are doing with Guida at this moment is more than just bringing her down. By equating her to a lowly murderer, they are toppling her from the pedestal of her authority and, simultaneously, declaring themselves free from her.

The Undoing of Guida

In the novel, every time a seemingly unsolvable problem arises, its solution is said to be usually at the capital of the state; more specifically, this solution is embodied in the priest Brasil. The non-coincidental nature of the priest's name need not be stressed here. The workings of his power, however, merit comment.

When Secundino arrives at the farm, he has been escaping the persecution from his uncles, who accused him of ordering the murder of his step-father (26). By crossing the frontiers between the states of Pernambuco and Ceará, Secundino is trying to obtain the protection of his other uncle, Quinquim. Guida immediately resolves to extend to him her sympathy: "Secundino was persecuted by justice; he was weak." Because of this, she was even willing to demand that her husband give comfort and protection for the criminal: "Belmiro was Quinquim's brother. Did the boy order his death? Actually, that was hard to swallow. But, if it was all among people of the same blood. . ." (31). The protection Guida extends to Secundino, however, does not surprise anyone, since she is accustomed to giving support to people in his situation, at least when this protection binds people to her in ties of loyalty. Later on, when her husband, Quinquim, needs protection, he cannot get it from her, because she herself is inflicting harm on him.

The name for the solution is Padre Brasil, because "there are certain things that he can [do], especially when it is a matter of honor" (110). Quinquim does go to the capital, where he speaks to Padre Brasil about his divorce. The priest, significantly also a friend of Quinquim's, tells him that he could only approve the divorce "if no reconciliation was possible" (122). But, besides the matter of harmony between husband and wife, Brasil is worried about something else: "it would be more convenient" that he take measures to prevent Guida from selling properties "before the decision of the Church judge," because if that happened, she "would have the right to ask for alimony in court, [in which case] the judge could penalize [Quinquim] to pay a considerable sum in alimony" (122).

This is, of course, sound advice, and it addresses not only a moral sense (reconciliation), but a financial one meant to enable the keeping of property as well. To avoid having to pay alimony, Brasil seems to be suggesting, some arm twisting might do. But whose arm is available for twisting when, it seems, Guida herself has built a large constituency of people who will be loyal to her? She is virtually shielded by her slaves whom she protects and who protect her in turn; she has the love of the *retirantes* whom she gives food and shelter; she feels she can count on Secundino and Lulu, to whom she gives food and protection from the law. She is, especially, a "worthy citizen," "mother," and "dona." Unlike Padre Brasil, however, Guida lacks practical sense, or a view of the ultimate implications of her acts: she keeps her slaves as slaves; she sends the *retirantes* off to the coast, even though she knows that her generous action will be undone when they starve on the roads or in the capital; she protects Secundino and Lulu against the law and later this will implicate their protection in her own condemnation. Where, one must ask, does Guida herself obtain guidance and protection?

One important detail of the novel is the absence of Guida's mother. She is, clearly, her father's daughter, because she continues the political reign he nurtured during his life. However, because she is a woman, her keeping of the power engendered by a man encounters many problems. As pointed out by Flora Süssekind, "Guidinha . . . does not reproduce her father's *hereditary* characteristics. [She] reproduces and transforms *social* traits of the masculine behavior" (*Tal Brasil, qual romance?* 150). For Süssekind, Guidinha, like Luzia of *Luzia-Homem*, a novel written some years after *Dona Guidinha do Poço*, belongs in the category of the "warrior-damsels"(*donzelas-guerreiras*), who "escape from the habitual destiny of their sex. They obtain positions of authority, but see themselves barred from marriage—as what happens to Luzia— or from maternity, as it happens to Guida, [who is] sterile" (146).

Indeed, Guida does not give birth to any child; however, she cannot be said to have been barred from maternity. The whole structure of Poço da Moita is a maternal project which enables Guida's feminine style of power and her nurturing, maternal characteristics. In fact, it is the immense power which is centered on Guida, and the peculiarly feminine characteristic of this power which doom her. Or, perhaps, which has necessarily to be doomed so that a new order can be born.

One of the first characteristics of this feminine, maternal, power is that it is primarily centered on Guida's ability to *feed* people. When the "retirantes" appear on her farm, "Margarida [is] extremely generous" with them. She has "two slaves in charge of serving them, of giving milk to the little children . . . of giving them jerked beef, manioc flour and brown sugar" (17). Later on, she is the one around whose table people gather to eat; at her table, enemies reconcile, friends talk, young men and young women congregate in complete harmony, and pleasure beyond the oral sense is obtained: these gatherings both at Guida's house or under Guida's influence, become oral pleasures which point to Guida as their distributor. It seems that this oral pleasure, since it is directly related to Guida, is the sound of her very heartbeat, soothing the infants—or infantilized adults—she is feeding. Of course, in what we might term this preoedipal phase, the body of the mother, or, in this case, Poço da Moita, is the all-encompassing universe which on the one hand provides nurturance, and on the other does not provide a space for sexual difference. That explains the reason why Guida orders castrations both of bulls and men. Once "neutered" both can be sent back to a pre-sexual phase.

Poço da Moita has always been an exclusively feminine space: Guida has been raised not by her father, but by her grandmother who, "if the father happened to reprimand the little thing, the old woman soon complained, raising her eyeglasses: —Leave the girl alone, Lau! Guidinha, come here close to me" (14). Her father's role in the farm seems to have been the same as Quinquim's; that is, both represent merely empty male figures who perform the role of token men. The mother figure—Guida and, before her, her grandmother—do not need men as sexual partners. Between Guida's father and her grandmother there is the interdiction of incest; and between Guida and Quinquim the text implies that nothing sexual happens;[7] that is, although the institution of marriage is approved (and applauded) within the political symbolic of Cajazeiras, and although Guida, according to the customary ritual, takes Quinquim's name just as she had previously been given her father's name, for her marriage does not affirm nor redeem

---

[7]The text says that Guida, whose father wanted her to be a man, had many suitors, whom she prodigalized "liberties," "and did not even save the little caresses which a maiden on her right mind can concede without harm to her physical integrity" (15). However, indiscreet as the narration is about Guida's sex life before her marriage, it shies away from any more details afterwards. It does not shy away, however, from a dubious comment: "When she married Major Joaquim Damião de Barros . . . she took the name of Margarida Reginaldo de Oliveira Barros. If, upon receiving the husband's name, she did everything else the Holy Church orders, only God knows" (16).

her sexual difference from Quinquim.[8] She, therefore, seems to occupy a limbo of sexual undifferentiation where the only factor to rescue her from fatally becoming the man her father wanted her to be is to have children.

As a woman reared to be the proprietor of a large estate, Guida is inescapably involved with the masculine realm of economics. The systematic negation of her femininity both by her father and by her grandmother who raised her as a tomboy, may explain her assuming her maternity with a vengeance. She seems to want to rid herself completely of the male influence in the world where she dwells with her "children." It seems that the figure of the mother, embodied in Guida, wants to revolve in an ideal world where only herself and her dependent infants live. Poço da Moita is, therefore, a utopian world, a *locus amoenus*, where men as differentiated sexual beings have no place and where Guida presides as the all-powerful Mother.

Julia Kristeva, on her article "Stabat Mater," writes that motherhood as it is represented in Western culture "is a *fantasy* that is nurtured by the adult, man or woman, of a lost territory [that] involves less an idealized archaic mother than the idealization of the *relationship* that binds us to her" (*The Kristeva Reader* 161). This relationship, in *Guidinha do Poço*, is one of bliss, eternal feeding, abundance even in the times of draught, and, especially, of deliverance from the terrors of the adult world. That explains the many feasts Guidinha promotes not only for the people of her house, but for all townspeople as well. In the parties, there is good food, good music, and fun. The horrors of the drought do not disturb these feasts, as long as Guida is willing to slaughter yet another animal for beef—and she is *always* willing to. Furthermore, there is a sense in which, at the same time Guida feeds the people, she also feeds on them—she needs

[8]Discussing the matter of naming in Lacan, Jane Gallop states that "[i]n Lacan's writing, the Name of the Father is the Law. The legal assignation of a Father's name to a child is meant to call a halt to uncertainty about the identity of the father. If the mother's femininity (both her sexuality and her untrustworthiness) were affirmed, the Name-of-the-Father would always be in doubt, always be subject to the question of the mother's morality. Thus the Name-of-the-Father must be arbitrarily and absolutely imposed, thereby instituting the reign of patriarchal law" (*The Daughter's Seduction* 39). For the purposes of the understanding the matter of naming in Dona Guidinha do Poço, it is interesting that, despite the fact that Guida is given her father's name at birth, and later on takes up her husband's name, she is known not by these names, but by the name—Poço—which, as my discussion of the term shows, displaces the patriarchal law and inscribes Guida as an eminently feminine figure.

them to be able to play the role of mother, in a symbiotic relationship. It is no coincidence, therefore, that in the last pages of the novel, when she enters Cajazeiras escorted by the police, she refers to those who are insulting her as "this hospitable people of my country!" (138). Also, Guidinha "delivers" her children from the danger of entering a sexed life: she castrates (benefits) whatever males—human or animal—need this castration in order to be happier or more adapted to life as Guida deems convenient. There is a price to be paid to remain in paradise; Guida sets the price.

However, in her handling of her maternal power, Guida commits three mistakes: she takes as a lover one of the young males she feeds, and she unmans her husband, who is ultimately in charge of keeping at least the appearances of some balance between male and female power within the politics of Poço da Moita. The third mistake is her belief that, by feeding her people, she would keep them always in a preoedipal phase, free from the encounter with the Law of the Father. By transforming her essentially nurturing role into an erotic role in her relationship with Secundino, Guida brings about her damnation, her separation from her people, and ultimately their entrance into the oedipal phase, where they have to contend with a world ordered not according to Guida's specifications, but according to Padre Brasil's determinations. Padre Brasil is the symbolic order—the Law of the Father—that intervenes in the dyadic mother-child relationship and recovers the child for the world of adulthood.

For these reasons, I disagree with Süssekind when she says that Guida was barred from maternity; rather, I would say, Guida embodies an enormously powerful and castrating mother whose powers, if not checked, will both lock her children in an eternal preoedipal phase and will prevent the father's authority to be heard in the children's education and transformation into "citizens."

More important, there is also a political reading to the same matters. The absent Padre Brasil may be taken to allegorize[9] the very centralizing republican

---

[9]The word "allegory" is very complex and has been the subject of study by several scholars. See especially Jameson, "Third-World Literature in the Era of Multinational Capitalism"; Ahmad, "Jameson's Rhetoric of Otherness and the 'National Allegory'; and Sommer, "Love and Country: An Allegorical Speculation" in *Foundational Fictions*. For my purpose, Sommer's crisp definition of allegory, "a narrative structure in which one line is a trace of the other, in which each helps to write the other" (42) is very appropriate. As we have seen throughout the discussion of Paiva's novel, fictional and historical "lines"—episodes, in this case—are seen in tense interaction because one needs the other to exist both in textual and historical form.

forces the author of the novel admires but fears. In 1889, Manoel de Oliveira Paiva wrote about the new regime's applicability in the Northeast: "If we resort to the municipal archives which portray, albeit in a simple way, the administration, the policing, and the justice . . . we will have lots of advantages in getting to know the mass, the raw material that we have to *mold* to the republican regime" ("Apresentação" 8, my emphasis). Like Guida, who is forced to send the *retirantes* to look for salvation on the coast, "*because that was the only place the Queen cared for*" ("Apresentação" 17, emphasis in the original), Manoel de Oliveira Paiva also resents this official favoritism for the coast: "What good exists (in the country)—I'd rather it didn't— . . . is the monopoly of the coast and the most alarming neglect for the *real* Brazil, which is the central territory" ("Apresentação" 17, my emphasis). These centralizing forces, coming "from the coast"—Fortaleza, the Capital of Ceará, where Padre Brasil lives, is on the coast—will mold the interior according to designs established elsewhere. The new regime, incarnated in Padre Brasil, becomes a form of paternalism.[10] The previous state of the nation constitutes a stage of pre-political consciousness in which all differences dissolve under the power of an all-nurturing mother. The newly inaugurated regime, the republic, whose beginning was historically operated by the army, destroys the power represented by the mother and establishes a new order. Obviously, this new order, embodied in Padre Brasil—and in the republic—brings forth the entrance of Brazil in twentieth century capitalism under the cloak of a religious male figure. This, ultimately, will replace the dependency on the mother for the dependency on the father who, himself, is dependent on a chain of other fathers.

Change, the text seems to be implying, is inevitable: just as a child has to be weaned from the mother's breasts, Brazil has to be weaned from its mixed origins centered around a feminized original space represented both by the farms named after religious, African and Indian figures, and by Guida herself. At this new moment for the definition of Brazil as a nation, the State, in its most masculine form, is going to, at once, take over the differences and unite them in a

---

[10]Sennett has a very clear explanation of the term "paternalism" which helps us understand this moment in *Guidinha do Poço*: "in a paternalistic society, males continue to dominate. The domination is based on their roles as fathers, protectors, stern judges." Priest ("padre," "father") Brasil protects Quinquim, or at least what Quinquim represents, and at the same time dispenses judgment on the situation as the friend presents it. As Sennett argues and *Dona Guidinha do Poço* exemplifies, "paternalism may seem the only form of male dominance possible in a society of great change like that of the 19th century" (53-54).

common symbolic form: a "Brazilian," and not an "Indian," or "African," or "Portuguese."

Fate would have it that the manuscript of *Dona Guidinha do Poço* should remain unpublished for almost sixty years, and that it would be recovered by a woman, the critic Lúcia Miguel Pereira. Although extra-literary causes determined that this should be so, the text's history is all too fitting with the discussion the novel puts forth. *Dona Guidinha do Poço*, the novel, and Guidinha, the character, were left silent, unable to represent themselves in the new, patriarchal order brought about in the Republic. The recovering of the text and its publication in 1952, although noted only by a few scholars at the time, work in Brazilian literature as the identification of an aporetic moment. Lost to its time, but not lost to all times, *Dona Guidinha do Poço*, still remains a "sharp blade" which cuts through the flesh of the patriarchal system of the end of the nineteenth century and longingly points to a time and order now vanished.

CONCLUSIONS

Although *Bom-Crioulo* is the last naturalist novel to be written in the nineteenth century, it is not the last Brazilian naturalist novel. In 1905 Domingos Olímpio published *Luzia-Homem*, and other writers adopted a revised form of naturalism during the 1930s and the 1970s. Massaud Moisés writes that "the realist, naturalist and impressionist patterns will not completely disappear after the publication of *Canaã* in 1902; actually they continue until 1922, mixed with symbolist elements, and they continue to a degree in the Northeastern fiction of the 1930s" (*Romantismo* 330). Flora Süssekind takes the point a little further when she says that, besides the naturalist episode of the 1930s, also in the 1970s there were naturalist novels such as Aguinaldo Silva's *O crime antes da festa*, José Louzeiro's *Acusado de homicídio*, and Renado Pompeu's *Quatro-Olhos*. Süssekind analyzes these distinct occurrences of naturalism which she calls *"studies of temperament,"* *"cycles,"* and *"journalistic novels."*

Süssekind discusses these three phases of naturalism and links them with the sciences they are related to. In the end of the nineteenth century, she says, there is "one sole and indisputable knowledge: physiology" (*Tal Brasil, qual romance?* 173). In the naturalism of 1930, on the other hand, the "theme" is not the cure of a diseased body, but "the possession of the land" (151); that explains why these "ciclos" have either names of agricultural products—"*cacau*" (cocoa), "*cana*" (sugar cane)—or of organized struggles for the possession of the land—"*cangaço*" (banditism), "*misticismo*" (mysticism; 151). According to Süssekind, "the effects of analogy and of tranquillity in the novel of the thirties find support in the social sciences" (161). The last phase of naturalism, Süssekind maintains, is a direct result of the repressive politics at work during the military dictatorship: "the new naturalism emphasizes more the *information* than the narration" (174), and it is based on the "sciences of communication" (173).

This division in three phases serves the purpose of showing that naturalism was not just an isolated incident at the end of the nineteenth century, but it has been the choice of writers of subsequent decades. Yet, I believe that Süssekind misinterprets a very important political aspect which can be said to be the common denominator for all these phases. She affirms that "the naturalist ideology works . . . on the aesthetic plan, as a kind of *band-aid* for a society whose divisions are clear. . ." (174). My point is exactly the contrary: naturalist ideology functions precisely as an uncovering of divisions, ruptures and discontinuities of the Brazilian society. Elsewhere, Süssekind makes some contradictory statements: "The frame of naturalism is narrow. In it there is no room for fragmentation. In it there is no room for doubts and divisions." However, she immediately goes on to say that "[t]he *naturalist image* reconstitutes with microscopic fidelity a fractured identity and tries to reinvigorate the weakened breasts of an Iracema-America which it tries to, if not revive, at least to picture" (198). If naturalism leaves no room for doubts, divisions and fragmentation, how can it at the same time be able to reconstitute a "fractured identity"? But Süssekind does not seem to see the contradiction. For her, what matters is that there is a "dreamed America" which exists exclusively as "echoes which can be heard only by an acculturated ear[,] . . . [which can be] loving to 'the speeches of other races,' of other cultures. One looks at América, at 'the things of the land,' but the optic instruments are provided by a distant, European father" (197). The role of the literature produced in America, she says, is to picture a "national utopia" in such a way that "it *will seem* that it has identity, specific regional and ethnic characteristics," and in a way to show that from it "divisions and ambiguities are absent" (197, my emphasis). However, for Süssekind, naturalism falls short of the task: "If the model is full of fractures, no problem: the picture gives it unity" (197).

Two points especially solicit my attention in Süssekind's explanation; first, her assertion that naturalist fiction does not revive, just *pictures*; and second, her apparent assumption that the life portrayed in naturalist fiction is something which belongs to "the past" ("echoes"), to the "dreamed America" which can only be recovered by acculturated ears. As I have contended throughout this book, naturalist fiction does more than picture: it analyzes, suggests reasons, portrays the ambiguities and the fractures, and finally proposes new ways of understanding the new country to be born out of the political turmoil. How else can we understand Azevedo's portrayal of the power of the community being subsumed by the power represented and organized around the Church in *O mulato*? Or how are we to understand a more general naturalist awe before the realignment of gender roles and family ties in *A carne*, *O cortiço*, *Bom-Crioulo* and *Dona Guidinha do Poço*? These novels constitute in Brazilian literary history, even today, some of the most radical texts yet produced. They represent a monumental space for those voices silenced during all periods of movement towards a national "consensus." In this sense, yes, naturalist works are "utopic," because, as we have seen in the subsequent years after their appearance, those voices they portrayed were, in most cases, silenced, suffocated, written out of history. On the other hand, as Süssekind herself affirms, since the naturalist moment recurs in Brazilian literary history, it is possibly less a "device" for looking at "the past" than a subtle, complex mode of explanation for how the "present" is available as a way of reading any future. The voices continue, even if in mutated form, to claim attention, recognition, space, the chance to be part of Brazil.

It is interesting to see how, in another book, Süssekind herself gives us a very illuminating example (and changes her position on the subject). Commenting on Roberto Schwarz's remarks on singer Caetano Velloso's decision to sing in English,

> ("Accused by the 'nationalists,' he answers that he was not the one who brought the Americans to Brazil. He always wanted to sing in this language, which he heard on the radio since he was a child. And it is clear that [because] he sings in English with a Northeastern accent, he registers a substantial moment of our history and imagination"). (*Ao vencedor as batatas* 56)

Süssekind says:

> The appropriation of foreign materials by the *tropicalista* group, criticized at the time, did not indicate solely an attempt at being in tune with the European or North American artistic avant-garde;] *on the contrary, in this juxtaposition of "autochthonous" and "imported" elements, rigid delimitations are broken, the idea of the national is discussed*[;]

and, she continues, it expresses

> *the contradictions of the Brazilian development as well as [it exposes the fact that] the left allied to the (national) bourgeoisie . . . could not stand the sound of (foreign) guitars*. (*Literatura e vida literária* 28, my emphasis)

What Süssekind deplores in the naturalists, namely their adoption of a foreign generated aesthetics, is the same thing she accepts in Caetano Velloso. Further ahead, Süssekind herself informs that these divisions, which reveal the "ideological and aesthetic fractures in the group of cultural producers in the period" (29), were abruptly cut by the *AI-5* (Institutional Act number 5), which enabled the military authoritarian government to violently censor and persecute all artists and intellectuals alike. In other words, it is not acceptable that present-day artists who have become superstars be persecuted on the basis of their adoption of a foreign-born form of artistic expression. Caetano Velloso's decision to sing in English signals, I think (and believe Süssekind would agree), to the "foreign within" which all Brazilians have to contend with. Unfortunately, Süssekind does not extend the same understanding to the naturalists.

One last point about Süssekind's remarks. In *Tal Brasil, qual romance?* she seems nostalgic for a time when Brazil was not the child of Iracema and an European father. She seems to believe that Brazilian's "acculturated ear" somehow constitutes an obstacle to the understanding of Brazil. I would argue, very much to the contrary, that Brazil, as a nation, can only be understood as an acculturated entity; in other words, there is no other Brazil. This acculturation, however, was not processed by the "European father" alone. There is no such a thing as Brazil before the Portuguese; there never has been. There were Indian peoples on the land; these Indians had their property, liberty, culture and lives taken by the Portuguese. However, the Indians never constituted a pure, primeval Brazil coerced into acculturation. The "Indians" have been appropriated at different times—always with ideological or more explicitly political purposes—as a symbol of Brazil. But they, alone, cannot and do not represent Brazil. The Africans, who arrived later and against their will, also do not represent Brazil. Neither do the white Europeans. No one single group, alone, can represent Brazil. To believe so, and to long for a non-acculturated Brazil, is ultimately only to reinforce racist and "centralist" ideas which would determine that this Indian voice, or that African language, or that White cultural trait, is *the* accepted one (in detriment to others which do not have power to represent themselves). Given the very real conditions of the colonization and settlement of the country, there is, I believe, little doubt about *which group* would arrogate to itself the right to speak for, and as, the non-acculturated Brazil.

However, there have been many times in Brazilian history when it seemed that Brazil, or rather, "Brazil," could be embodied in one subject. These occasions have always happened during times when the Brazilian State has needed a "unified front" by means of which it can more easily address, control and punish those Brazilian subjects that do not conform to the established norm. For the purposes of my discussion, one of these occasions was the end of the monarchic and beginning of the republican regime. The other occasions have been during the 1930s and the 1970s, when the country was ruled by military dictatorship. What Süssekind seems to fail to realize is that these three occasions were exactly the times when naturalist fiction appeared in what we may agree for the moment were its three different dispensations: studies of temperament, cycles—"regionalist literature"—and journalistic narrative. We will not adequately understand the very phenomenon of naturalism until we ask why this fiction appears at these specific times in Brazil.

That is, we need, first of all, to understand a more searching relationship between State institutions and ideology before we presume to understand how fiction participates in the negotiation. This is of course a daunting task. Let me give the following crucial passage from Foucault as offering some indication about what conceptual stratifications need to be considered. In this passage, Foucault is discussing the problem of the establishment of the functions of surveillance, normalization and control, a linkage instituted in the seventeenth century, and which later comprised the additional functions of punishment, correction, education and so on. For him, if the phenomenon of power is considered as dependent solely on the State apparatus, it will inevitably transform the State into an essentially repressive—punitive—instance of the relations of power. What he proposes, instead, is that relations of power, and "the analysis that must be made of them, necessarily extend beyond the limits of the State" (*Power/Knowledge* 122). This is so because, Foucault says, for all omnipotence of its apparatuses, the State "is far from being able to occupy the whole field of power relations, and further because the State can only operate on the basis of other, already existing power relations" (122). The State is, then,

> superstructural in relation to a whole series of power networks that invest the body, sexuality, the family, kinship, knowledge, technology and so forth. True, these networks stand in a conditioning-conditioned relationship to a kind of "meta-power" which is structured essentially round a certain number of great prohibition functions; but this meta-power with its prohibitions can only take hold and secure its footing where it is rooted in a whole series of multiple and indefinite power relations that supply the necessary basis for the great negative forms of power. (*Power/Knowledge* 122)

For my more immediate purpose, I will not take up the question of how an idea of power, or rather, Power, may be mystified here. The significant thing is that Foucault's "State" is neither a sovereign nor a total entity. It is pervasive and comprehensive but its final force is in a sense almost crude and prohibitive. "Relations" more diffuse and enabling circumscribe the State, and investments more elusive and foundational articulate the basis for its sway. *Bom-Crioulo*, *O cortiço* and *Dona Guidinha do Poço* are exemplary for the demonstration of this point. In these novels there is a very clear dramatization of how the "field of actual power relations" is not embodied in one single, superstructural instance; rather, these relations are present at all levels, and the negotiations among these levels make the dispensation of power at once diffuse and complex. But it is essential to my argument that naturalism be the name of that Brazilian literary practice which has been recurrently employed to address the perception of a national entity—the State—which has attempted to arrogate to itself the entire space of power relations.

As I hope I made clear in the Introduction, the State does not appear as "itself" in the words of the Rio de Janeiro professoriate that criticized and regulated the reception of naturalist fiction either in the nineteenth or the twentieth century. Rather, in the nineteenth century this professoriate provided a series of norms for the understanding of literature, and those norms, *in themselves*, because originated in the capital of the empire, were taken as a standard idea of what Brazilian literature was, as if "by consensus." The measure of how this consensus has taken hold is the fact that twentieth century critics continue echoing the norms of a century ago. Of course the idea of this consensus, as it has been handed down in history, has not been made to disclose its own internal ideological operation. That is, the conditions of the intellectual life in the end of the nineteenth century have been, for the most part, understood as localized disputes aimed at addressing either merely personal dislikes or blind allegiances to one of the several philosophical currents popular at the time.

Naturalism, as I understand it, is nothing but the literary practice which has addressed the rifts, discontinuities and contradictions the Brazilian nation has faced in several moments of its history. It of course addresses power in its forms of relations and prohibitions. It is central to the practice that this address be oblique, confused, and even incomplete. In the nineteenth century naturalism, in *Bom-Crioulo*, for example, the seemingly least powerful character, Aleixo, after being seduced and transformed into a sexual object by both a man and a woman, starts reproducing the repressive features of nineteenth-century sexual behavior. By trying to control Carolina, Aleixo relives in this heterosexual relationship a relay of power very difficult to characterize, much less locate as a model, although this power shapes both his homosexual relationship with Bom-Crioulo and his professional relationship with the navy. The navy, in fact, provides the most obvious site of a governing structure, but it does not constitute a central, seamless set of power relations, nor is the navy defined in the text as an institution in any way under direct governmental control. Instead, to take just one example, although the navy is "officially" heterosexual and administers physical and moral punishment to the homosexual sailors, it has a homosexual officer in its high ranks. More contradictory still, the homosexual captain dotes on some sailors and does not shy away from favoring them as much as he pleases, while "stray homosexual acts" by other sailors are punished with whippings. These physical punishments, however, are not administered by the officer himself, but by another sailor, who takes the opportunity to enjoy his power by handling the instrument of torture. For their part, the other sailors beat up their peers each time they are challenged over either their masculinity or their objects of desire. There is power everywhere in *Bom-Crioulo*, in other words, but it leaks away, like masturbated sperm, and it does not recreate itself at higher, more supervening levels.

Similarly, in *O cortiço*, the vexing complexity of power relations is dramatized both within and without the tenement house. Pombinha and João Romão, for instance, generate their "economy" of power through procedures which sometimes align and sometimes oppose them to other characters inside the universe of the tenement house and in the financiers' corner (for João Romão) and in Léonie's house (for Pombinha). Pombinha's very personal brand of power is obtained through the negotiation of her adolescent sexuality with Rosa Baiana's, Léonie's and her mother's. João Romão's power derives both from his exploitation of his tenants and from his cunning with his stocks. There is a sense, however, in which both Pombinha's and João Romão's power is embedded in a much wider network of power relations which, because of its diffusiveness and multiplicity, cannot be embodied simply in the State, even if, as Foucault stipulates, a State needs to insinuate itself into tenant farming, stock market, and even sexual politics in order to take hold.

Yet, if the power of the State is always capable to operate because it occupies the whole field of actual power relations, how can we understand the appearance of an antagonist literature such as naturalism? In my view, the naturalist moment arose in Brazil at a moment when the Brazilian nation, or, in Anthony J. Cascardi's words, "its political analogue, the autonomous State," was in complete disarray. Before the fifteenth of November of 1889, when Deodoro da Fonseca proclaimed the republic and expelled the imperial family, the political struggles leading to—or opposing—that moment had waged long and bitter struggles throughout the country. After Deodoro da Fonseca left the government, the same political climate continued unabated. In *Os sertões*, Euclides da Cunha gives an account of the chaotic internal situation. About the government of Floriano Peixoto, Deodoro da Fonseca's successor, Cunha writes: "having been born out of a triumphant blow against a *coup d'etat* which violated the constitutional guarantees, it created the process of suspension of these guarantees; [because this government] tenaciously embraced the Constitution, it choked it, thus transforming legality into a synthesis of his designs . . . and transforming [Brazil] into a lawless land." About the civilian government which followed Peixoto's in 1894, Cunha writes that it "did not have the essential basis of an organized public opinion. It found the country divided into victorious and defeated [factions]. And [because] it was incapable of correcting a situation which was neither openly revolutionary nor normal, it equally repelled [both] extreme recourses [to use] force and the serene influx of laws" (*Os sertões* 201). The country was, to put it in other words, in "dead gear."

We know that modern Brazil, like so many other nation-states, is fundamentally the product of the end of the nineteenth century. I do not see how we can avoid describing "the whole field of actual power relations" which at this time came officially to produce the Brazilian nation under the sovereignty of the republican State without employing the more familiar notion of "ideology," a term dating from the initial usage of Marx and Engels to mean "irrational or illusory thinking produced by class interest and the social formation" (Brantlinger, *Crusoe's Footprints* 80). Such a usage has been modified into this century, where, among other developments, ideology acquires the more inward force of something which most people, most of the time, are not aware of; in other words, ideology is unconscious and unwilled. For the purposes of my discussion here, Sacvan Bercovitch's discussion of the problem of ideology in American literary history is very useful because of the contrasts it provides with the Brazilian instance.

Bercovitch writes that ideology is "the ground and texture of consensus." But, in terms of the turbulent Brazil of late nineteenth century, the idea of a consensus seems far-fetched, strained. To recall some aspects of this turmoil: a new set of recently freed Brazilians required admittance to the nation's citizenship; a sixty-year-old monarchical regime could not keep its grip on power under the new social and philosophical times, and newly arrived European workers settled in several regions of the country and created new pressures on the job market and on the policies of land distribution. Everything was fluid, volatile. Changes of the deepest political nature were being processed. What could the ideology of this time be?

Bercovitch again:

> In its narrowest sense [ideology] may be a consensus of a marginal or maverick group. In the broad sense in which I use the term here (in conjunction with the term "America"), ideology is the system of interlinked ideas, symbols, and beliefs by which a culture—any culture—seeks to justify and perpetuate itself; the web of rhetoric, ritual, and assumption through which society coerces, persuades, and coheres. ("The Problem of Ideology" 635)

Let's assume for a moment that the naturalists were one of such marginal groups. What kind of consensus did they have? As we have seen throughout this discussion, naturalists were posed against both the outside—represented by the nationalistic professoriate and critics of the capital—and against themselves. Even their allegiance to foreign aesthetics was, in itself, fractured and fraught with contradictions. Yet, they had a quarrel, a fight, with some "other." It may be that, unlike their North American counterparts who, Bercovitch says, had nothing *but* America to quarrel about (645), these naturalist writers had *nothing* to quarrel about. To borrow Doris Sommer's expression, they were pulling the mask away from the masquerader (*Foundational Fictions* 30-31). The problem is that the masquerader had no face, *yet*. The confusion and fluidity that the Brazilian nation faced at that moment resembled a group of atoms, in the moment before they combine and cohere to create a body: the elements existed in a state of suspension. Some exterior factor would determine the form. The naturalists wanted to be that factor, or at least a constitutive element in the eventual final form.

In other words, Brazil had to be invented all over again. Naturalist fiction, as I see it, struggled to maintain in the nation's nascent self those disparate representations of willful, independent women, homosexuals, blacks, and mulattoes, who were all in imminent danger of being written out and off the new political order. Can the question of when an ideology is decisive only be answered retrospectively? For my own more specific concerns about the formation of national subjectivity, I find the following articulation by Antonio Gramsci most useful:

> . . . to the extent that ideologies are historically necessary they have a validity which is "psychological"; they "organise," human masses, and create the terrain on which men move, acquire consciousness of their position, struggle, etc. To the extent that they are arbitrary they only create individual "movements," polemics and so on (though even these are not completely useless, since they function like an error which by contrasting with truth, demonstrates it). (*Selections from the Prison Notebooks* 377)

What I find most compelling about Gramsci's particular emphasis is that it is founded upon a distinction between historical necessity and arbitrariness. It is exactly at the juncture between the two—never easy to represent, and perhaps not even possible at any one moment in time—where I wish to locate the naturalist moment. It has been conventionally given in Brazilian literary history as devalued, or, one could say, polemical at best, in the sense of being a negative to some more confident positivity. Whether one wants to name this positivity, in turn, as an hegemonic ideological formation or just, more bluntly, the State, the important thing about naturalism is that it confounds the unity of certain specific periods in Brazilian history by exposing this unity to the lived experience of individual marginality, contradiction, and instability.

This is not to say that naturalism is itself free from ideology. Indeed, precisely because ideological structures are the only ones we have in order to imagine any identity at all, we can recognize registers of subversion or resistance in the naturalist text because it expresses these structures. What makes naturalism so powerful is the very thing which has always made it a contested site as well as a problem for literary periodization: its multiple narratives, its obscenities, its gender fixations, its exaggerations—its "non-Brazilianness." We might recall Richard Sennett's discussion of authority, especially his term "disobedient dependence" at this point. Brazilian naturalists of the nineteenth century, although writing an antagonist literature, could only do so as long as they had "Brazil" as their general discursive framework; after all, it is this "Brazil" that enabled their cultural existence. However, the Brazil that there was was about to dissolve, fade out exactly as Guidinha do Poço's farms are destroyed. Their historic moment kept in suspended state the "necessary basis for the great negative forms of power."

In his essay on Adorno in *Marxism and Form*, Jameson has a lovely phrase to describe one perspective on modern music: "willed ugliness" (23). I believe this expression is appropriate for Brazilian nineteenth-century naturalism too. Naturalism, we might say, provides the will, while ideology provides the context for its reception as ugly. Of course ideology changes. The key Gramscian idea of "hegemony" I take to express the constellation of power in terms of class hierarchies as it is produced at various points in history. Naturalism, on the other hand, is hegemony's rebuke, because it discloses within any hegemony counter-hegemonic energies based on social groups who are insufficiently subordinated or incompletely assimilated. On the basis of such a disclosure, what was heretofore disposed as historically inevitable stands forth, on the contrary, as something that can be understood instead as accidental or contingent. If naturalism has had an ideology of its own, it would be necessarily determined from within the encompassing ideology espoused at the moment by the State. To be against, is, in itself, no separate ideology. However, the space provided by this "against," especially in the case of nineteenth century naturalism, which was nascent, incomplete, and divided against itself, is a crucial one, because it allows for the recuperation of the network of power relations at work in a political and historical moment that also needs to be comprehended as against itself.

To make a very large claim: whether one is considering Aluísio Azevedo, Júlio Ribeiro, Adolfo Caminha, Manuel de Oliveira Paiva, and then later, Graciliano Ramos or José Lins do Rego, and later still, José Louzeiro or Aguinaldo Silva, what we continually find in Brazilian naturalism is the central Brazilian State dissolved back into regions, these regions dissolved further into ranches or houses, and these houses dissolved even further into individuals. These elements, like in the cinematic effect of "fade out," were, necessarily, the elements of which Brazil was constituted. It is as if there is not so much a nation as what Neil Larsen terms a "nation-effect" (74).

Similarly, before there is a self constructed in the social realm, and then a social role that eventually functions in terms of a national identity, there persists in the naturalist text the presence of a selfhood that is not recuperable by either society or nation, and which does not contribute to the "master narrative" of the state. This selfhood is not bourgeois, nor is it the inversion of the bourgeois. What is it then? Can it be defined in class or even ideological terms? I have argued throughout that such a selfhood—especially when impossibly male and female, or equal parts black and white—has always been a scandal to Brazilian critics, anxious, every one, to have everything absorbed into its due coherence, whether in a narrow literary sense or in a more broad ideological one. I hope that it is clear that my own presentation of naturalism is in sharp contrast to such a notion. To dismiss naturalism because it does not somehow "fit," or else, as Süssekind, to see it too comfortably because of its utopian potential, or, worse, to call it a "kind of *band-aid*," is only to rob naturalism of its recurrent power, which is available in Brazilian literary history especially when there is a need for dislocation, conflict, and incoherence.

BIBLIOGRAPHY

Ahmad, Aijaz. "Jameson's Rhetoric of Otherness and the 'National Allegory'." *Social Text* 17, 6.2 (1987): 3-25.

Alencar, José. *O guarani.* 14th ed. São Paulo: Editora Ática, 1988.

—. *Iracema, Lenda do Ceará.* Ed. Silviano Santiago. Rio de Janeiro: Francisco Alves, 1988.

—. "A língua portuguesa no Brasil." *Obra completa.* Rio de Janeiro: Editora José Aguilar, 1958. 3:305-20.

Althusser, Louis. "Ideology and Ideological State Apparatuses (Notes Towards an Investigation." *Lenin and Philosophy.* Trans. Ben Brewster. New York: Monthly Review Press, 1972. 127-86.

Anderson, Benedict. *Imagined Communities; Reflections on the Origin and Spread of Nationalism.* New York: Verso, 1987.

Andrade, Olímpio de Souza. *O livro brasileiro.* Rio de Janeiro: Editora Paralelo, 1974.

Araripe Júnior, Tristão de. *Obra crítica.* 2 vols. Rio de Janeiro: Casa de Rui Barbosa, 1958; Rio de Janeiro: Ministério de Educação e Cultura, 1960.

Aronowitz, Stanley. "On Intellectuals." *Intellectuals Aesthetics Politics Academics.* Ed. Bruce Robbins. Minneapolis: U Minnesota P, 1990. 3-56.

Assis, Antônio Maria Machado de. *Crítica literária.* Ed. M. de Alencar. Rio de Janeiro: Guarnier, 1924.

—. *Helena. Iaiá Garcia.* 5th ed. São Paulo: Editora Cultrix, 1968.

—. *Philosopher or Dog? (Quincas Borba).* Trans. Clotilde Wilson. New York: Avon Books, 1954.

Azevedo, Aluísio. *O cortiço.* 4th ed. 1890. São Paulo: Editora Ática, 1976. Trans. as *A Brazilian Tenement.* Trans. Harry W. Brown. New York: H. Fertig, 1976.

—. *O mulato.* 1881. São Paulo: Editora Ática, 1988. Trans. as *Mulatto.* Trans. Murray Graene MacNicoll. Rutherford: Farleigh Dickinson U P, 1990.

Bakhtin, Mikhail. *The Dialogic Imagination.* Trans. Caryl Emerson and Michael Holquist. Austin: U Texas P, 1983.

—. *Problemas da poética de Dostoiéviski.* Trans. Paulo Bezerra. Rio de Janeiro: Forense Universitária, 1981.

—. *Rabelais and His World.* Trans. Hélène Iswolsky. Cambridge: MIT Press, 1979.

Barbosa, João Alexandre. Introdução. *José Veríssimo; teoria, crítica e história literária.* Ed. João Alexandre Barbosa. Rio de Janeiro: Livros Técnicos e Científicos Editora, 1978. IX-XXXVII.

Barman, Roderick J. "Politics on the Stage: The Late Brazilian Empire as Dramatized by França Júnior." *Luso-Brazilian Review* 13.1 (Summer 1976): 244-60.

Bello, Andrés. "Discurso pronunciado en la instalación de la Universidad de Chile." *Obras Completas. Opúsculos literarios y críticos.* Santiago de Chile: P. G. Ramirez, 1881-92. 303-18.

Bello, José Maria. *A History of Modern Brazil: 1889-1964.* Trans. James L. Taylor. Stanford: Stanford U P, 1966.

Bercovitch, Sacvan. "The Problem of Ideology in American Literary History." *Critical Inquiry* 12.4 (Summer 1986): 631-53.

Brantlinger, Patrick. *Crusoe's Footprints.* New York: Routledge, 1990.

Brookshaw, David. *Race and Color in Brazilian Literature.* Metuchen, N.J.: Scarecrow Press, 1986.

Burns, E. Bradford. "The Enlightenment in Two Colonial Brazilian Libraries." *Journal of the History of Ideas* 25 (1964): 430-38.

—. "The Intellectuals as Agents of Change and the Independence of Brazil, 1724-1882." *From Colony to Nation: Essays on the Independence of Brazil.* Ed. A. J. R. Russell-Wood. Baltimore: The Johns Hopkins U P, 1975. 211-46.

Bushnell, David, and MaCaulay, Neil. "The Rise of the Brazilian Monarchy (1822-1850)." *The Emergence of Latin America in the Nineteenth Century.* Oxford: Oxford U P, 1988. 146-79.

Butler, Judith. *Gender Trouble; Feminism and the Subversion of Identity.* New York: Routledge, 1990.

Caesar, Terry. "Beasts Vaulting among the Earthworks: Monstrosity in *Gravity's Rainbow.*" *Novel* 17.2 (Winter 1984): 158-70.

Caldwell, Helen. *Machado de Assis, The Brazilian Master and His Novels.* Berkeley: U California P, 1970.

Caminha, Adolfo. *Bom-Crioulo.* 1895. São Paulo: Editora Ática, 1983. Trans. as *Bom-Crioulo: The Black Man and the Cabin Boy.* Trans. E. A. Lacey. San Francisco: Gay Sunshine Press, 1982.

Cândido, Antônio. *A educação pela noite.* São Paulo: Editora Ática, 1987.

—. *Formação da literatura brasileira (momentos decisivos).* Rev. ed. 2 vols. São Paulo: Livraria Martins Editora, 1964.

—. "Literature and the Rise of Brazilian national Self-Identity." Trans. Charles L. Eastlack. *Luso-Brazilian Review* 5.1 (June, 1968): 27-43.

—. "A obra de Sílvio Romero e o seu momento." *O método crítico de Sílvio Romero*. São Paulo: FFCL da Universidade de São Paulo, 1963. 123-139.

—. *Teoria literária e literatura comparada*. São Paulo: FFCL da Universidade de São Paulo, 1963.

Carvalho, José Murilo de. "Elites and State Building: Brazil." *Comparative Studies in Society and History* 4.3 (July 1982): 378-99.

Carvalho, José Murilo de, et al. *Sobre o pré-modernismo*. Rio de Janeiro: Fundação Casa de Rui Barbosa, 1988.

Cascardi, Anthony J. *The Subject of Modernity*. Cambridge: Cambridge U P, 1992.

Castello, José Aderaldo. *Aspectos do romance brasileiro*. Rio de Janeiro: MEC/Serciços de Documentação, 1961.

Castoriadis, Cornelius. *A instituição imaginária da sociedade*. 2nd ed. Rio de Janeiro: Paz e Terra, 1986.

Coelho, Jacinto do Prado. *Dicionário de literatura portuguesa, brasileira e galega*. 3rd ed. Porto: Figueirinhas, 1985.

Coleman, Alexander. *Eça de Queirós and European Realism*. New York: New York U P, 1980.

Collichio, Therezinha Alves Ferreira. *Miranda Azevedo e o darwinismo no Brasil*. Belo Horizonte: Editora Itatiaia, 1988.

The Compact Edition of the Oxford English Dictionary. Glasgow: Oxford U P, 1971.

Conrad, Robert E. "Neither Slave nor Free: The *Emancipados* of Brazil, 1818-1868." *The Hispanic American Historical Review* 53.1 (February, 1973): 50-70.

—. "The Planter Class and the Debate over Chinese Immigration to Brazil, 1850-1893." *International Migration Review* 9.1 (Spring 1975): 41-55.

Costa, Emília Viotti da. "Brazil: The Age of Reform, 1870-1889." *The Cambridge History of Latin America*. Ed. Leslie Bethell. Cambridge: Cambridge U P, 1983-86. 5.725-78.

—. "The Political Emancipation of Brazil." *From Colony to Nation*. Baltimore: The Johns Hopkins U P, 1975. 43-88.

Coutinho, Afrânio. *Introdução à literatura brasileira*. 7th ed. Rio de Janeiro: Editora Distribuidora de Livros Escolares, 1972.

Cunha, Euclides da. *Os sertões; campanha de Canudos*. 33rd ed. Rio de Janeiro: Livraria Francisco Alves Editora, 1987.

Curtin, Phillip D. "Benjamin Kidd and *The Control of the Tropics*." *Imperialism*. Ed. Phillip D. Curtin. New York: Walker, 1971. 33-40.

Dayan, Daniel. "The Tutor Code of Classical Cinema." *Movies and Methods*. Ed. Bill Nichols. Berkeley: U California P, 1976. 438-51.

Dean, Warren. *Rio Claro: A Brazilian Plantation System, 1820-1920*. Stanford: Stanford U P, 1976.

Domingues, Heloísa Maria Bertol. "Os intelectuais e o poder na construção da memória nacional." *Revista Tempo Brasileiro* 87 (out.-dez., 1986): 43-57.

Dudley, William S. "Institutional Sources of Officer Discontent in the Brazilian Army, 1870-1889." *Hispanic American Historical Review* 55.1 (February, 1975): 44-65.

Eddy, Williard O. "The Scientific Bases of Naturalist Literature." *Western Humanities Review* 8 (Summer, 1954): 219-30.

Eksteins, Modris. "History and Degeneration: Of Birds and Cages." *Degeneration; The Dark Side of Progress*. Eds. J. Edward Chamberlin and Sander L. Gilman. New York: Columbia U P, 1985. 1-23.

Eliade, Mircea. *The Myth of the Eternal Return*. New York: Princeton U P, 1971.

Elshtain, Jean, ed. Introduction. *The Family in Political Thought*. Amherst: U Massachusetts P, 1982. 1-30.

Foster, David William. "Adolfo Caminha's *Bom-Crioulo*: A Founding Text of Brazilian Gay Literature." *Chasqui* 17.2 (November, 1988): 13-22.

Foucault, Michel. *Discipline and Punish*. Trans. Alan Sheridan. New York: Vintage Books, 1979.

—. *The History of Sexuality*. Vol 1. Trans. Robert Hurley. New York: Random House, 1978.

—. "The Order of Discourse." *Language and Politics*. Ed. Michael Shapiro. New York: New York U P, 1984. 108-38.

—. "The Subject and Power." *Critical Inquiry* 8 (Summer 1982): 777-95.

—. "Truth and Power." *Power/Knowledge; Selected Interviews and Other Writings by Michel Foucault*. Ed. Colin Gordon. New York: Pantheon Books, 1977. 109-33.

Fraser, Nancy. "On the Political and Symbolic: Against the Metaphysics of Textuality." *Boundary 2* 14.1-2 (Fall, 1985-Winter, 1986): 195-209.

Frazer, James George. *The Golden Bough*. New York: Macmillan, 1937.

Frieiro, Eduardo. *O diabo na Livraria do Cônego*. Belo Horizonte: Itatiaia, 1957.

Gallop, Jane. *The Daughter's Seduction; Feminism and Psychoanalysis*. Ithaca: Cornell U P, 1982.

—. "Of Phallic Proportions: Lacanian Conceit." *The Daughter's Seduction*, q.v., 15-32.

Galloway, J. H. "The Last Years of Slavery on the Sugar Plantations of Northeastern Brazil." *Hispanic American Historical Review* 51.4 (November, 1971): 586-605.

Gardner, Augustus K. *History of the Art of Midwifery*. New York: Stringer & Townshend, 1852.

Gilman, Stuart C. "Political Theory and Degeneration: From Left to Right, From Up to Down." *Degeneration: The Dark Side of Progress*. Eds. J. Edward Chamberlin and Sander L. Gilman. New York: Columbia U P, 1985. 165-98.

Girard, René. *Violence and the Sacred*. Baltimore: The Johns Hopkins U P, 1977.

Gluckman, Max. "Gossip and Scandal." *Current Anthropology* 4.3 (1963): 307-16.

Gonzaga, Sergius. *Manual de literatura brasileira*. Porto Alegre: Mercado Aberto, 1985.

Goodrich, Diana S. "From Barbarism to Civilization: Travels of a Latin American Text." *American Literary History* 4.3 (Fall, 1992): 443-63.

Gordon, Jan B. "A-filiative Families and Subversive Reproduction: Gossip in Jane Austen." *Genre* 21.1 (Spring, 1988): 5-46.

Gramsci, Antonio. *El "Risorgimiento"*. Buenos Aires: Granica, 1974.

—. *Selections from The Prison Notebooks*. Trans. Quintin Hoare and Geoffrey Nowell Smith. London: Lawrence and Wishart; New York: International Publishers, 1971.

Greenfield, Gerald Michael. "The Great Drought and Elite Discourse in Imperial Brazil." *Hispanic American Historical Review* 72.3 (August, 1992): 375-400.

Guimarães, Aquiles Cortes. "O espírito do positivismo na cultura brasileira." *Revista brasileira de filosofia* 36.145 (jan.-março, 1987): 25-30.

Gutiérrez Nájera, Manuel. "El movimiento literario en México." *Obras*. México, D.F.: Universidad Nacional Autónoma de México, 1959. 1:189-92.

Hallewell, Laurence. *O livro no Brasil*. São Paulo: EDUSP, 1985.

Hollanda, Sérgio Buarque de. *Raízes do Brasil*. Rio de Janeiro: Livraria José Olympio Editora, 1936.

Hostos, Eugenio María. *La peregrinación de Bayoán.* 1863. Puerto Rico: Instituto de Cultura, 1970.

Houaiss, Antonio. *Estudos vários sobre palavras, livros, autores.* Rio de Janeiro: Paz e Terra, 1979.

Hulet, Claude L. *Brazilian Literature 2; 1880-1920, Naturalism Realism-Parnassianism Symbolism.* Washington D.C.: Georgetown U P, 1974.

Jameson, Fredric. *Fables of Aggression; Wyndham Lewis, the Modernist as Fascist.* Berkeley: U California P, 1979.

—. *Marxism and Form.* Princeton: Princeton U P, 1971.

—. *The Political Unconscious; Narrative as a Socially Symbolic Act.* Ithaca: Cornell U P, 1982.

—. "Third-World Literature in the Era of Multinational Capitalism." *Social Text* 15, 5.3 (1986) :65-88.

Kalcic, Susan. *Ethnic and Regional Foodways in the USA.* Knoxville: U Tennessee P, 1985.

Kidd, Benjamin. *The Control of the Tropics.* London: Macmillan, 1898.

Kowarick, Lúcio. *Trabalho e vadiagem: A origem do trabalho livre no Brasil.* São Paulo: Editora Brasiliense, 1987.

Kristeva, Julia. "Stabat Mater." *The Kristeva Reader.* Ed. Toril Moi. New York: Columbia U P, 1986. 161-85.

LaCapra, Dominick. *Rethinking Intellectual History.* Ithaca: Cornell U P, 1983.

Larsen, Neil. *Modernism and Hegemony; A Materialist Critique of Aesthetic Agencies.* Minneapolis: U Minnesota P, 1990.

Layoun, Mary N. "Fictional Formations and Deformations of National Culture." *The South Atlantic Quarterly* 87.1 (Winter, 1988): 53-74.

Lima, Luiz Costa. *O controle do imaginário.* São Paulo: Brasiliense, 1984. Also as *Control of the Imaginary.* Trans. Ronald W. Souza. Minneapolis: U Minnesota P, 1988.

—. *Dispersa demanda: ensaios sobre literatura e teoria.* Rio de Janeiro: Livraria Francisco Alves Editora, 1981.

Lins, Álvaro. "Dois naturalistas: Aluísio Azevedo e Júlio Ribeiro." *O romance brasileiro (de 1752 a 1930).* Ed. Aurélio Buarque de Hollanda Ferreira. Rio de Janeiro: Edições O Cruzeiro, 1952. 151-65.

—. *Literatura no Brasil. II, Realismo, Naturalismo e Parnasianismo.* Rio de Janeiro: José Olympio Editora, 1955.

Loos, Dorothy Scott. *The Naturalistic Novel of Brazil.* New York: Hispanic Institute in the United States, 1963.

Lopes Júnior, Francisco Caetano. "*Bom-Crioulo*: Between Love and Death." *Proc. of the Conference "The Black Image in Latin American Culture."* Slippery Rock: Slippery Rock University, Pennsylvania, November 1989. 230-40.

Lousada, Wilson. Nota bibliográfica sobre José Veríssimo. José Veríssimo, *História da literatura brasileira.* 5th ed. Rio de Janeiro: Livraria José Olympio Editora, 1969. ix-xii.

Lukács, Georg. *Writer and Critic and Other Essays.* Trans. Arthur Kahn. London: Merlin Press, 1970.

Macedo, Sérgio D. T. *Crônica do negro no Brasil.* Rio de Janeiro: Distribuidora Record, 1974.

Marotti, Giorgio. *Black Characters in the Brazilian Novel.* Trans. Maria O. Marotti and Harry Lawton. Los Angeles: U California P, 1987.

Martí, José. *Obras completas.* La Habana: Editorial Nacional de Cuba, 1963-65.

Martin, Ronald E. *American Literature and the Universe of Force.* Durham: Duke U P, 19981.

Martins, Cláudio, et al. *O pão.* Edição Facsimilar. Fortaleza: Imprensa Universitária da Universidade Federal do Ceará, 1982.

Martins, Wilson. *A crítica literária no Brasil.* Rio de Janeiro: Francisco Alves, 1983.

Marx, Karl. "The 18th Brumaire of Louis Bonaparte." Karl Marx and Frederick Engels. *Collected Works.* London: Lawrence and Wishart, 1979. 11:103-97.

Marx, Leo. *The Machine in the Garden.* New York: Oxford U P, 1964.

Mérian, Jean-Yves. *Aluísio Azevedo: vida e obra (1857-1913).* Rio de Janeiro: Espaço e Tempo Banco Sudameris—Brasil; Brasília: INL, 1988.

Merquior, José Guilherme. *De Anchieta a Euclides.* 2nd ed. Rio de Janeiro: Livraria José Olympio Editora, 1979.

Miceli, Sérgio. *Intelectuais e classe dirigente no Brasil (1920-1945).* São Paulo: Difel, 1979.

Michaels, Walter Benn. *The Gold Standard and the Logic of Naturalism; American Literature at the Turn of the Century.* Berkeley: U California P, 1987.

Miller, D. A. *The Novel and the Police.* Berkeley: U California P, 1988.

Mitchell, Lee Clark. *Determined Fictions.* New York: Columbia U P, 1989.

Moisés, Massaud. *Realismo.* 2nd ed. São Paulo: Editora Cultrix, Editora da Universidade de São Paulo, 1985. Vol. III of *História da literatura brasileira.*

—. *Romantismo, Realismo.* São Paulo: Editora Cultrix, 1984. Vol. II of *História da literatura brasileira.*

Nachman, Robert G. "Positivism, Modernization, and the Middle Class in Brazil." *Hispanic American Historical Review* 57.1 (February, 1977): 1-23.

Norris, Frank. *The Octopus; A Story of California.* New York: New American Library, 1960.

Novak, Barbara. *Nature and Culture; American Landscape Painting 1825-1875.* New York: Oxford U P, 1980.

Nunes, Maria Luísa. *The Craft of an Absolute Winner; Characterization and Narratology in the Novels of Machado de Assis.* Westport, Conn.: Greenwood Press, 1983.

Oliveira, Cândido de. *Súmulas de literatura brasileira; testes e questões objetivas à maneira de provas e concursos.* 14 ed. São Paulo: Gráfica Biblos, n.d.

Ortiz, Renato. *A moderna tradição brasileira; cultura brasileira e indústria cultural.* São Paulo: Editora Brasiliense, 1988.

Paiva, Manoel de Oliveira. *Dona Guidinha do Poço.* 1952. São Paulo: Editora Ática, 1981.

Pang, Eul-Soo, and Secklinger, Ron L. "The Mandarins of Imperial Brazil." *Comparative Studies in Society and History* 14.2 (March, 1972): 215-44.

Patai, Daphne, and Murray Graeme MacNicoll. Introduction. Aluísio Azevedo, *Mulatto.* Cranbury, N.J.: Associated U P, 1990. 7-26.

Pereira, Lúcia Miguel. *Machado de Assis. Estudo crítico e biográfico.* 5th ed. Rio de Janeiro: José Olympio, 1955.

—. *Prosa de ficção (de 1870 a 1920).* Rio de Janeiro: José Olympio, 1950. Also Belo Horizonte: Itatiaia; São Paulo: Universidade de São Paulo, 1988.

Pierson, Colin M. "José de Alencar: Realistic Dialogue and Characterization in the Anti-Slavery Thesis Play." *Luso-Brazilian Review* 18.1 (Summer, 1981): 161-71.

Pinto, Rolando Morel. "Apresentação." Manuel de Oliveira Paiva, *Dona Guidinha do Poço.* São Paulo: Ática, 1981. 5-10.

Poovey, Mary. "Cultural Criticism: Past and Present." *College English* 52.6 (October, 1990): 615-25.

Queirós, Eça. *Cousin Basílio.* Trans. Roy Campbell. New York: The Noonday Press, 1953.

Queirós Júnior, Teófilo de. *Preconceito de cor e a mulata na literatura brasileira.* São Paulo: Editora Ática, 1982.

Rabassa, Gregory. *O negro na ficção brasileira; meio século de história literária.* Trans. Ana Maria Martins. Rio de Janeiro: Edições Tempo Brasileiro, 1965. Orig. an unpublished Ph.D. dissertation, Columbia University, 1954.

Ramos, Julio. *Desencuentros de la modernidad en América Latina.* México, D.F.: Fondo de Cultura Económica, 1989.

Ramos, Julio. "Fragmentación de la república de las letras." *Desencuentros de la modernidad en América Latina; literatura y política en el siglo XIX.* México, D.F.: Fondo de Cultura Económica, 1989. 50-81.

Reis, Arthur Cezar Ferreira. *Aspectos da formação brasileira.* Rio de Janeiro: Livraria José Olympio; Brasília: Instituto Nacional do Livro, 1982.

Renault, Delso. *A vida brasileira no final do século XIX; Visão sócio-cultural e política de 1890 a 1901.* Rio de Janeiro: José Olympio Editora, Instituto Nacional do Livro, 1987.

Ribeiro, Júlio. *A carne.* 1888. São Paulo: Editora Saber, 1975.

Ribeiro, Luís Felipe. "A mulher no romance brasileiro: trajetória de uma ideologia." *Revista tempo brasileiro* 80 (jan.-março, 1985): 3-33.

Ridings, Eugene W. "Business Interest Groups and Communications: The Brazilian Experience in the Nineteenth Century." *Luso-Brazilian Review* 20.2 (Summer, 1983): 241-57.

Romero, Sílvio. *Ensaios de crítica parlamentar.* Rio de Janeiro: Moreira, Maximiano, 1883.

—. *História da literatura brasileira.* 5 vols. 1888. Rio de Janeiro: José Olympio, 1949.

—. "A prioridade de Pernambuco no movimento espiritual brasileiro." *Revista brasileira.* segunda fase, 2 (1879): 486-96.

—. *Retrospecto literário, história da literatura brasileira.* 3rd ed. Vol V. Rio de Janeiro: Livraria José Olympio Editora, 1946.

—. *Teoria, crítica e história literária.* Ed. Antônio Cândido. São Paulo: Editora da Universidade de São Paulo; Rio de Janeiro: Livros Técnicos e Científicos, 1978.

Rosa, Alberto Machado da. *Eça, discípulo de Machado?* 2nd ed. Lisboa: Editora Presença, 1946.

Russell-Wood, A. J. R. "Preconditions and Precipitants of the Independence Movement in Portuguese America." *From Colony to Nation; Essays on the Independence of Brazil.* Ed. A. J. R. Russell-Wood. Baltimore: The Johns Hopkins U P, 1975. 3-40.

Rycroft, Charles. *A Critical Dictionary of Psychoanalysis.* New York: Basic Books, 1968.

Said, Edward. *The World, the Text, and the Critic.* Cambridge: Harvard U P, 1983.

Sant'Anna, Affonso Romano de. *Análise estrutural de romances brasileiros.* Petrópolis: Editora Vozes, 1979.

Santiago, Silviano. *Vale quanto pesa.* Rio de Janeiro: Paz e Terra, 1982.

Santos, Afonso Carlos Marques dos. "Memória, história, nação: propondo questões." *Revista tempo brasileiro* 87 (out.-dez., 1986): 5-13.

Schwartz, Stuart B. "The Manumission of Slaves in Colonial Brazil: Bahia, 1684-1745." *Hispanic American Historical Review* 54.4 (November, 1974): 603-35.

Schwarz, Roberto. "As idéias fora do lugar." *Ao vencedor as batatas; forma literária e processo social nos inícios do romance brasileiro.* São Paulo: Duas Cidades, 1977: 13-28.

Schwarz, Roberto. *Ao vencedor as batatas; forma literária e processo social nos inícios do romance brasileiro.* São Paulo: Livraria Duas Cidades, 1981. 13-28.

Sennett, Richard. *Authority.* New York: Vintage Books, 1980.

Silva, Hélio. *O poder civil.* Porto Alegre: L & PM Editores, 1985.

Skidmore, Thomas. *Black into White, Race and Nationality in Brazilian Thought.* New York: Oxford U P, 1974.

Sklair, Leslie. *The Sociology of Progress.* London: Routledge & Kegan Paul, 1970.

Sodré, Nelson Werneck. *História da literatura brasileira; seus fundamentos econômicos.* 4th ed. Rio de Janeiro: Edição Civilização Brasileira, 1964.

—. *História militar do Brasil.* Rio de Janeiro: Edição Civilização Brasileira, 1965.

—. *O naturalismo no Brasil.* Rio de Janeiro: Edição Civilização Brasileira, 1965.

Sommer, Doris. *Foundational Fictions; The National Romances of Latin America.* Berkeley: U California P, 1991.

—. "Irresistible Romance: The Foundational Fictions of Latin America." *Nation and Narration.* Ed. Homi Bhabha. New York: Routledge, 1990. 71-98.

Stepan, Nancy. "Biological Degeneration: Races and Proper Places." *Degeneration; The Dark Side of Progress.* Eds. F. Edward Chamberlin and Sander L. Gilman. New York: Columbia U P, 1985. 97-120.

Süssekind, Flora. *Literatura e vida literária; polêmicas, diários e retratos.* Rio de Janeiro: Jorge Zahar Editor, 1985.

—. *Tal Brasil, qual romance?* Rio de Janeiro: Achiamé, 1984.

Topik, Steven C. "Brazil's Bourgeois Revolution?" *The Americas* 48.2 (October, 1991): 245-71.

Veríssimo, José. "Campanha de Canudos." *Estudos de literatura brasileira. 5a. série*. Rio de Janeiro, Paris: Guarnier, 1905. 59-87.

—. "Das condições da produção literária no Brasil." *Estudos de literatura brasileira. 3a. série*. Rio de Janeiro, Paris: Guarnier, 1903. 35-82.

—. *História da literatura brasileira*. 5th ed. 1916. Rio de Janeiro: Livraria José Olympio, 1956.

—. "O modernismo." *Teoria, crítica e história literária*. Ed. João Alexandre Barbosa. Rio de Janeiro: Livros Técnicos e Científicos Editora, 1978. 169-78.

—. "Questões da língua portuguesa." *Estudos de literatura brasileira. 6a. série*. Rio de Janeiro, Belo Horizonte: Editora Itatiaia; São Paulo: Editora da Universidade de São Paulo, 1977. 33-76.

Wasserman, Renata R. Mautner. "Lima Barreto, the Text and the Margin: On *Policarpo Quaresma*." *Modern Languages Studies* 22.3 (Summer, 1992): 53-69.

Weber, Max. *Economy and Society*. Eds. Guenter Roth and Claus Wittich. Berkeley: U California P, 1978.

—. *The Protestant Ethic and the Spirit of Capitalism*. Trans. Talcott Parsons. New York: Scribner's, 1958.

Webster's New Collegiate Dictionary. 2nd ed. Springfield: G. & C. Merriam, 1956.

Westbrook, Perry D. *Free Will and Determinism in American Literature*. Rutherford: Fairleigh Dickinson U P; London: Associated U P, 1979.

Williams, Raymond. *Keywords: A Vocabulary of Culture and Society*. New York: Oxford U P, 1976.

Zaretsky, Eli. *Capitalism, the Family, & Personal Life*. New York: Harper & Row, 1976.

Zola, Émile. *The Experimental Novel and Other Essays*. Trans. Belle M. Sherman. New York: Haskell House, 1964.

INDEX